AMERICAN CITIES AND TOWNS

AMERICAN CITIES and TOWNS

Historical Perspectives

★ ★ ★

Edited by Joseph F. Rishel

DUQUESNE UNIVERSITY PRESS
Pittsburgh, Pennsylvania

Published by:

Duquesne University Press
600 Forbes Avenue
Pittsburgh, Pennsylvania 15282-0101

Library of Congress Cataloging-in-Publication Data
American cities and towns: historical perspectives/edited by
    Joseph F. Rishel.
        p. cm.
    Includes bibliographical references and index.
    ISBN 0–8207–0239–0 (cloth)
    1. Cities and towns—United States—History.   2. City and
town life—United States—History.   I. Rishel, Joseph Francis.
1945–HT123.A6617   1992
307.76'0973—dc20   92–20597
                                                          CIP

Printed in the United States of America.

Contents

Introduction

Joseph F. Rishel

Cities and towns have always been important in American history. They have been centers of politics, commerce and culture from the Puritans' time to the present. The momentous economic and social changes, and the political reform movements of the nineteenth and twentieth centuries have largely been spearheaded by cities. Therefore, to understand American history, we must learn more about urban places and how they developed.

This book presents new historical perspectives on urban places in the United States. It is not a textbook or a collection of primary source documents, nor is it intended to be a series of impressionistic essays. Instead, it presents articles on cities and towns in a variety of contexts and geographic areas in every period from 1630 to 1983. *American Cities and Towns: Historical Perspectives* does this through 11 separate articles, each of which forms a chapter. These articles are not intended to cover every aspect of the urban experience; rather, they seek to shed light on topics that urban historians have largely ignored. In most cases, however, they expand upon or reinterpret the extant body of historical literature.

This introduction will identify each chapter in the book and acquaint the reader with related work already done by scholars in the field. In some cases, these chapters explore entirely new ideas. Thus, the historiography is correspondingly small. In other cases, these articles challenge longstanding interpretations, requiring a more lengthy

1

treatment of the existing body of historical literature.

In the first of these articles, "Plantation to City Charter: The Rise of Urban New England, 1630–1873," Harold A. Pinkham, Jr. builds partly on Jon C. Teaford's *The Municipal Revolution in America* (1975). Teaford examines the sometimes tortured courses of municipal governments in the middle and southern provinces as they were challenged by the egalitarian and libertarian promises of the Revolution. In contrast to the frequently obstructionist tactics of municipal leaders in the urban centers to the south of New England, Boston's selectmen and town meetings were far more accommodating to revolutionary ends than city mayors and aldermen. Thus, in the half century before 1825, when the democratic revolution was completed in virtually all American cities, town government in Boston brought greater flexibility and broader participation by the citizenry in urban decision making.

In 1977 Bruce Daniels published the first of a series of studies on New England town development. During the next decade, he examined the processes of town growth, highlighting Connecticut and Rhode Island communities. In his view, town government was far more complex than commonly believed, especially with the increased diversity and population growth of the eighteenth century. Some changes seem to suggest the emergence of a gradual process of maturation in the more populated towns: plantation proprietors separating from the townspeople, parishes subdividing, decentralizing of the method for admitting new freemen, and the increasing number of town officers. These changes suggest the possibility of a preurban process, stages through which each town that was destined to become an urban center would pass.

The title of chapter 1, "Plantation to City Charter," implies that such an urbanization process existed in the towns of New England. While the histories of many communities suggest that numerous localities were exposed to much the same stimuli, few appear to have completed the requisite stages to actually become urban centers and receive city charters. The acquisition of a city charter,

Pinkham avers, was a symbolic right of passage, the literal manifestation of urban success.

In chapter 2, "The Great Brothel Dousing: Leisure, Reform, and Urban Change in Antebellum Pittsburgh," Scott C. Martin breaks new conceptual ground by examining the ways in which leisure activities framed and helped define cross-class interactions. Leisure received increased attention from historians in the 1980s, who expanded upon and refined the pioneering work of Foster Rhea Dulles's *America Learns to Play: A History of Recreation* (1940). In *Eight Hours for What We Will: Workers and Leisure in an Industrial City, 1870–1920* (1983), Roy Rosenzweig demonstrated the importance of leisure in the development of the Worcester, Massachusetts, working class. In a similar vein, Steven Ross depicted the role leisure activities played in promoting class consciousness and shaping the political agenda of Cincinnati workers in *Workers on the Edge: Work, Leisure and Politics in Industrializing Cincinnati, 1788–1790* (1985). Patricia Click also addressed the issue of class and leisure in *The Spirit of the Times: Amusements in Nineteenth Century Baltimore, Norfolk and Richmond* (1989), noting that leisure activities varied between socioeconomic groups over time. Martin builds on these works but focuses on how leisure promoted class formation and definition by articulating urban class ideologies. In examining the interaction of social and ethnic tensions, "The Great Brothel Dousing" rejects the notion that reform was invariably an attempt at social control of one class by another. Rather, Martin views leisure reform as one of the dynamics of urban change: a cross-class phenomenon with a continuum of tactics ranging from moral suasion at one end to vigilante action at the other.

In chapter 3, "Mobility and a Catastrophic Event: Who moves After the Town Burns Down?", Robert M. Preston treats the question of geographic mobility. In 1969 Stephan Thernstrom's pioneering work, *Poverty and Progress: Social Mobility in a Nineteenth Century City*, helped launch a plethora of studies of the social, occupational and geographical mobility of Americans. Many of these works, including those by Peter Knights, Clyde and Sally Griffen, Paul E. Johnson, and Stuart Mack Blumin, center on specific northeastern cities. But until well into the twentieth century, a majority of Americans lived in rural areas and small towns like Emmitsburg, Maryland, the town that Robert M. Preston selected for study. However, the characteristic of being a small town does not, of itself, make this research worthwhile for those interested in mobility analysis.

While many researchers have considered occupation, ethnicity, race, and economic and social status as factors affecting geographic mobility, Preston adds a single catastrophic event as an independent variable. Thus he tests the strength of a set of interdependent variables that many other scholars have identified as causal elements in geographic mobility. Given the frequency of fires in nineteenth century urban America, this phenomenon seems an important one to consider.

In chapter 4, "Beyond the Great City: Finding and Defining the Small City in Nineteenth Century America," Maureen Ogle also treats the small city, but here the focus is municipal services. Observing that the great body of extant literature is overwhelmingly devoted to large cities, she seeks to fill the void through this study of four smaller and widely separated communities in the late nineteenth century.

Urban historians have generally asserted that the modern city, with all of the services that city government performs through large bureaucratic structures, was created almost solely due to the impact of massive immigration and industrialization. Necessity forced them to do what they did, otherwise it would not have been done. All of the general urban histories convey this message in one form or another. Books such as those by Zane Miller and Patricia Mooney (*The Urbanization of Modern America: A Brief History* [1987]), Howard Chudacoff and Judith Smith (*The Evolution of Urban America* [1987]) and Raymond Mohl's survey of late nineteenth century urban America (*The New City: Urban America in the Industrial Age, 1860–1920* [1985]) create a picture of an urban America in which the large cities, especially New York, dominate historical inquiry to an inordinate degree.

Even studies devoted to the evolution of city services rely almost exclusively on evidence drawn from large cities. This is true of Nelson Blake's *Water for the Cities* (1956) and *Garbage in the Cities* (1981) by Martin V. Melosi. Studies of smaller communities—those with a population under 20,000—tend to treat the urban place as a kind of laboratory where family and kinship ties, local politics, ethnicity, etc., can be easily studied. The sweeping sketches by Page Smith in *As A City Upon A Hill: The Town in American History* (1966) and Lewis Atherton in *Main Street on the Middle Border* (1954) constitute virtually the only extended forays into small city history. Both, however, tend to speak in generalities rather than specifics, treating the nebulously defined small town as a cultural institution embodying all the appropriate values associated with the antithesis of the evil big city.

Two other more recent histories examine the small city more factually and more specifically. In his *River Towns in the Great West: The Structure of Provincial Urbanization in the American Midwest, 1820–1870* (1990), Timothy R. Mahoney examines the city as a part of a region. Mahoney's concern is the ways in which these smaller cities influenced and were influenced by their surrounding areas. Although Lawrence H. Larsen's *The Urban West at the End of the Frontier* (1978) gives a clearer picture of the small city, much remains to be done, for the small city is not merely a microcosm of the metropolis. In this chapter, Maureen Ogle looks beyond the great city and offers interesting alternatives in analyzing urban growth.

In chapter 5, "The Other Migration: The Foundations of African American Suburban Settlement, 1880–1930," Leslie E. Wilson and Valerie Hartman present a discussion of a long-neglected aspect of American suburbanization. Although this is now attracting scholarly attention, there is, at this writing, no volume solely concerned with the outward movement of blacks in the first half of the twentieth century. Several authors—including Earl Hutchinson, Philip Clay, Harold Connolly, Harold Rose, William Pendleton, Leo Schnore, Harry Sharp and Harlan Paul Douglass— have discussed this phenomenon but only in a cursory fashion. Moreover, such discussion as does exist is mostly concerned with the later period and the larger legacy of black urban deconcentration.

The first notice of early black suburbanization appeared in Harlan Paul Douglass's *The Suburban Trend* published in 1925. In observing this, Douglass relied on the census of 1920. Nearly 50 years later, in 1973, Harold Connolly also used the census, but concluded that there were other sites of black settlement besides those listed by Douglass. His article, "Black Movements Into the Suburbs: Suburbs Doubling Their Black Population During the 1960s," focused on the recent period, but directed attention to the differences between the two eras. Commentary by Pendleton, Schnore, Sharp and Rose acknowledged the black migration, but suggested that pre-World War II suburbanization was vastly different. Their works were followed by the writings of Thomas Clark, Avery Guest and the team of Harvey Marshall and John Stahura. (Wilson and Hartman have included extensive historiographic information on the above-named authors in their notes.) Each supports the belief that historians have overlooked this phase of black migration and all aver that white and black suburbanization were different. Black suburbanization was, so they claim, principally a search for employment, not a push by the affluent seeking to escape the city. Some assert that this was not true suburbanization, since it did not match the suburban myth and existing historical literature. Wilson and Hartman concur with at least some of these findings, but they view this migration as the forerunner of modern black suburbanization. The suburbs selected by blacks in 1910 and 1920, for instance, are the same ones that are resettled by a further influx six decades later. Yet this early period is also unique. Wilson and Hartman propose new interpretations of this period and find continuing patterns with modern black migration.

In chapter 6, "Middletown Reindustrializes," Dwight W. Hoover examines the changing economic base of a mid-sized Indiana city in the first quarter of the twentieth century. More specifically, Hoover discusses the introduction of the automobile industry to Muncie, a city that already possessed an industrial base.

Historians have most often assumed industrialization to be a one-time phenomenon or else a progressive one. This is commonly supposed to have occurred in the time period from about the Civil War to the 1920s. It is described by Maury Klein and Harvey A. Kantor in their book, *Prisoners of Progress: American Industrial Cities, 1850–1920* (1976) and by Raymond A. Mohl in *The New City: Urban America in the Industrial Age, 1860–1920* (1985). Perhaps the classic study of industrial development is Allan Pred's *The Spatial Dynamics of U.S. Urban-Industrial Growth, 1800–1914,* published in 1966. The period embraced by this study ends at about the same time that Muncie's automobile industry was taking off. For the period following World War I, the attention of urban historians shifts away from industrial development to such matters as suburbanization, transportation, city planning and ethnic unrest.

With the exception of Detroit, the historical treatment of the automobile tends not to focus on the impact of the industry on a particular city, but rather on how the use of the new transportation medium affected the lives of urban residents. This focus is quite old. It was followed by Robert S. and Helen M. Lynd in their celebrated study, *Middletown,* published in 1929. In this book the Lynds do not discuss how the automobile industry made possible the prosperity they found in Muncie in the twenties. Instead, they detail how the automobile changed the mores of Muncie by giving more freedom to the young via liberalized sexual practices, and by diverting attention from the significant urban problems brought on by industrialization.

This neglect of the industrial base was noted in Leon Mandel's *Driven: The American Four-Wheeled Love Affair* (1977), but Mandel does not explore the base either. In a chapter titled, "Middletown Transformed," he chronicles the close attraction the car had for Muncie residents and their dependence upon it for transportation as well as for personal satisfaction. Much the same interpretation is given by James J. Flink in his books, *America Adopts the Automobile, 1895–1910* (1970) and *The Car Culture* (1975), and by John B. Roe in *The Road and the Car in American Life* (1971). Even works on specific cities neglect the industrial impact of auto production. Two of the more notable books are *Automobile Age Atlanta: The Making of a Southern Metropolis, 1900–1935* (1979) by Howard L. Preston, and *The Automobile and Urban Transit: The Formation of Public Policy in Chicago* (1983) by Paul Barrett. Due to the surprising lack of attention paid by historians to this vital part of twentieth century American manufacturing, the chapter presented by Dwight W. Hoover assumes greater significance, and Muncie provides a laboratory-like environment for study. Thus, "Middletown Reindustrializes," enters heretofore unexplored territory in urban-industrial history.

In chapter 7,"An Urban-Rural Dimension of the Scopes Trial," Burton W. Folsom presents a radical departure from the commonly accepted interpretation of that famous case. In what has become standard fare offered by historians, the Scopes trial was a revealing portrait of rural-urban tensions in 1920s America. Big-city reporters and lawyers descended on Dayton, Tennessee for a trial involving the teaching of evolution. Clarence Darrow, the Chicago criminal lawyer, the symbol of enlightened modern urbanism— so the interpretation goes—defended John Scopes's right to teach evolution in the public schools of Tennessee in violation of a recently passed state law. William Jennings Bryan, the folksy politician from Nebraska, the symbol of fundamentalist antiscientific rural America—so the interpretation continues—defended the Tennesseans' right to control what was taught in their classrooms.

Popular historical accounts of the trial by Ray Ginger, *Six Days or Forever?* (1958) and L. Sprague DeCamp, *The Great Monkey Trial* (1968), emphasize an urban-rural split at the trial. In this view, Bryan was fighting a rearguard action to protect the traditional values of rural America from modern scientific thinking. This view was reinforced in biographies of Bryan by Lawrence Levine in his *Defender of the Faith* (1965), by Louis Koenig's political biography in *Bryan* (1971), and by Paolo Coletta in *Political Puritan* (1965). And it is likewise reinforced in biographies of Darrow by Irving Stone in *Clarence Darrow for the Defense* (1971), and Kevin Tierney in *Darrow* (1979).

More recent studies by Robert Cherny, *A Righteous Cause: The Life of William Jennings Bryan* (1985) and George Marsden, *Fundamentalism and American Culture* (1981), also stress the urban-rural tension displayed in the Scopes trial. Cherny says that "when the iconoclasm of the Chicago lawyer met the piety of the Miami Sunday school teacher, the clash pitted science against religion, urban sophistication against rural innocence, academic freedom against antiintellectualism." According to Marsden, "the rural setting, so well-suited to the stereotypes of the agrarian leader [Bryan] and his religion, stamped the entire [antievolution] movement with an indelible image."

In "An Urban-Rural Dimension of the Scopes Trial," Burton Folsom challenges this traditional view. He reviews what Bryan himself said, which is so often falsely represented by historians, and he reexamines statistics on evolution referenda and presents suprising data on the relationship between rural-urban voting behavior.

In chapter 8, "Mistaken Identity: Putting the John Reber Plan for the San Francisco Bay Area in Historical Context," David R. Long presents a city-region plan that is both descriptive and analytical in its treatment. Long juxtaposes this plan to those of Daniel Burnham and Thomas Adams, the two recognized leaders of the infant and early adolescent American city planning field. In physically comparing John Reber's plan with the works of his contemporaries, this article relies heavily on two works: *Burnham of Chicago: Architect and Planner* (1979) by Thomas Hines and *Thomas Adams and the Modern Planning Movement* (1985) by Michael Simpson. The theoretical analysis draws primarily upon Mellier Scott's *American City Planning Since 1890* (1969) and

M. Christine Boyer's *Dreaming the Rational City: The Myth of American City Planning* (1983). These latter sources are used to illustrate how John Reber intuitively drew upon themes from both of the dominant urban planning schools of his era: the City Beautiful and the City Functional. There is little disagreement among scholars concerning what these two movements actually were, although Boyer adds a Marxist spin to her analysis.

Historians are also in agreement concerning the nature of these early planning endeavors. In large part, they were intellectual exercises. The actual construction that they envisioned was often limited or nonexistent, hence Boyer's title. And so it was with the Reber Plan. Despite its revolutionary nature, the Reber Plan was very much like contemporary plans, and despite a concerted effort on the part of its supporters, the project failed to reach fruition.

In chapter 9, "Preparing for Armageddon: The Role of the City in Civilian Defense Planning During World War II," Robert Earnest Miller bases his research largely on primary materials in the Office of Civilian Defense Papers (Record Group 171) and the Office of War Information Papers (Record Group 208) in the National Archives, on the Fiorello H. LaGuardia Papers at the New York City Municipal Archives, and on the Eleanor Roosevelt Papers at the Franklin D. Roosevelt Library in Hyde Park, New York.

The unpublished work by Elwyn A. Mauck, the staff historian for the Office of Civilian Defense (OCD), *Civilian Defense in the United States, 1941–1945* (1944) and the government-sponsored weekly newsletter, *Defense* (Washington, 1940-1945 [renamed *Victory* in 1943]) are valuable sources on the development of civilian defense policies at the federal level. From these and other sources, historians have uncovered at least parts of the government's efforts in urban civil defense during World War II. While general studies of the homefront by John Morton Blum, Richard Polenberg and Allan M. Winkler offer only fleeting glimpses of civilian defense activities, Richard R. Lingeman's *Don't You Know There's A War On?: The American*

Home Front, 1941-1945 (1976, 2nd ed.) and Lee Kennett's *For the Duration: The United States Goes to War, Pearl Harbor— 1942* (1985) devote full chapters rich in anecdotal evidence about the OCD's civilian protection policies. Biographies of top OCD administrators such as Donald A. Ritchie's *James M. Landis: Dean of the Administrators* (1980) and Thomas Kessner's *Fiorello H. LaGuardia and the Making of Modern New York* (1989) provide good accounts of the inner workings of the OCD. Except for Phillip J. Funigiello's *The Challenge to Urban Liberalism: Federal-City Relations During World War II* (1978), which devoted a full chapter to Eleanor Roosevelt's nonprotective community service programs, and Robert Miller's own dissertation, "The War that Never Came: Civilian Defense, Mobilization, and Morale During World War II," (University of Cincinnati, 1991), very little has been written about this important aspect of civilian defense.

In chapter 10, "A Clash of Priorities: The Federal Government and Dallas Airport Development, 1917–1964," Robert B. Fairbanks builds on several historiographic traditions in raising new perspectives on the history of the city. Although very different in its approach and topical venue from chapter 9, this article also treats federal-city relationships.

In their examination of this connection, historians have studied the twentieth century almost exclusively, and most of their efforts have stressed the impact of New Deal policies on urban politics. More recent scholarship has also investigated the social and economic impact of New Deal programs on cities as exemplified by Kenneth T. Jackson's work on suburbs and housing, and Jo Ann Argersinger's work on the New Deal's role in community building in Baltimore. Roger Lotchin and Gerald Nash each examine the role of the military and World War II on urban development. Carl Abbott in *The New Urban America: Growth and Politics in Sunbelt Cities* (1987) and Richard M. Bernard and Bradley R. Rice, eds., in *Sunbelt Cities: Politics and Growth Since World War II* (1983) emphasize the positive impact that the federal government had on sunbelt urban development. In the article on a sunbelt city presented here, Fairbanks suggests that federal involvement sometimes helped urban boosters reach their goals of growth and development, but at other times the conflicting priorities of the federal government and city government appeared to thwart those goals.

This theme touches on another recent tradition in urban history literature, what is commonly called planning history. Much of planning history has attempted to examine specific urban planning trends, such as William Wilson's *The City Beautiful Movement* (1989). Other studies by Christopher Silver, *Twentieth-Century Richmond: Planning, Politics, and Race* (1984) and Carl Abbott, *Portland: Planning, Politics, and Growth in a Twentieth-Century City* (1983), have focused on politics and planning in particular cities. Although Fairbanks's article is also concerned with a single city, with the topic of planning and the role of federal-city relations, it seeks to implement and combine these themes in novel ways. This chapter also calls attention to a much neglected part of urban history, the role of the airport. Except for Thomas J. Noel, "Unexplored Western Skies: Denver International Airport" (*Journal of the West* 30: 90–100), this topic has received scant attention from scholars. As a result, this article attempts to delineate, via the Dallas experience, the importance that cities placed on airport development. The few studies of airport development from an urban perspective are often airport biographies, as in *A Dream Takes Flight, Hartsfield Atlanta International Airport and Aviation in Atlanta* (1989) by Betsy Braden and Paul Hagan. More analytical studies include an examination of airport planning by Paul Barrett, "Cities and Their Airports: Policy Formation, 1926–1952," in *Journal of Urban History* (Nov. 1987), and a study in the exercise of power and group dynamics by Jameson W. Doig, "Coalition-Building by a Regional Agency: Austin Tobin and the Port of New York Authority," in *The Politics of Urban Development* (1987), Clarence N. Stone and Heywood T. Sanders, eds. In "A Clash of Priorities," Robert Fairbanks differs from his predecessors in his examination of the relationships between the federal and city governments over an extended period of time.

In chapter 11, "Erastus Corning 2nd and Democratic Politics in Albany, New York: 1942–1983," Ivan D. Steen shows how a political organization—and an individual politician—can stay in power for a very long time. While the literature on municipal politics is extensive, it is less so using the methodology employed by Steen. Owing to the paucity of diaries or revealing letters written by local politicians, scholars have turned to the still relatively new approach of compiling oral history. A major study using this approach in writing the biography of a local politician is *Don't Call Me Boss: David L. Lawrence, Pittsburgh's Renaissance Mayor* (1988), by Michael P. Weber.

Since Albany, from a political standpoint, is essentially an Irish town, studies of Irish political organizations were useful. Edward M. Levine's *The Irish and Irish Politicians: A Study of Cultural and Social Alienation* (1966) shows how Irish local politicians perceive themselves and how they operate. Steven P. Erie, a political scientist predicting the demise of Albany's Irish machine, wrote *Rainbow's End: Irish-Americans and the Dilemmas of Urban Machine Politics, 1840–1985* in 1988. In researching this, Erie used Frank S. Robinson's *Albany's O'Connell Machine: An American Political Relic* (1973). Robinson sees the Albany Democrats remaining in power primarily through corrupt practices rather than, as Steen concludes, that they "pleased most of the people most of the time." Ivan Steen sides primarily with those who see political machines as not necessarily all bad, while recognizing that their methods are not always in strict conformity with the law. Through an examination of the longest mayoral reign in American history, he shows the ingredients of successful political domination.

These chapters show the new directions that historians are taking in their study of urbanization in America. These authors help focus attention on the key roles that cities and towns have played in shaping economic, political and cultural life for more than three hundred years. *American Cities and Towns: Historical Perspectives* is a contribution to a significant and growing field in American history.

1

Plantation to City Charter

The Rise of Urban New England, 1630–1873

Harold A. Pinkham, Jr.

Few who have studied early New England communities have considered the transition of particular communities into cities. Rather, they have tended to ignore the urban growth that began as early as the seventeenth century.[1] William Haller, a historian writing in 1951, reflected this view when he stated that "plantations and towns which became too populous for their circumstances had a tendency either to split in two or produce offshoot plantations as an outlet for population growth."[2] Neither Haller nor other writers have explained how expanding population and functions led to the rise of urban centers. The colonial legislatures of New England were unprepared to grant municipal status to any of their towns.

By contrast, in the colonies to the south, where counties as well as townships were the basic vehicles for settlement, the "municipal revolution in America" as identified by Jon C. Teaford, had begun.[3] Crown and proprietary officials recognized the uniqueness of selected urban centers with grants of city and borough government. New York and Pennsylvania granted municipal government before the end of the seventeenth century: Manhattan in 1665, Albany in 1686 and Philadelphia in 1691. Ten additional municipal grants followed between 1701 and 1736: New Jersey with four, Pennsylvania three, Virginia two and Maryland one.[4]

The dominant Puritanical and agricultural interests of

New England, as reflected in its legislatures, ignored a dynamic and ongoing process in community development—the urbanization of some of its towns. Although urban localities began to evolve quite early within the coastal plantations of eastern Massachusetts and New Hampshire, a lengthy adjustment process involving several steps would occur before legislatures would recognize the urban characteristics of these sites and grant city charters.[5] Because plantations, the earliest units for ordering social and political life, tended to be large, they were susceptible to subdivision from the start. Ideally, the adjustment process—which began with the incorporation of the plantation as a town—ended when the town ceased to subdivide and the central core had achieved its optimum concentrations of population and functions. In Massachusetts, a population of 10,000 was set by that state's Constitutional Convention of 1820.[6] Thus, ideally, the lawmakers needed to keep the ongoing urbanization process continually monitored, ready to grant or deny incorporation to towns, boroughs or cities as time and circumstances warranted.[7]

Among the thousand or so New England towns existing at the end of the Revolution, only 45 had developed patterns of growth distinctive enough between 1784 and 1873 to receive city charters from state legislatures. However, the charge of the representatives went beyond that of merely granting city charters; they were also concerned with the incorporation of approximately 110 towns that separated from the parent plantations and were thus instrumental in the formation of cities. In the early going, legislative representatives encountered stiff resistance to change. Their actions were inhibited by many factors, including: fear of the loss of newly won liberties and rights, conflict of economic interests between representatives of farm towns and the commercial urban centers, and inadequate legislative models for the creation of cities and towns.

Chronologically, the responses of government authorities to the mounting urban challenge divided into five phases: periodic efforts by Boston merchants to secure a city charter during the colonial period; hesitant experiments by Connecticut and Rhode Island lawmakers from 1784 to 1821; a modest sized Boston-stimulated charter movement from 1822 to 1836; rapid expansion of municipal government from 1836 to 1866; and, finally, Boston's annexation of its neighbors from 1867 to 1873.[8]

CONNECTICUT AND RHODE ISLAND INITIATE THE REVOLUTION

Cities were slow in coming to New England. The first phase of the movement toward city government occurred in the second half of the seventeenth century in Boston. The town meeting filed separate petitions for municipal government with the General Court in 1650, 1659, 1661, 1662, 1663 and 1677. On each occasion the legislature, preferring to keep the town subordinate to county and province, failed to act through its procrastination, hesitation and delay.[9]

Despite a strong decade-long movement starting in 1779 that resulted in 25 charters in the Colonies, New Englanders remained reluctant, responding late and accounting for only six of that total. New charters caught the spirit of the Revolution, reducing restrictions on individual ambition and removing the granting of exclusionary rights to municipalities, but New Englanders remained suspect of the power of city government. Only after 11 charters had been issued in Virginia, South Carolina, Pennsylvania and New Jersey, did New England establish its six municipal charters.

Connecticut, which chartered five of the new cities, showed an ambivalance toward municipal authority, placing its new cities—Hartford, New Haven, Middletown, New London and Norwich—within the confines of existing larger towns. A sixth locality—Newport, Rhode Island—unlike its Connecticut counterparts, whose territorial adjustments would lie in the future, had already lost its outlying subcommunity in 1743. The leaders in Newport were far less equivocal than those in Connecticut; when they charted their first city, it encompassed the boundaries of the town that it replaced.[10] Boston, despite its eventual leadership role in the "municipal revolution," appears to have offered few precedents as guides for Connecticut and Rhode Island legislators in 1784.[11] Regardless of its sizable population (17,000) compared to the average of 5,000 people for the Connecticut and Rhode Island localities, Boston continued with town government.

Despite the plethora of new charters in states to the south, for New Englanders the established levels of government—state, county and township—were seen as quite adequate for the rural society at the time. That selected towns could be elevated above their sister localities to become cities posed serious jurisdictional issues within the general courts, where towns were the essential base of power for the deputies. The issue seems to have been no less acute for the counties, which would have to forge a new relationship with municipalities.[12]

By placing cities within existing towns, a move to placate rural elements, Connecticut's deputies created an unprecedented duality between the prerogatives of town and municipal power and responsibility. Inhabitants of the new municipalities were legal residents of *both* city and town, while the townspeople living outside the city's boundaries lacked the dual residency of the urban dweller. Judicial and police functions of the five cities were separated from those of the county, as the city court and the two sheriffs were granted county powers.[13] The mayor, however, was subject to removal by the legislature.[14]

The evidence suggests that legislators were premature in granting such charters in 1784. The towns would lose additional subcommunities, and the central cores would remain underpopulated and underdeveloped, not exceeding until 1850 the average population minimum of 10,000 set by Massachusetts in 1820. The Quinnipiac plantation (New Haven) had yet to lose subcommunities as of 1784, but would have five outlying areas separate by 1822.[15] The remaining Connecticut towns and their cities would not lose as many subcommunities as New Haven, but their boundaries would adjust as their central sections grew.[16]

Connecticut lawmakers, continuing to face mounting resistance from their rural members who were dissatisfied with the autonomy granted to the first five cities, tried a new approach. They introduced the borough—Bridgeport— in 1800 and placed it within two existing towns. This was unprecedented because the borough had customarily been given county authority and thereby placed above the towns.[17] Bridgeport was originally carved from Fairfield and Stratford. The inhabitants of the borough, however, became official residents only of Stratford. Limited authority over the everyday workings of government and the maintenance of law and order were granted to an elected warden and six burgesses. However, such traditional township powers as those of confirming the tax recommendations of the warden and burgesses, recognizing new freemen and approving ordinances of the warden and burgesses, resided firmly with the legal freemen's meeting. In a concession to the county, judicial decisions of the warden and burgesses could be appealed to the county Superior Count.[18]

After the Constitution of 1818, Connecticut legislators reaffirmed their dualistic structure, reenacting in 1821 their statutes of 1784 and 1800.[19] Also that year they added another layer of complexity to their dualistic structure, incorporating Bridgeport as a town and thus transferring the borough to the new town and severing its ties to Stratford.[20] Despite providing for the election of officials at an annual meeting of residents, the Connecticut enactment for Bridgeport made no allowance for public approval of the new borough, nor was the election of burgesses through equal wards included.[21] The wards that were created appear to have been for maintaining peace and order, the wardens having the powers of justices of the peace.

In 1787, only three years after the charter was introduced, a populist revolt in Newport forced a return to town government. In the view of the petitioners, city government was too novel for "Free Republicans" and imposed "indignities to their property and civil liberty." Furthermore, in their opinion, it enabled "a few influential men" to control the election of mayor, aldermen and Commonmen, who in turn appointed officers "independent of the suffrage of the people." To them, the municipal corporation created was too powerful, threatening and wasteful, the power of the corporation being "indefinite and therefore dangerous."[22]

The heavy-handedness of charter advocates, more than traditional resistance to change by rural legislators, appears to have been the primary reason for the downfall of city government in Newport. Charter provisions reveal serious shortsightedness by local advocates and legislators alike. Considering the lofty republican principles still fresh in the American mind following the Revolution, the failure to allow for local approval, while placing arbitrary power in the hands of a small, self-perpetuating clique of merchants, was the most serious general flaw. Newport would not receive another charter until 1853.[23]

BOSTON SETS THE PACE

Advocates of city government in Boston also had begun their work in 1784. A small but influential group of Boston merchants launched a three-pronged movement—constitutional revision, legislative enactment and town meeting acceptance.[24] The merchants persevered, undaunted by three prevalent conditions: a lack of authorization for cities in the Massachusetts Constitution of 1780, a powerful town meeting tradition, and a legislature that reflected the interest of a rural majority. Nagging questions as to appropriate strategy persisted: should they win local acceptance first and then address the constitutional and legislative challenges, or should the revision of the constitution be paramount? In the end, a coordinated pursuit of all these issues led to success.

The struggle in Boston to culminate the "municipal revolution" would occupy 38 years, lasting until 1822.[25]

Although successive petition drives met with increasingly better results, the crucial majority at town meeting could be acquired only after a three-day debate in December 1821, and then only after the constitutional convention had given permission for city government earlier that year.[26] In the long run, local opposition would prove far more formidable than constitutional revision or legislative enactment because state leaders made it clear that no city would be created without prior approval by the residents of the town.

During the next five years, legislatures in Connecticut and Rhode Island became active once again. Connecticut turned to borough government repeatedly during the 1820s and 1830s, but few boroughs were to become cities. Of the 11 boroughs created by 1836, only Bridgeport became a city.[27] To further illustrate the tenuous nature of its three-stage process to cityhood—town, borough, and city—only three of the 16 boroughs incorporated up until 1870 had achieved municipal government. Only Waterbury (1853) and New Britain (1870) would join Bridgeport as cities by that date. However, before dismissing Connecticut's role in the "municipal revolution" too readily, one should consider the fact that another four communities that became boroughs by the 1850s received city charters later in the century.[28]

The Rhode Island General Assembly in 1830, avoiding the mistakes of its disastrous earlier Newport grant, provided for local approval in making Providence a relatively autonomous city modeled after the more liberal Boston design.[29]

In the early 1830s, Maine legislators caught the fever. Their first two charters—Portland in 1832 and Bangor in 1834—adhered to the main elements of the Boston arrangement, allowing the inhabitants greater involvement. The Boston experience was reflected in many major provisions: common boundaries between town and city; equally apportioned wards, which provided the basis for representation on common councils; prior approval of city government by the residents of the town in question; and concurrent votes by boards of aldermen and commonmen in making ordinances and approving appointments.[30]

In 1836 the transitory phases in the emergence of city government ended with the general acceptance of the Boston approach. That same year Connecticut made the borough of Bridgeport a city, following the outlines of the Boston scheme. However, the new city remained within the town of Bridgeport.[31] In 1836 Massachusetts deputies reaffirmed their commitment to the Boston system in granting comparable charters to Salem and Lowell.[32]

A look at the maturity of the cities emerging during this phase reveals that each one—Boston, Salem, Lowell, Providence, Portland and Bangor—by 1836 had made major territorial adjustments in their emergence from the plantation stage.[33] Boston, Salem and Portland systematically lost subcommunities as population and urban functions grew dramatically on their central peninsulas.[34] Lowell, receiving predetermined boundaries in 1822 as a planned site for a future industrial city, had attained a population second only to that of Boston by 1836.[35] Providence had passed systematically through its plantation phase, having been transformed from a county to a consolidated town and having lost the last of its seven subcommunities by 1765.[36] Bangor, a modest sized plantation from the beginning, seemed quite premature by contrast, losing its only subcommunity in 1853, 19 years after becoming a city.[37]

PROLIFERATION OF THE BOSTON MODEL

Lingering vestiges of the plantation structure disappeared rapidly after 1836, as 32 new cities were carved from a nearly equal number of towns. They ranged from oversized towns barely out of the plantation stage—such as Hallowell, Maine and Waterbury, Connecticut—to adjusted and mature towns such as Worcester, Massachusetts and Portsmouth, New Hampshire. This four-stage process in urban transformation featured, sequentially, a decade-long respite from charter writing; a second decade of rapid proliferation, 1846 to 1855; 11 years of retrenchment, lasting to 1866; and, finally, six annexations by Boston.

Once the respite had ended in 1846, a surge in charter writing ensued; outlines of the Boston plan were endorsed in each new charter.[38] Chronologically, only 14 charters had appeared in the first 62 years, while 25 were written in the decade beginning in 1846.[39] Geographically, 22 of the cities were located as follows: seven in eastern Massachusetts, six along the northeastern coast of New England, five on the Merrimack River, and four on the Kennebec River. On a state-by-state basis during the decade, Massachusetts incorporated ten cities; Maine, eight; New Hampshire, five; and Connecticut and Rhode Island, one each. In terms of their frequency, 16 cities were chartered in two periods of equal output, from 1848 to 1850 and from 1853 to 1855.

The Massachusetts and Maine legislatures dominated the proliferation period. Lawmakers applied increasingly more egalitarian versions of the Boston model to their 25 new municipal charters. Unlike the previous Boston-Salem-Lowell instruments of government, Roxbury's charter of 1846 initiated the procedure of electing the aldermen from representative wards, rather than at-large.[40] Furthermore, unlike Boston's charter, Roxbury's document restricted the powers of the wardens, provided for appeal to county government, and established police and city courts.[41] Thus Roxbury became the first of the suburbs of Boston's "urban fringe," identified recently by Henry C. Binford, to receive a municipal charter (1846).[42] Ironically, it also became the first of the communities so heavily impacted by mass transportation and residential migration that is was annexed (1867) to Boston, thus becoming the first of Sam Bass Warner's "streetcar surburbs."[43]

By 1854 with the passage of the charter for Fall River, the General Court restored the provision calling for general meetings of the legal residents when necessary, also seen in the Biddeford charter of 1855 and other Maine statutes.[44]

Another problem was halfheartedly addressed at this time—that of the mayor's lack of power. Apparently reacting to the frustrations reported by Boston's mayor,

Josiah Quincy, and his immediate successors to strengthen the executive power of the office,[45] the Maine legislators sought to correct the imbalance in a modest way. Several Maine charters attempted to strengthen the prerogatives of the mayor by means of a veto on money bills. The veto, however, could be overridden by a simple majority of the aldermen and council.[46]

The pace of charter granting fell off drastically in the decade after 1855, when only seven charters were granted throughout New England. Massachusetts chartered two (Chelsea and Taunton), Maine two (Lewiston and Sacco), Connecticut two (Meriden and New Britain) and Vermont one (Burlington).[47] As in the proliferation phase, Boston's instrument of government provided the guidelines. Uncertainties raised by events related to the oncoming Civil War were undoubtedly a factor in the retrenchment.

After the experimentation seen in the first 62 years, which found Connecticut pulling in one direction, Rhode Island in another, and Massachusetts in a third, charter writing evolved more uniformly after 1846. Politically, the majority of the new entities had more in common. Each, with minor differences, reflected the Boston approach; they were separate and autonomous from any town, divided into equally populated wards, accepted by at least a majority of the residents, and granted little executive authority to the mayor.

THE DIFFERENCES BETWEEN PLANTATIONS

Two plantations in particular—Charlestown, Massachusetts and Hallowell, Maine—illustrate the need to delve below the surface to assess readiness for municipal government.[48] On the surface, the two towns had much in common, being extremely old and initially large plantations, having been founded three years apart in the early settlement period, receiving their city charters within three years of each other in the mid-nineteenth century, and spawning new cities from seceding subcommunities.

A close examination of the two plantations, however, reveals some fundamental differences. On one hand, Charlestown, as an "urban fringe" suburb, expanded steadily in population and functions from the beginning while undergoing balanced territorial adjustment.[49] As a plantation it lost three of its outlying communities between 1642 and 1842. Two of the subcommunities, paralleling the parent community in rate of development, would later become cities.[50] On the other hand, Hallowell would subdivide much more rapidly, four times between 1771 and 1852. One subcommunity—Augusta—became a city in 1849, a year before its parent community.[51] Such a rapid pace of town incorporation and city chartering indicates a basic prematurity. Maine, it appears, was not developed sufficiently demographically, economically or socially to warrant the creation of seven subdivisions within the Hallowell plantation.

The similarities between the enormous plantations of Charlestown and Hallowell masked important differences in urban maturation, and such was the case in smaller plantations as well. It might appear that Roxbury and Worcester, Massachusetts, and Belfast and Calais, Maine, in shedding only one or no subcommunities over many years, were at a seemingly appropriate size and level of maturity and needed no further adjustment before being given charters by their respective legislatures.[52] But that was not the case; location was paramount. Roxbury, adjacent to Boston, grew rapidly, as did Worcester, which served to funnel traffic between Boston and Springfield. Belfast and Calais, receiving charters prematurely from overly optimistic legislators were in relative decline, having fallen victim to diminishing coastal carrying trade and declining shipbuilding industries.

BOSTON ANNEXES ITS NEIGHBORS

Because of economic expansion following the Civil War, the pace of urban adjustment and maturity increased dramatically. While the need for subdivision and secession as a means for urban adjustment diminished, a new mechanism entered the scene—annexation. Boston launched itself down the road of urban imperialism by annexing Roxbury in 1867.[53] Within the next five years, four additional localities had been annexed and thus became "streetcar suburbs"—Dorchester (1869), Brighton (1873), West Roxbury (1873) and Charlestown (1873).[54]

For Roxbury, annexation may seem upon first reflection as diametrically opposed to the trend outlined in this essay, that of concentrating population at the center while shedding lesser populated subcommunities on the periphery. Yet a closer examination reveals the basic logic of the phenomenon, that the central core—Boston—had absorbed all the inhabitants that it could accommodate comfortably and was seeking relief through territorial expansion.

2

The Great Brothel Dousing

Leisure, Reform and Urban Change in Antebellum Pittsburgh

Scott C. Martin

At about 10:00 P.M. on Wednesday, 1 June 1842, a fire alarm sounded in the streets of Pittsburgh. Within minutes, a number of the city's "energetic firemen" assembled at a frame house on Fourth Street, near the corner of Grant Street. The house, one of a number known to the local populace as "Aristocracy Row," was owned by Samuel Diehl—more commonly known as "Blind Sam, the fiddler"—and occupied by "Polly Varner, the Latimores, and other degraded creatures,—and frequented by persons no less degraded." Despite the fact that Blind Sam's establishment was not ablaze, the firemen directed a stream of water through the front windows, causing great commotion inside, with "many of the inmates making a sudden exit the back-way, several *en-deshabille.*" Ignoring Blind Sam's protests ("'The rascals are ruinin' all my property— I'll *see* about this tomorrow!'"), which included "a stream of curses as heavy as that of water which was directed against his dwelling," the firefighters proceeded to "render the building rather an uncomfortable dwelling place for its inmates" before retiring for the evening.[1]

The following evening a similar assault occurred at the "indomitable Crow's Nest," a tenement off Wood Street on Virgin Alley, long noted as "the scene of every vice, and the rendezvous of thieves and criminals of every description." As with the dousing of Blind Sam's, the firemen ignored the owner's protest and directed a stream of water through the front windows, giving the "smiling faces of Mrs. Murphy and Hannah Johnson" a "refreshing shower."

> The door was then closed, and the whole nest, of all colors, fledged and unfledged, drunk and sober, took a flight the back way. The retreating squad was headed by a Maria Ramsey, in the ranks were old Mother Murphy, Hannah Reams, and Hannah Johnson, or Williams, while Henry Johnson, the husband of the last named, commonly known as the *Irish Nagur*, (accompanied by a few "nice young men;") brought up the rear! The besieged thus effected a retreat with flying *colors*.[2]

The next night, Pittsburgh's firemen desired "another frolic": the "cry of fire was raised and the Engines again hauled up to the 'Crow's Nest' but the Mayor came and *persuaded* them to desist."[3]

Community action against brothels was no novelty in America, either in the colonial or early national era.[4] What made the brothel dousings in Pittsburgh significant was their position in the context of urban development. The purification of morals in 1842 reflected and expressed many of the tensions and problems confronting both the general populace and government in the rapidly expanding urban area. Pittsburgh, which 50 years earlier had been little more than a frontier trading town, underwent great change during the first four decades of the nineteenth century. Growing from a town of 1,565 in 1800 to a city of 21,515 in 1840, Pittsburgh's population would more than double to 46,601 by the end of that decade.[5] Many of these new residents were neither native Americans nor of Scots-Irish descent, as were most early settlers. By 1839 *Harris' Directory* estimated that with Irish, German, African and other ethnic immigrants swelling the population, less than 50 percent of the Pittsburgh area's population had been born in the United States.[6]

Economic growth as well as demographic increase and ethnic diversification transformed Pittsburgh during the early decades of the nineteenth century. By 1812,

rudimentary class divisions had already emerged; as com-
mercialization and industrialization proceeded, these divisions developed further and solidified.[7] Expanding industry and commerce produced a varied, transient
workforce that was no longer controlled by an apprentice
and journeyman system of supervision. The city's emergence as a transportation center, especially during the
years of the canal boom, brought hordes of transient
workers and "vagabond laborers" both for construction
and shipping duties.[8] Combined with the gradual breakdown of the apprentice system and the increasing size and
diversity of the population, this transience made it more
difficult than ever before for the community to exercise
necessary social control over its members.

As the decades passed, changes in Pittsburgh's population and workforce eroded customary methods of the
communal control of behavior. Familial influence, informal
social pressure and ostracism by the "respectable" portions
of the community no longer sufficed to keep the peace in
Pittsburgh's streets. Whether the problem was conceived
as juvenile delinquency, organized criminal activity or
simple rowdiness,[9] Pittsburgh had, by all accounts, a major
law and order problem by the mid-1830s. Pittsburgh mayor
Jonas R. McClintock expressed community concern in 1836
when he warned the city's combined councils that a "spirit
of lawless misrule seems to have spread itself over many
sections of our heretofore happy country." McClintock
reminded the councils that Pittsburgh's provisions for public
safety were the product of its incorporation in 1816, "a
period when we were much less liable, owing to the
absence of our present facilities for transportation, to be
troubled with the visits of desperate characters."[10] Altered
conditions, McClintock argued, necessitated renewed vigi-
lance and stronger measures to insure public safety.

Much of the community's concern centered on the objectionable or immoral leisure practices that were fast
becoming widespread among transient laborers and some
segments of the working poor.[11] It was easy enough to
know how to deal with murder or robbery; chronic drunk-

enness, fighting, disorderly conduct, false alarms and prostitution were other matters entirely. Though clearly a threat to the city's safety and morals, vice was often a victimless crime, and thus difficult to eradicate. Middle class reforms like temperance and moral societies preached primarily to the already converted, and action by the authorities was usually slow, difficult and ineffective.

When customary methods of social control failed, Pittsburgh had no effective formal apparatus to replace them. For instance, neither professional fire nor police services existed in antebellum Pittsburgh. In the village, borough and early city, volunteer departments saw to fire protection. With the city's incorporation in 1816, the councils established a small night watch, but no real police force. Insufficient funds proved a chronic and vexing problem: the watch established in 1816 was abolished a year later when a depression hit the region, and subsequent efforts at police control also suffered because of the city government's lack of money. Some Pittsburghers proposed a volunteer night watch, similar to the volunteer fire system, but this too proved impractical.[12]

The costly, ineffectual police force motivated many Pittsburghers to turn to the traditional practice of communal vigilantism to remedy social nuisances and moral evils. The mayor's election day in early January was an annual occasion for extra-legal action against various groups and leisure practices. It was well known, noted one newspaper editor, that

> previous to the institution of the City Watch the citizens of Pittsburgh were in the habit of abating certain nuisances themselves, without the intervention of law, and that election nights were set apart for the destruction of houses of ill-fame, two of which, established by a notorious courtezan [sic], were burnt to the ground on as many election eves, by the aid of skiffs filled with tar-barrels, and other combustible matter, which were deposited in the halls of the buildings thus purified by fire.[13]

The problem with this type of nuisance abatement was that it lent itself to excess. Often the vigilantism became worse than the problems it purported to cure, becoming itself an excuse for lawlessness and violence. In 1828 Pittsburgh's election night was "attended by riotous proceedings, such as shoutings, burning tar barrels, firing crackers, throwing fire balls, & c." When the mayor and City Watch attempted to arrest the rioters, they "were violently assailed, and some of the officers badly hurt by missiles thrown by no boyish hands. . . . At one time the Court House was set on fire, by a flaming ball thrown on the roof."[14] Pittsburgh lawyer Charles B. Scully captured the mood of the city on another election night in the early 1840s in his diary, noting that

> the whole city is ringing like a Bedlam with the 'feu de joie' of the Clay men, all the Engines are out and there's a 'd——d fuss generally.'—there is an 'interregnum,' and the whole City is rollicksome, the ordinances of peace and good order are pro tem suspended, & blackguardism is rampant everywhere.[15]

This was the type of behavior Jonas R. McClintock hoped to eliminate by improving police services in the mid-1830s. By "throwing his personal action and influence into the organization, and coupling it with a sternness and moderation suited to the circumstances," McClintock hoped to convince the "Saturday night *regulators* that *personal liberty* did not contemplate the right to inaugurate the Sabbath by an appeal to the boatmen's horn, the horse-fiddle, or the sentimental discords of 'nice young' serenaders."[16] Though McClintock succeeded for a time, the financial, economic and demographic forces already mentioned doomed his halting efforts to failure. By 1842, financial considerations motivated Pittsburgh's councils to reorganize the City Watch of 22 men into the "night police" of 11, a savings of more than half the original cost. For Pittsburghers who took a dim view of the City Watch to begin with, this reduction of personnel was symptomatic of the city's inability to suppress crime and vice. The old watch, they noted, was "strong enough to prevent the destruction by the mob of such infamous haunts [i.e., brothels], yet too weak, or perhaps unwilling to suppress them themselves."[17]

Into this morass of vice, violence and civic impotence stepped the city's volunteer fire companies. Their attack on Blind Sam's and the Crow's Nest in 1842 was an attempt to adapt a traditional communal organization to a new purpose. If the night police could not combat vice and immorality, then the people of Pittsburgh could fall back on the energetic firemen of their volunteer companies. Long a staple of community life,[18] fire companies served important leisure functions for both their members and the community at large. As Charles Dawson noted, fire companies were less efficient in the early city, but

> they had any quantity of fun. Then fire companies took the place in street pageants and parades now occupied by some of the benevolent orders. They gave banquets, and were banqueted in turn, and a public demonstration was imperfect indeed without the volunteer firemen as active participants.[19]

In the face of widespread dissatisfaction with the "inefficiency of the police of Pittsburgh,"[20] city residents looked enthusiastically to a traditional organization with approved leisure functions to reform the objectionable leisure of threatening outsiders.

This solution to the problems of vice and law enforcement was appealing for two reasons. First, the excesses of mob action could be avoided: the fire companies were, after all, organized groups with at least a modicum of discipline and civic responsibility. Their voluntarism and social club ethos made them less offensive to the public's sensibilities than an armed police force. Second, using fire companies for moral reform promoted a sense of continuity with the past and with customary methods of addressing community problems. Rather than depending on an expensive, professional police force, the community relied on its tradition of voluntarism, expressing communal solidarity and minimizing the divisions wrought by class formation and demographic change. In a sense, then, the brothel dousing of 1842 was both an attempt to abate a serious moral nuisance and to deny that Pittsburgh had changed so much that spontaneous communal action could no longer solve its urban problems.

In another sense, however, the brothel dousings revealed *exactly* the changes Pittsburghers sought to deny through recourse to traditional communal action. Though popular for their leisure and instrumental functions, fire companies were by the 1840s far from model civic organizations. Because they drew their membership from an expanding, diversified population to meet increasing needs for fire protection,[21] volunteer companies themselves were caught up in many of the same processes and practices they aimed at curtailing through vigilante action. Drinking, fighting between rival companies, racing through crowded streets to and from fires, and setting false alarms to provoke fights or races were common practices among firefighters, reflecting an increasing working class presence and influence among the volunteers. Fighting between rival companies, which reached its peak around 1840,[22] often stemmed from contests over which company would be the first to "throw water" on a fire. Companies throwing bricks and stones at each other on the way to throw water was a regular occurrence, and if a company could damage the "apparatus of a company for the time being regarded as an enemy, it was accounted an achievement of great merit." Sometimes volunteer firemen turned in false alarms or started small fires to keep up their company's *esprit de corps* by providing an opportunity for group action.[23]

Maintaining this *esprit de corps* made many volunteer companies resemble gangs more than public service organizations by the 1830s. As the city's elite gradually lost influence among the volunteers, rowdy elements gained majorities in many companies, and the *raison d'etre* of some volunteer units seemed to be drinking, fighting and racing rather than extinguishing fires. David Kay, an axeman of the period, remembered that the South Side's (then Birmingham's) Hydraulic Company "was no fire company; it was just a lot of young rascals who ran with the machine, fought one another and the other companies, and squirted more water on the spectators for the fun of the thing than on the fire."[24] William G. Johnston, a volunteer during the 1840s, agreed. In "every organization of firemen," he wrote, "a rowdy element managed to get a foothold, and it was ever the delight of this class to keep a pot of strife boiling." This rowdy element, which Johnston took pains to differentiate from the companies' respectable middle and upper class members, believed that "fighting was no small part of the duties of a fireman."[25]

In this light, the brothel dousing appears to be an attempt by the volunteer companies to rehabilitate their public image. To deflect criticism from their own questionable practices, some volunteers took the objectionable leisure of others to task, satisfying both the community's desire for moral reform and their own inclination for property destruction and riotous behavior. By channeling their propensity for rowdiness into a socially acceptable crusade, Pittsburgh's volunteers showed the city that despite their shortcomings, they were still public-spirited citizens and guardians of the community's physical and moral safety.

The acquiescence of Alexander Hay, Pittsburgh's mayor, as well as some other leading citizens, to the brothel dousings illuminates another aspect of urban change: the development of municipal government in the face of population growth and expanded suffrage. As several newspaper accounts pointed out, Hay's attempts to stop the dousings and to prevent further incidents were half-hearted at best. The *Morning Chronicle* reported that it knew

> on good authority, that a member of the Select Council, who was present at the late attack on the "Crow's Nest," spoke in favor of giving the inmates of that house "a good drenching," and that the Mayor of the city objected *only* to the throwing of stones at the house, and not to the original flooding that it received.[26]

Charles Dawson also noted that attacks on the brothels were "winked at by the authorities," and that at one such dousing, "one of the leading citizens of the times held the nozzle under the supposition that there ought to be a fire in the den if there was not." Further, at an 8 June meeting of firemen convened to deny charges of riot and dereliction of duty, Hay and other prominent citizens lent their un-limited support to the volunteers.[27] This support for vigi-lante justice appears misplaced unless it is examined in the context of Pittsburgh's governmental development.

At issue in the early 1840s was the emergence of the office of mayor as a powerful political post, especially in relation to the Select and Common Councils. During Pitts-burgh's town and borough days, the councils were ad-equate to govern its citizens, and even after incorporation in 1816 the newly created position of mayor lacked any real power. The Councils' motivation in appointing a mayor—the mayor was selected by Council from the city's aldermen until 1834, when he was popularly elected—was judicial convenience, not administrative necessity. For many years the mayor's chief duty was presiding over the Mayor's Court, a judicial body intended to reduce the Court of Quarter Session's unmanageably large case loads.[28]

Charismatic young mayors like Jonas R. McClintock and Samuel Pettigrew altered this arrangement in the 1830s by exercising civic leadership and effecting needed reforms in the rapidly growing city. In the process, they gained popular favor and support, thereby enhancing the mayor's political position in relation to the councils. After the shift to popular election in 1834, many citizens, particularly workers, threw their new electoral weight behind mayoral and council candidates who courted their support. Prominent among these citizens were the city's firemen. In 1838, for example, a "meeting of the Firemen and Citizens" nominated William Little, a young Pittsburgh businessman, for mayor. A shocked Pittsburgh *Gazette* reported that "our city presents this remarkable spectacle, of the 'Firemen of the city,' most of them very young, and some of them little more than boys, nominating a candidate for the chief magistracy of the city and the candidate accepting."[29] If the nomination seemed remarkable, the election must have been astounding: Little won in a close election, apparently largely due to the firemen's votes. Whatever their age, experience or conduct, the firemen could no longer be ignored as political force in the city.

The firemen's emergent political clout brings Mayor Hay's actions in the brothel dousings and their aftermath into clearer focus. Changes in the police force were the responsibility of the combined councils' Police Committee; the mayor's function was largely to approve the Committee's choice. A few months before the brothel dousings, however, "Mayor Hay undertook to assert his power to act independently of councils in the choice of night-watchmen" by rejecting their choice for chief of the watch. The Police Committee, through City Solicitor Andrew J. ("Mandamus") Wiley, took Hay to court and forced him to accept the councils' choice. This failed attempt to enhance mayoral power, the *Mercury* noted, was "to the last degree mortifying to the Mayor and those political bigots whose humble instrument he is."[30]

In the wake of this defeat, Hay and his supporters sought new ways to enhance their power and discredit their opponents in the councils. Supporting the fire companies' actions filled the bill admirably. Hay capitalized on his popularity with the city's firemen—before his tenure as mayor he had been president of the Eagle Engine and Hose Company and Second Chief Engineer of the city's Fireman's Association[31]—and also discredited the police force appointed by council. Hay and his supporters, the firemen, and two Pittsburgh papers laid the blame for the dousings squarely at the door of the police and their Council superiors. The *Chronicle* of 10 June, for example, opposed "mob-law" but emphasized that "we consider those who, having the law to protect them in so doing, have neglected to suppress the houses of ill-fame, . . . as much more culpable than those who destroyed them without law." A few days later, the *Chronicle* went even further, contending that the police themselves had instigated the riots.[32] The brothel dousing, then, was more than nostalgia for a simpler, more familiar form of communal action: it was also a salvo in the unfolding political struggle for control of Pittsburgh's developing municipal government. In addition, it was a denial that class formation and expanded suffrage had altered Pittsburgh's social and political relations, for it joined prominent citizens and common firemen in a united defense of traditional community values.

The suitability of the brothel dousings to this purpose reflected still another aspect of urban change in Pittsburgh: the increasing presence of racial and ethnic minority groups in the city. The attacks on Blind Sam's and the Crow's Nest were attempts at moral reform, but were also expressions of hostility toward the Germans, blacks and Irish who comprised much of Pittsburgh's growing lower class. Brothels and disorderly houses were numerous in Pittsburgh; the firemen might have attacked any number of such establishments, but they chose the two most glaring examples involving objectionable minorities. The minority aspect was important, for it allowed Pittsburghers the fiction that alien cultures, and not internal social and economic processes, were responsible for the perceived increase in immorality.

Accounts of Pittsburgh vice and crime commonly reported and emphasized the ethnic and racial characteristics of participants. An account of a fight at Blind Sam's published in March 1842, for example, reported in detail the occupations and ethnicity of the combatants; disturbances at the Crow's Nest earlier in the year yielded court testimony of "scenes of amalgamation that would have disgraced a slave plantation." Reporting on the brothel dousing itself, the *Morning Chronicle* observed that the Crow's Nest was owned by Hannah Murphy, who kept a grog-shop downstairs, and occupied by "the Irish nagur and a degraded *white* woman, who lives with him as his wife, together with such females as can be induced to live in such a sink of filth and wretchedness—amalgamation and crime!" Even the *Manufacturer*, which was hostile to the mob action, noted puckishly that the "purifiers" of the Crow's Nest made "Molly Murphy the 'Irish Nigger,' the 'Bay Nigger,' & every other kind of niggers fly from the premises in quick time."[33] The dousings' appeal to a public nostalgic for a simpler, more homogeneous community, and to office-seekers eager to make political hay, lay partly in their targets: the city's disdained—and feared—minority groups. Support of the firemen's actions by community and government thus expressed both a denial that the community had changed and anger at the groups whose presence seemed to threaten change.

The brothel dousings revealed a city struggling with the problems generated by urban growth and change, but they also demonstrated the impracticality of clinging to out-moded methods of addressing those problems. The firemen's vigilantism was acceptable as long as it served the public interest and partook of the leisure, social club ethos of the volunteer companies; this was not long the case. On the night of 4 June, three days after the first dousing of Blind Sam's, the seductiveness of mob rule overpowered whatever good intentions the purifiers had originally had. That night the city witnessed the "crowning scene of this mob purification," in the destruction by fire of 17 buildings in the Fifth Ward for the purpose of "punishing a Mrs. Turney, who kept a disorderly house in the neighborhood." Though the city's firemen later vehemently denied any complicity in or knowledge of the affair, it appears that some volunteers set a fire at Mrs. Turney's, which spread rapidly and destroyed the homes of 22 "poor but honest" families. Even more damning was the report that during the blaze, *"none of these firemen,* except a few attached to the Niagara, used any exertions to arrest its progress."[34]

If the brothel dousings and their destructive climax pointed to the urgent need for professional police and fire services in Pittsburgh, they also revealed the tenacity with which its residents were clinging to past methods of protecting the community. As the riots, races and other excesses of the volunteer fire system grew worse,[35] the understaffed police force proved unable to suppress them. Some Pittsburghers began to call for abolition of the volunteer system and the establishment of a professional fire bureau. This proposal evoked acrimonious rejection from many quarters: the *Iron City*, for example, insisted that the devotion of volunteers was inherently superior to the efforts of mere "hirelings."[36] Despite frequent problems with both fire and police departments and numerous failed efforts at reform, Pittsburghers retained volunteer fire companies and an inadequate city watch until the late 1860s,[37] when large territorial additions forced them to realize that their city was no longer the small town their ancestors had known.

3

Mobility and a Catastrophic Event
Who Moves After the Town Burns Down?

Robert M. Preston

As Richard Jensen has pointed out, American social historians are perhaps concentrating a disproportional amount of time, energy and attention on a very small segment of the population—that is, the large city, urban population.[1] The cities of Philadelphia, Pennsylvania; Salem, Massachusetts; Kingston, New York; Pittsburgh, Pennsylvania and Poughkeepsie, New York have all been scrutinized in major studies that have contributed much to our knowledge of nineteenth century urban life. But each of these cities had an 1860 population of 13,000 or more, and each was among the 75 largest cities in America. The problem with concentrating upon such populous areas is that less than 15 percent of the population in 1860 lived in such places.[2] If historians are to understand America in the twentieth century, the appreciation of the urban experience is imperative. Thus, to study cities *is* important. But to understand the experience of the majority of the American population in the late nineteenth century, to understand the many and not just the few, one must study small towns and rural areas.

This study is concerned with the massive geographical mobility that Emmitsburg, Maryland experienced between the 1860 census year and the 1870 census year. Emmitsburg, a town in northcentral Maryland, with an 1860 population of less than 1,000, experienced a great fire in 1863. The ultimate question is: did this small town experience a massive geographical immigration because of the same factors that urban historians have found to be operative in large cities at this time, or did this town experience this migration due to the catastrophic event of a great fire?

The Battle of Gettysburg was fought along the Emmitsburg Road during July 1863. The town of Emmitsburg, just eight miles to the south, saw numerous Union and Confederate troops pass through its streets before and after the Gettysburg Campaign. The summer of 1863, however, was remembered for years by the Emmitsburg townspeople as a dreadful time, not because of the bloody battle, but because of the great fire of Emmitsburg.

The fire started in the loft of the Beam and Guthrie Livery Stable about 11:00 P.M. on Monday, 15 June 1863.[3] According to town gossip, the fire was the work of an arsonist, the "mean devil" Eli Smith.[4] The fire spread eastward along Main Street until it reached the town's square and then continued for two blocks, jumped Main Street and then burned westward toward the square again. This left three of the four corners of the town's square blackened by the fire. In all, 28 houses and nine business establishments were damaged or destroyed.

The last structure to burn was the town's largest hotel. This hotel, along with a few other inns in Emmitsburg, were integral parts of the town's economy.[5] Emmitsburg, a rural preindustrial town of 973 persons in 1860, was situated along one of the main commercial arteries between the growing industrial city of Baltimore and Pittsburgh, one of America's gateways to the agricultural west. Many wagons coming from the east and west stopped at Emmitsburg in the 1860s. Nineteen percent of the town's workers were employed in transportation as wagonmakers, wheelwrights, blacksmiths, saddlers and drivers.[6]

Not only did the fire interrupt this economic life of the town, but its affect on individuals was awesome. About 20 percent of the town's population—128 persons—were victimized by the fire through loss of homes, furnishings, farm animals, business inventories or business establishments. Forty-two fire victims who were property owners suffered loses totaling almost $82,000, or 22 percent of the value of all the property (real and personal) owned by citizens of Emmitsburg in 1860.[7]

After raging all night, the fire was finally brought under control after dawn with the help of the townspeople and students from nearby Mount Saint Mary's College and Seminary. Wet blankets were placed on the roof of the building on the only corner of the square that did not burn; this was credited with containing the fire.[8] Emmitsburg did not yet have a municipal water system; instead a common well in the town square served as the water source for firefighters.

Migration from Emmitsburg caused the town's population to fall 27 percent, from 973 in 1860 to 706 in 1870. That decline, however, represents more than simply 267 persons leaving Emmitsburg in the decade of the 1860s. By tracing the adult males listed in the 1860 census, we find that 71 percent of them do not reappear in the 1870 census. If we can assume that the entire population was moving in a manner similar to that of the adult male population, then we can calculate the minimum number of persons who moved in and out of Emmitsburg in the 1860s.

As 71 percent of the adult males left Emmitsburg during the 1860s out of a population of 973, this means that 691 persons would have left Emmitsburg in the 1860s, and 424 had to move into Emmitsburg for the population to reach 706 by 1870. Thus 1,115 persons moved in and out of Emmitsburg in the decade. This is only an estimated minimum, because those who moved in and out between the census years (as did seven of the property—owning fire victims) are not considered.

This massive 1860s migration of Emmitsburg townspeople, however, included only a minority of those who were directly affected by the great fire. Presumably, one would think, since the town experienced a massive migration, the victims of the fire would surely be numbered among the migrants. After tracing the history of the 32 families who were present in Emmitsburg in 1860 and who were victimized by the great fire, one finds that less than a third (31 percent) actually left Emmitsburg within seven years after the fire. This is contrasted sharply with the nearly three-quarters (71 percent) of the town's adult population as a whole who left.

The 69 percent of the fire victims who remained in Emmitsburg throughout the 1860s had reported the value of their property to be $45,400 in the 1860 census. In the 1863 fire, they lost $32,900 worth of that property, or 72 percent of their 1860 property. Despite this huge loss, though, they remained. Beyond this, a comparison of the fire victims to the population of the town as a whole suggests that the victims possessed certain social and economic characteristics that may have led them to see a bright future in Emmitsburg, even while they were standing in the smoldering embers of their ruined past.

After applying the same mobility methodology to the study of Emmitsburg in the 1860s that other historians have applied to the analysis of mobility in cities,[9] such as Pittsburgh, Salem, Boston, Newburyport, etc., it becomes obvious that social and economic factors, rather than the great fire, were the dominant causes of geographical mobility in Emmitsburg in the 1860s.[10] Occupation, wealth and familial status have all previously been identified as characteristics that distinguished those people who left a city or town from those who remained.[11]

During the 1860s in Emmitsburg there was, first of all, a similarity between the adult male fire victim who remained and the adult males in the population as a whole who remained. Table 1 shows that both a majority of these fire victims and these adult males in the town were generally heads of households and property owners.

Table 1:
PERSISTENCY RATE, EMMITSBURG DURING THE 1860S
(PERCENTAGES)

	Adult male fire victims who remained	*All adult males in town who remained*
Heads of Household	100	55
Property Owners	77	58

The similarity between the adult male fire victims who remained and all adult males in Emmitsburg in the 1860s who remained is also demonstrated in Table 2. In each category—property owners whose property was valued in excess of $1,000, in excess of $500, less than $500, and the average value of real property—the adult male fire victims

Table 2:
PROPERTY OWNERSHIP AND VALUE, 1860 ADULT MALE HEADS OF HOUSEHOLD
(PERCENTAGES IN FIRST FOUR GROUPS)

Property Value	*Fire victims who remained*	*Townspeople who*	
		Remained	*Left*
Owned Property in Excess of $1,000	41	33	10
Owned Property in Excess of $500	55	48	17
Owned Property Less than $500	45	36	62
Owned Real Property Less than $500	50	44	73
Average Value of Real Property Owned	$2,814	$3,752	$1,255

are more similar to all adult males who remained than they are to the adult males who left the town.

There is also a similarity between the fire victims who remained and all adult males in the town who remained with regard to occupation classification. Of the fire victims who remained, 84 percent were professional or skilled workers. There were farmers, doctors, druggists, teachers, justices of the peace, merchants, tavern owners, shoemakers, carpenters, hatters, wheelwrights, plasterers, machinists and blacksmiths among them. In the town population in general, these were the types of workers that produced the highest persistency rates. In fact, 40 percent of all professionals, merchants, farmers, clerical and skilled workers remained in Emmitsburg in the 1860s. On the other hand, only 17 percent of the semiskilled and unskilled workers and unemployed remained. Again, the characteristics of the fire victims who stayed in Emmitsburg match those of the adult males in the population as a whole who stayed more closely than those of the townspeople who left Emmitsburg.

The minority of fire victims who left within the 1860s, and thus joined the majority of townspeople on the road out of Emmitsburg, were in some ways similar to the fire victims who remained. They too were property owners, heads of households, and numbered among the ranks of the skilled craftsmen and professionals. As such, it may appear that they "should have" stayed in Emmitsburg, if social and economic factors were indeed dominant, rather than the catastrophic fire, as the cause for migration. But a sampling of the circumstances faced by the fire victims who left suggest that even strong social and economic factors are occasionally overridden.

Daniel Wile, for instance, had been the owner of the large hotel on the square, the last structure to burn in the fire. If he concluded that Emmitsburg was a jinx for him, most would agree. He, his wife, Mary, and their children, Anna and Henry, moved to Emmitsburg in the 1850s. His family continued to grow, but his luck did not. In 1856 or 1857, Wile purchased the City Hotel. A few days after the purchase, the former owner and he were examining a gun. The gun accidentally discharged, and Wile was shot through the neck. After recovering, he decided to raze the hotel and build a new four-story structure. Four years later the great fire of Emmitsburg destroyed it, causing $10,000 worth of damage.[12] Wile, then, joined the majority of townspeople who were leaving Emmitsburg.

Some fire victims who left soon returned to the town. George Beam, for instance, whose farm animals and horses were destroyed in the stable where the fire started, left Emmitsburg after the fire, but he returned during the 1870s and continued his livery stable business into the twentieth century.[13] Another who returned was William Patterson, a medical doctor whose office was on one of the three corners of the town square that was destroyed. He was 61 years old at the time of the fire. Soon after leaving Emmitsburg, he returned in the 1870s and died there in 1876.[14]

Joshua Shorb is counted among those who left after the fire, but more than likely he did not leave *because of* the fire. He incurred a $4,000 loss when the fire destroyed his machine shop and foundry. But he rebuilt his business and not until 1868, four years after the fire, did he move his business to Westminster, a town east of and much larger than Emmitsburg.[15]

Some, like Charles Shorb, did seem to leave town in response to the catastrophe. Charles Shorb was just 31 at the time of the fire, but he and his wife had amassed considerable wealth, most of it invested in his store's inventory. In the fire he lost $12,000, or one-half of his 1860 wealth. Shorb and his wife, in fact, lost more than any other fire victims. This may have motivated them to leave the town that had given them a fortune, and then misfortune.[16]

But Charles Shorb and a few others were quite clearly in the minority. Most with social and economic backgrounds similar to Shorb's remained in town throughout the 1860s, whether or not they had been fire victims.

To explain why certain fire victims left Emmitsburg and

others did not, we should consider a possible economic reason: the type of property loss each victim suffered. About the same proportion of those who left had lost houses in comparison to those who remained; however, one-half of those who left had lost their business establishments and inventories in the fire, as opposed to less than a quarter of those who remained. Because so few of the fire victims left, the sample may be too small to draw any definitive conclusions. But paying attention to such an economic factor as the type of property lost would be wise in other studies of catastrophes. The fact remains, nonetheless, that the majority of fire victims remained, and at the same time matched the social and economic characteristics of those in the population as a whole who remained in Emmitsburg during the 1860s.

In his dramatic conclusion to his section on the great fire, James A. Helman, author of the 1906 *History of Emmitsburg, Maryland*, wrote: "Oh, the desolation a fire makes; most of the people lost their all, and never recovered."[17] Helman was a 23-year-old resident of Emmitsburg at the time of the great fire. It is difficult, and perhaps presumptuous, for a historian over a century after the event to say that an eyewitness was wrong. But the evidence, I believe, supports my conclusion.

Of the 42 who lost property in the fire, most lost much, and most recovered. Or, at least most of those who remained in the town recovered. By 1870, just seven years after the fire, three- quarters of those who had stayed in Emmitsburg were doing as well or better than they had been in 1860, according to the value of their property. By 1870, only two people who had remained seem to have suffered unrecoverable losses.

The personal progress each fire victim would have experienced in the 1860s if the fire had not occurred can never be known. But with the use of the mobility methodology that social historians have developed in recent decades, the *actual* progress the fire victims did experience can be known. The great fire of Emmitsburg was not a major factor causing people to move out of the town.

Instead, as the above evidence indicates, social position, such as one's occupation, and status as a property owner were dominant factors in determining whether individuals, regardless of having personally suffered the tragedy of a catastrophe, would remain or leave their home town.

This study is obviously indebted to the host of social historians who developed mobility methodology used here. Most of these social historians who have done mobility studies—Clyde and Sally Griffen, Peter Knights and many others—have analyzed growing industrial urban centers with massive immigrant populations. Oddly, some of the same social and economic causes of migration that these researchers of large, industrial, immigrant-crowded cities discovered were also operative in at least one small, preindustrial, rural town, whose population was 97 percent native-born. And, most importantly, these factors were even operative in the face of a major catastrophe, such as the 1863 great fire of Emmitsburg, Maryland.

This similarity between large cities, which have been brilliantly researched, and this small town, however, should not lead one to conclude that whatever is true for Boston and Philadelphia is necessarily true for every small town. Social historians need to study the small towns and their surrounding areas of late nineteenth century America, for that is where most Americans lived in that era. Indeed, no history of nineteenth century America will be complete until the history of America's small towns is more adequately known.

4

Beyond the Great City
Finding and Defining the Small City in Nineteenth Century America

Maureen Ogle

It is a truism that the history of nineteenth century urban America has been writ large; that is, the nation's largest cities have received the lion's share of historians' attentions. Small cities have been treated as dusty hamlets in which nothing ever happens and from which everyone longs to escape. Certainly it is true that in the last 30 years of the nineteenth century the majority of American urbanites lived in a handful of large cities. It is also true, however, that most cities were small, with populations under 20,000. This larger class of cities has received little attention from historians, but to ignore this facet of the American landscape is to pass over important features of America's urban experience, and thus to obscure the actual texture of its past.[1]

A case in point is the nationwide drive to develop municipal services that took place at the end of the nineteenth century. Historians have devoted much attention to this phenomenon, especially to its social, political and technological aspects. That attention, however, has been skewed largely toward the nation's largest cities. Municipalities with populations of 15,000 or less have received scant attention. That slant toward the large is unfortunate, for surely a story remains to be told about the small cities, too. In the last third of the previous century, small communities such as Boone, Iowa; Shreveport, Louisiana; Billings, Montana and Stockton, California, developed police and fire departments, sewer networks, waterworks and the like. If nothing else, the national scope and simultaneity of the phenomenon rouses interest, especially when one considers the ways in which historians have explained city-building in the large metropolises.[2]

There, the argument goes, the pressures of immigration, industrialization, rapid growth, pollution, crime, poverty and disease propelled municipal officials to respond with a host of urban services. Scholars have argued, for example, that the problem of overcrowding, coupled with new ideas about disease prevention, prompted Americans to build waterworks. Similarly, tightly packed wooden buildings plus rowdy gangs of hooligan volunteer firefighters caused the emergence of "professional" fire departments. Others claim that urban crowding and resulting pollution led urbanites to build large sewer systems.[3]

While these explanations may have validity for the histories of the nation's largest cities, they lack both potency and cogency when applied wholesale to the history of late nineteenth century urban America. Overcrowding, disease and industrialization—often cited as explanations for the national drive to build waterworks in the 1870s and 1880s—are not valid when applied to a small city like Shreveport, which built water works when its population was under 10,000. Similarly, the use of "rowdyism" to explain the emergence of professional and semiprofessional fire departments does not fit the case of Boone, Iowa, a city of less than 5,000 people, which organized a fire department without any evidence that rowdy volunteers threatened the safety of the city. Thus it may be that explanations for the emergence of municipal services in the big cities do not fit the histories of small cities.[4]

Put another way, there may be more to late century city-building than has so far met the eye. This essay will examine nineteenth century American ideas about "city," especially the relationship between small cities and large, and, using the examples of three small Iowa municipalities, suggest possible lines of research for small city history.

Certainly the great cities have played an important role in
America's social, political and economic history. But both
then and now, life in the nation's metropolises has been
far removed from the lives of millions of Americans who
have lived in small cities. A complete history of urban
America should address the milieu in which those people
have lived; as it is written now, that history obscures much
of its own complexity.

Defining Nineteenth Century Cities

A discussion of the development of municipal services
in these small cities may make more sense if first placed
within a general context of nineteenth century views of the
city. Throughout the century, Americans embraced a series
of changing ideas about and attitudes toward their cities.
Prior to the late 1830s, for example, Americans regarded
municipalities as all of a piece; charters, granted on a case-
by-case basis by state legislatures, endowed these corporations with more or less similar collections of broad police
powers. Typically these powers enabled cities to keep the
peace, to abate nuisances, and in general to act so as to
prevent chaos from disrupting the normal pursuit of private
enterprise. But beginning in the late 1830s and continuing
throughout the 1840s and 1850s, officials in some very
large cities petitioned state legislatures for an expansion of
those powers, in order to cope with what residents perceived as an ongoing state of chaos that threatened the
equilibrium of their cities.[5]

People of the time blamed this situation on immigrants,
immorality, disease, crime and poverty. None of these
problems was particularly new: since colonial times
American cities had faced poverty, crowded living conditions, crime, street filth and moral corruption.[6] What was
new in the mid-nineteenth century was the use of the
municipal corporation as an agency to cope with those ills
on a permanent basis. Expanded police and taxation powers enabled cities such as New York, Boston and Cincinnati

to support full-time police and fire departments, clean the physical city, and provide expanded charity services such as almshouses. However, contemporaries discovered these so-called "social evils" *only* in large metropolises: not every city required or asked for the kinds of legal and judicial powers granted to that special class of urban communities. It seemed that the mid-century malaise of urban chaos struck only the nation's largest cities and set those cities apart from others.[7]

At mid-century, as some cities demanded and received expanded municipal powers, some states also began altering the manner in which legislatures dealt with municipalities. Beginning in the 1850s, some states abandoned the practice of individual municipal incorporation and instead passed general incorporation laws, among them, Ohio in 1852; Iowa, 1858; Indiana, 1857; Kansas, 1859 and Pennsylvania, 1851. General incorporation acts allowed legislatures to forego the practice of writing special act legislation every time a new city was created or an old one demanded greater powers, since the acts spelled out exactly what powers were available to cities. These acts signified both the existence of a shared view of what constituted a "city" and the recognition that a city was a distinct element in society, different from, for example, the country and farm. Individual incorporation acts were no longer necessary because people had embraced a common view of what a city was and what powers it should have, regardless of where the city was located.[8]

As importantly, beginning in the 1850s and continuing throughout the century, many states formalized these distinctions among cities by enacting statutes delineating various classes of cities based on population, and granting specific powers to each. For example, the general incorporation acts for Ohio and Iowa established classes of cities. The Iowa law recognized three classes: those with populations of 15,000 and over comprised the first class; those with populations of 2,000–15,000 comprised second class cities; municipal corporations with populations under 2,000 were designated as towns. All three categories shared a general body of broad police powers, but first and second class municipalities enjoyed additional powers, different not only from those given to towns, but also from each other. For example, the law empowered cities of both classes—but not towns—to establish boards of health, police and fire companies, and markets. In addition, first class cities received extra powers in order to cope with the special problems posed by large numbers of people. The law authorized cities of that class to appoint boards of trustees to oversee public waterworks, superintend street work and improvements, establish "infirmaries" and "houses" of work, refuge, or corrections for the poor and to erect city prisons. Towns and second class cities, in theory unburdened by those problems, did not receive these powers.[9]

Iowa and Ohio were not alone. An 1874 Pennsylvania law recognized three classes of cities, as differentiated from towns. An 1877 Missouri law recognized four classes of cities. By the mid-1870s, Illinois, Minnesota and Kansas also had passed such laws; other states followed later.[10] These laws reflected a mid- to late century belief that even if the city differed from the farm, not all cities were alike, either: cities with many people faced different and more problems than smaller cities. That may seem like an obvious statement of affairs—as cities get bigger, problems arise—but in fact this explicit recognition, expressed in state law, indicates that Americans now perceived cities differently than they had earlier. That new view included the belief that cities were not all alike, and therefore should be treated differently.

Not surprisingly, then, during the last third of the century when Americans discerned yet another and different municipal crisis, these distinctions of size played a significant role. This new urban crisis had two faces: on the one hand, large cities—magnets for industry and commerce, immigrants and migrants, the poor and the rich—faced growth, crowding, pollution and social disorder. In short, they presented Americans with an unprecedented political and social challenge. On the other hand, efforts to cope with this challenge—by building or expanding municipal services such as waterworks, sewer systems, fire and police departments, and so forth—spawned an era of unprecedented political corruption and governmental mismanagement. Indeed, by the 1860s and 1870s, the administration of government in great cities had itself come to constitute a serious problem, one to which reformers addressed themselves with some vigor. Criticisms centered on the failure of city leaders to provide efficiently services that just a few decades earlier no city government would have been expected to offer.[11]

While the late nineteenth century era of bosses, political machines and reform movements in the United States has been well documented by historians, those reports seldom note that it was not cities per se that reformers decried, but rather a special class of municipalities, sometimes called the great cities, unique instances of political organization whose size and commercial influence made their "arrangement and management ... the most important of all the problems of social science."[12] By singling out this group of cities as especially problem-prone, contemporaries again acknowledged the existence of other classes of cities, namely those with smaller populations and fewer problems. Great cities, it seemed, were exceptional—and problematic—instances of political and legal organization, and therefore different from small cities. The reason was clear: residents of small cities and towns, their community life unburdened by a "swarm" of foreigners and incompetent voters, their characters untainted by the heterogeneity of the great city, simply did not face the kinds of problems to which great cities seemed naturally to give rise.[13]

In the 1870s and after, therefore, as Americans faced this new urban crisis and the need for reform, they focused on the serious problems of mismanagement in the great cities, rather than on cities in general. It was still possible to look to the nation's small cities and towns as workshops, clean slates, in which city services could be created and public works built in an atmosphere free of corruption. Indeed, some saw the small city or town—sometimes labeled the "country" and "suburb"—as the hope of the nation, offering an antidote to the corrupted atmosphere that plagued the great cities.[14] Only in the country could real homes be made, away from the brutal commercial hustle and bustle of city life. The city was for commerce; the country was— or could be—for living. In small cities and towns, "truth, purity, the holiest affects, the highest charities and healthful culture . . . united with a simplicity of life scarcely possible" in great cities, wrote Susan F. Cooper in *Putnam's Magazine.* "Today," she continued, "he is wise who goes to the city as to a market, but has a home in the country."[15]

Thus if the great cities wallowed in a morass of corruption and incompetence, the small town remained the workshop of American democracy. However, the fact that large cities received so much attention and dominated the concerns of reformers does not mean that small municipalities were themselves free from strife. Rather, as one observer noted in 1873, the problems facing great cities were "radically different" than those of small cities and towns. In particular, residents of small cities struggled with the problem of growth in a competitive economy. By the 1870s hundreds of small municipalities dotted the land, with more being created all the time as Americans moved west. As miles of railroad track wove the United States into an increasingly interconnected hub-hinterland complex, small towns and cities competed fiercely with each other and with larger metropolises for rail connections, manufacturing and people. The survival of small municipalities depended on their ability to attract and retain both people and industry, and to build reputations that set them apart from their counterparts just down the road. "Boards of trade," usually comprised of local businessmen, organized promotional efforts and recruited industry. Local "improvement societies" urged a general overhaul of village and town, in order to render life there more amenable and to prevent would-be migrants from moving to larger and more modern cities.[16]

It was in this context, then, during the 1870s and 1880s

that hundreds of small towns all over the United States sought to replicate the kinds of services that larger cities had begun offering during the 1840s and 1850s. Cities that prospered were those that offered a variety of amenities— adequate fire and police protection, paved sidewalks and streets, an abundant supply of pure water. Indeed, it seemed that no small town could hope to compete in the marketplace of cities unless it, too, offered citylike "improvements." It was not the need to combat "social evils" in the form of overcrowding, epidemics and rising crime rates that motivated the spate of city improvement in the small towns, but rather the desire to offer a variety of modern city services in order to create economic and population growth. In fact, it was the *desire for*, rather than the problems *created by*, growth that absorbed these cities in the late nineteenth century. A brief look at the case of three small Iowa communities will demonstrate the nature of the small city dilemma in the last third of the nineteenth century.

DEVELOPING URBAN SERVICES IN THREE SMALL CITIES

Iowa City, Marshalltown and Boone all had 1890 populations of 10,000 or under. Settled in the 1840s, late 1850s and 1860s, respectively, by the late 1860s all three had been designated as second class cities.[17] Two sat on rivers, and all three benefited from railroad service. The three shared a veritable mania for developing municipal services of the very kind that were proving so problematic in the great cities: within two decades beginning about 1870, city officials and voters in all three—either through direct action or by using municipal authority to aid private developers—built pressurized waterworks; developed hierarchical, semiprofessional fire and police departments; erected street lights; paved city streets and built city-wide sewer systems. They did so as a way to spur local development, in order to prevent their communities from becoming, as one Boone resident put it, "small way station[s] in the map of Iowa."[18]

The development of firefighting and water supply services illustrates this phenomenon. During the 1860s, when
fire erupted, men and women rushed to the scene and
worked together in ad hoc bucket brigades, hauling water
from cisterns or wells to flames, while others carried goods
from burning buildings. In the 1860s none of the three
cities owned much in the way of firefighting equipment:
Iowa City had a hand-operated pump truck, and all three
had a few ladders and buckets. Each city had passed "fire
ordinances" aimed at regulating the materials used in
constructing buildings, stoves and chimneys in the city
center. Thus, locals organized firefighting on an emergency-
to-emergency basis, and the municipal government played
only a minimal role in fire prevention.[19]

During the 1870s these methods of firefighting fell out
of favor. In each of the cities, local residents, city council
members and firefighters alike bemoaned the state of affairs.
A Marshalltown newspaper pleaded for a "fire king, whose
word shall be law at fires. . . ." Without an "efficient head,"
residents stood about at fires, and it was impossible to
move them toward "anything like an organized effort." In
Iowa City, too, residents and newspaper editors urged the
city council to act. After one fire that destroyed the only
city hotel, one newspaper lamented that "there was no fire
apparatus, no water, no nothing, and the people could
only fold their arms and watch the devouring element."
The only "proper way" to fight fires, commented one
citizen, was with a force of men supervised by a "com-
petent head," rather than with masses of unorganized
spectators.[20]

Each city acted upon these sentiments; by the mid-1880s,
each city fought fires in a radically different manner.
Bucket brigades had given way to well-trained formations
of men using a large assortment of tools, including hooks
and ladders, hand-pumped and steam engines, axes and
the like. Although firefighters were still volunteers, they
now wore uniforms and functioned in hierarchically organized task-specific companies directed by a chief who
dispensed his orders through a formal chain of command.

A sturdy rope cordoned the fire site, separating firefighters from onlookers, and a uniformed fire police brigade removed goods and protected busy firefighters from "well-meaning but ignorant on-lookers." Signaling systems informed firefighters where the blazes would be found and notified waterworks employees to raise the water pressure. City firefighters belonged to state and national professional organizations, and worked out regularly in practice drills.[21]

The new methods ensured efficiency, regularity and order, the hallmarks of a late nineteenth century up-to-date city. Task-specific firefighting and fire police companies eliminated chaos at fires and made the job of firefighting more effective; alarm signals hastened the firemen to the site; practice drills eliminated disorder. All of these reassured local property and business owners that their investments would be relatively safe, at least safer than if firefighters relied on informal bucket brigades. An efficient and permanent firefighting force boosted the cities' reputations, and was perceived as an attractive inducement to potential settlers and investors. As importantly, however, at no time did the three cities see semiprofessional formal fire departments as a solution to problems of volunteer rowdyism; indeed, prior to the formation of the hierarchical organization described above, the only complaints both townspeople and firefighters alike had about local fire services were that they lacked efficiency and were not in keeping with what one could expect in an up-to-date city.[22]

The construction of water supplies followed much the same path. During the 1870s, residents of Iowa City, Boone and Marshalltown gradually rejected the use of cisterns and wells; digging wells, noted one Iowa City newspaper, was "the work of villages. ... Waterworks is the work of a city." A Marshalltown newspaper prodded locals to act, arguing that water would reduce fire hazards and insurance rates, as well as promote "cleanliness, health and comfort, and manufacturing interests." Acting on the belief that an ample and reliable supply of water would attract industry, by the mid-1880s the cities had expanded both the supply of public water and the uses for which it was intended. By that date, each city had abandoned its publicly owned wells and cisterns in favor of centralized waterworks stations. Now water intended for firefighting, industry and domestic use traveled through a citywide network of pipes, mains and hydrants. Full-time works managers and employees kept the plants operating and ensured a steady supply of water. First bells, then telegraph wires, and finally a telephone connected the waterworks to firehouses. Night or day, winter or summer, firefighters could expect to have water. Without reliable supplies, the city could not guarantee local property owners, or prospective owners, that their investments would be safe from disaster.[23]

More importantly, each city expanded the range of uses for a public water supply. City councils used water to flush creeks and sewer trenches, and to remove the wastes of hotels and breweries, making it easier for those small local industries to function. They also promised a bonus of free piped water to industries willing to locate there. By offering more than a collection of cisterns and wells, these three cities made important strides to ensure their own survival. The important point, however, is that a citywide waterworks system did not alleviate prior problems of polluted or scarce water supplies; rather it staved them off, thereby, residents believed, ensuring the cities' reputations and facilitating economic growth. Nor did "city" water serve as a solution to rampant disease; rather, residents believed that ample water would prevent disease from creating the havoc it did elsewhere.[24]

These urbanites also added other municipal services so that their cities would more fully reflect contemporary ideas about what constituted an up-to-date "businesslike" city. By the early 1890s, for example, all three cities boasted "permanent" paved streets and sidewalks, electric street lights, uniformed full-time police forces, and citywide sewer systems that replaced the sewer fragments built earlier. "Businesslike" management and government aided the city-building process. Good management resulted from expert advice, such as that given by engineers and "professional" firefighters. Local property and business owners who served on city councils also brought businesslike expertise to municipal government; government by expert was preferable to the kind of corrupt government found in very large cities, where greedy politicians and "rings" had the run of city councils. In addition, local businessmen, in conjunction with the city councils, developed packages of amenities with which to lure various industries, such as meatpackers, rendering plants, oil processing mills and the like. Cities offered tax exemptions to companies that settled within the city borders, promised that water would run regularly, and assured prospective investors that paved streets, regular police service, and efficient firefighting would make the cities safe and healthy sites for business.[25]

By the late 1880s and 1890s, however, municipal services notwithstanding, the belief that small cities differed from large was even more sharply defined than it had been earlier. It had become clear to these Iowans that successful municipal government required not just information and expertise but also an awareness of the small city's limitations. Indeed, residents and lawmakers in the three cities became increasingly self-conscious about those limitations. Two events illustrate this point: the Iowa City fire department's late 1880s efforts to obtain horse-driven trucks for its equipment, and the late 1890s formation of the Iowa League of Municipalities.[26]

In 1887 Iowa Citians attempted to persuade the city council to provide "better facilities" for hauling equipment to fires; what residents wanted were horses to pull the engine and hose wagons. Petitioners from the fire police, from three of the fire companies, and from a specially called citizens' meeting inundated the city council with petitions. Expressing fears that city-owned teams would provide unfair competition to other citizens, the council reluctantly referred the matter to a special committee for further study.[27]

The committee responded with a resounding no, arguing that the city could not maintain "necessary and just control" over the animals and yet allow the fire companies to retain their status as quasi-independent arms of city government.[28] Nor was the threat of fire itself sufficient to sway the council, as petitioners had hoped. In the event of conflagration, noted the report, horse carts would be of little use, and, except for the business section, Iowa City's "detached system of buildings" diminished the possibility of catastrophe. In addition, the committee calculated that only half the city's average of six fires each year occurred at night. Since "customary horse conveyance" was readily available during the day, the committee did not think six fires or less a year justified the enormous expense being demanded.[29]

This last was the telling point. It would be desirable, concluded the report, if the city "control[led] the affairs of a city large enough to need and able to purchase" the equipment requested. State law prohibited second class cities from levying a special tax for the support of fire departments, and the city finances were not up to the task. "Let us not . . . become the laughing stock of the world by trying to swell our fire department to those maintained by cities of many times our population and wealth," urged the council committee.[30]

Clearly, then, there was a limit to just how far the small city could carry its quest for growth. The potential for ridicule itself was sufficient to slow the small city, but the Iowa City council's rejection of the request for horses and wagons implied something more: if the city bit off more than it could chew in terms of city services—and it had clearly heaped its plate full during the 1870s and 1880s— it faced the threat of chaos in management and finances, chaos of the sort that energized municipal reformers in the great cities during the same period. Iowa Citians surely were aware of the ills that troubled their larger counterparts, and these council members apparently wanted none of the same disrupting the progressive serenity of their city. If Iowa Citians had once sought the station their city "ought to fill," for these council members that place had been attained. Striving for more would only lead to problems and threaten the progress that had been made toward establishing a prosperous and up-to-date community.[31]

The Iowa City decision occurred in an atmosphere that was, in fact, becoming increasingly problematic. Ironically, during the 1890s the three cities' success at luring business and developing services finally engendered an "urban crisis" of the sort that historians usually tout as the *cause* for developing municipal services in the large cities. Successful development forced each city to cope with various managerial, technical and financial problems. Large paving and sewer projects strained municipal budgets; utilities management overwhelmed available personnel and local expertise; court decisions and new legislation alternately aided or strangled the process of city-building. Moreover, municipal improvements and the subsequent industrial development spurred by those improvements did not always produce the intended effect. Often lured with free water, local manufacturers polluted streams, wasted water, and forced the cities to expand existing water and sewer systems.[32]

In facing the problems generated by growth, however, the three cities once again followed a path uniquely designed to meet the needs of the small municipality; and, once again, the great city best served the small as a counterexample. In 1898 five Iowa mayors, including those from Iowa City and Marshalltown, attended the second convention of the League of American Municipalities, held in Detroit. Organized by and dedicated to the needs of city officials, the League's object was to allow members to "learn and teach the best practical methods of securing improved public service," and its members focused on information gathering and dissemination, rather than reform.[33]

But even there, it seemed, the differences between the small city and the great loomed large. Marshalltown mayor Frank Pierce recalled later that while the LAM meeting was of the "greatest interest," the Iowa mayors came away "convinced that there was little in common" between the administrative problems and issues facing New York, Chicago, Boston and the other large cities represented at the convention, and those of the cities of Iowa, most of which had populations under 15,000 and only one of which had over 50,000 people. As a result, the five mayors called on their colleagues throughout the state to organize an Iowa "league" within which the state's municipal leaders could discuss the problems and issues peculiar to smaller cities. In October 1898, 35 delegates from 23 Iowa cities gathered in Marshalltown and organized the Iowa League of Municipalities.[34]

The group drafted a constitution declaring its intention to "disseminate information and experience upon, and promote the best methods to be employed in the management of municipal departments" and to pursue legislation advantageous to the state's cities. Not intended as a reform group, the League's primary purpose was the self-education of its members; the goal was to manage city growth and avoid the problems that urban reformers in big cities aimed to solve. Many small Iowa cities could not afford to hire full-time experts to guide city leaders through the process of installing desirable waterworks, electric plants and other urban services. League members proposed to use annual conventions and committees to achieve these aims. Starting in 1900, the Iowa League also published a monthly journal, *Midland Municipalities*, which served as a clearinghouse of information for those leaders. Local and national experts contributed articles that discussed everything from water purification to garbage disposal to street paving. By 1909 almost 200 Iowa cities and towns had joined the League, and municipal leaders in the neighboring states of Nebraska, Minnesota and Kansas had organized similar groups dedicated to the needs of the small city.[35]

By the end of the century, then, these three cities had donned city-like garb and placed themselves firmly within a hierarchy of cities. Between about 1870 and 1890, Boone, Iowa City and Marshalltown underwent radical transformations, not due to rapid growth or industrialization, but due to services such as firefighting and waterworks that residents believed *would engineer such a transformation.* Consequently, city-building efforts took place not in an atmosphere of crisis generated by booming population or rapid industrialization, but within a context of *planned action designed to spur growth.* If there was an urban crisis, it was one engendered by the fear of declining population, or, by the end of the century, one generated by the growth spawned by successful municipal development.[36]

In each case it appears that these urbanites acted in accord with a set of ideas about what a late nineteenth century city should have and what it should do: in an up-to-date city, residents enjoyed paved streets and running water, citywide sewer systems and full-time police protection. The point of obtaining all the "adjuncts which go to make up a first class city, [sic]" as one Iowa Citian phrased it, was to attract manufacturing and industry. That was, claimed a Boone newspaper, the only "firm basis on which a town [could] be built." Or, put another way, the development of city services served as a spur to economic development, rather than as a cure-all for overpopulation, ethnic diversity, disease, bad housing, corruption and the like. What these Iowans demanded from city government in 1890 was quite different from what Iowans had expected in the 1850s and 1860s. Simply put, what they wanted—and got—were the kinds of services and amenities found in the nation's largest metropolises, but without the political chicanery, rampant corruption and inefficiency that plagued the larger cities.[37]

TOWARD A HISTORY OF SMALL CITIES

Obviously the examples of three cities alone do not make the case for a bona fide and distinct small city history. The available evidence indicates, however, that the municipal development process in these three cities was not unusual. For example, in the last quarter of the century, popular magazines and professional journals such as the *Atlantic Monthly*, the *North American Review*, *Harper's* and the American Public Health Association's journal often included articles on the subject of "improvements" in the small cities, serving up fairly technical discussions of waterworks and sewer systems, or reporting on the latest efforts in various "village improvement societies." The more technically oriented journal *Plumber and Sanitary Engineer*, first published in 1878, was a virtual self-help manual for the small city, devoting considerable space to the construction of "public works" in small municipalities. Two characteristics of these articles provide insights into the history of late nineteenth century American cities. First, their authors clearly distinguished between very large cities and the more typically sized city of a few thousand, and second, they expressed the view that small cities could and should be equipped with urban services. This marked a distinct departure from what people had believed about cities several decades earlier.[38]

While evidence from journals is useful, truly substantive documentation must come from the cities themselves. Unfortunately, that evidence is less than abundant, a fact that should surprise no one, since historians rarely consider small cities to be worthy of study. However, the limited evidence available indicates that Boone, Iowa City and Marshalltown were not alone in their endeavors. The 1880 census survey of cities, for example, includes limited information about municipal improvements in a number of small cities nationwide. Census takers found that many municipalities with populations just at or well under 15,000 had already initiated, or were considering implementing, municipal services such as waterworks, formally organized fire and police departments, or citywide sewer systems.

Chattanooga, Tennessee firefighters, for example, worked in task-specific companies with equipment quite similar to that found in the three Iowa cities. In Stockton, California, hydraulic pumps, wells and a reservoir tower provided water service similar to Boone's. Officials in Atchison, Kansas; Rockford, Illinois and Kalamazoo, Michigan all reported that their cities provided police and fire departments as well as waterworks or sewers or both. Evidence beyond the census is both harder to come by and more limited: the few available studies of small cities tend to focus on waterworks, to the exclusion of other services. In the 1880s and with a population just at 10,000, Shreveport residents built a waterworks. The burgeoning municipality of Billings, Montana, also introduced water in that decade, while one observer claimed that Leadville, Colorado had a waterworks as early as the 1870s. Letty Donaldson Anderson has tracked the emergence of waterworks in a number of New England communities. Moses Baker's exhaustive surveys of waterworks indicate that cities with populations as small as 2,000 built works in the last third of the nineteenth century.[39]

Did residents in these other cities share the same motives as the people of Boone, Iowa City and Marshalltown? As yet the evidence is too circumstantial to say. The census takers, for example, recorded only the bare facts, leaving out the emotional, social and economic climate in the cities studied. Moreover, in studies of individual cities, historians often focus not on the services themselves, but on the political wrangling that accompanied their introduction. For the present, then, the available evidence must remain a skeleton of facts; a greater understanding of its meaning requires that historians look beyond the great city to that part of urban America about which little is known.

In the case of the three cities discussed here, however, it appears that, during the last quarter of the century, the creation of municipal services preceded rapid municipal growth, and certainly preceded the kinds of problems that earlier had prompted larger cities to develop similar services. Their example demonstrates, too, that not all cities were New York; the path traveled by the small city was necessarily not the more tortuous one trod by the nation's great cities. If the latter were "conspicuous failures," as one contemporary observer remarked, then the small cities, as exemplified by Boone, Marshalltown and Iowa City, were, to borrow another phrase, "unheralded triumphs." The pattern of development in these three Iowa cities may serve as trailmarkers for possible research into the nature of the emerging late nineteenth century urban system, and the distinct and discrete nature of its components. America, it seemed, was to be a nation of cities, both large and small; so, too, the histories of those cities may be written both large and small.[40]

5

The Other Migration
The Foundations of African American Suburban Settlement, 1880–1930

Leslie E. Wilson
and Valerie S. Hartman

The migration of African Americans from the urban core to the periphery has been a subject of debate for nearly five decades. This debate has focused on the origins of this suburban migration; scholars have suggested several possible dates for its beginning. Based on his examination of the 1920 census, in 1925 Harlan Paul Douglass discovered the presence of blacks in suburbia, but he attributed it to the need for service workers.[1] In 1973, after rediscovering the work of Douglass, Harold Connolly suggested that blacks have always had a suburban presence. It is his contention that African American suburban migration has been a continuous process, but it was not noticed until the late sixties, when the black suburban population increased faster than the migration of all other racial groups.[2] In separate studies, others, including Donald Bogue, Avery Guest, Leo Schnore, Henry Sharp and Reynolds Farley, have challenged these notions, and have suggested that while this process might have begun prior to World War II, true middle-class African American suburbanization did not occur until the late fifties or early sixties as a result of the Civil Rights movement.[3]

Although the process of black urban deconcentration was well established before 1880, the period from 1880 to

1930 is crucial to a greater understanding of this trend. During this era, blacks became a noticeable presence on the city's outer rims. Although this era is generally referred to as the "Great Migration" in reference to the large influx of blacks in cities, suburbia experienced a great migration of its own. In many suburban communities, especially in metropolitan New York, Chicago and Los Angeles, the African American population doubled or tripled between 1900 and 1930. Within this era, African Americans created their own suburban model and left a firm foundation for the next generation of black suburban settlers.

Prior to 1880, the black presence in suburbia was merely a reflection of the evolution of the suburbs. As most American suburbs were not built for the affluent, blacks were typical of their environment. Like average suburbanites, they were poor, not well educated, and toiled as laborers or farmers. Though not a large contingent of the suburban population, blacks settled in numerous suburban communities throughout the nation. They were urban refugees and suburban pioneers, at first seeking the confines of the periphery to escape the reigns of slavery, overbearing slave masters, and urban racism, and later, following emancipation, in search of greater degrees of opportunity and equality.

However, with the development and progression of the "modern suburb" between 1860 and 1880, blacks suddenly were not the social equals of their white counterparts. The modern suburb was the picturesque community designed for the wealthy.[4] Its residents commuted to the cities and chose to live on the urban fringe to escape the ills of the metropolis. As land resided on by the poor was claimed to house the wealthy, effective attempts were made to relocate the black population.

In several regions, particularly in several southern states, suburban areas with visible black populations were annexed by urban governments.[5] Often these suburbs were poor communities with predominantly black populations.

They were annexed amidst fears raised by the adjacent white populations. As a result, black suburbanization declined in the South during the first half of the twentieth century. While there were prosperous African Americans living in distinctive communities, most of these were within the city limits. The remaining predominantly black communities along the urban fringe were not regarded as suburbs. These communities, due to their racial, social and economic status, were referred to as *all-black towns*.[6]

In other regions of the nation, annexation alone did not resolve this problem. Along the developing waterfront— whether it was an ocean, river or lake—blacks were often encouraged to sell their land to speculators at low prices, or were evicted from their rented homes.[7] And in areas where blacks were not perceived as a threat, restrictive covenants and neighborhood property associations were used to limit future black encroachment. Even forms of violence were used to encourage blacks to relocate. As a result, from 1880 to 1900, as the status of suburbia began to change, the lifestyles of those blacks who remained in suburbia were severely altered. However, this suburban growth was never a uniform process. For example, New York's Westchester County grew dramatically from 1880 to 1900. During this period, the white population nearly doubled, increasing from 106,364 to 178,742. The black population more than doubled, rising from 2,585 to 5,318. Across the Hudson River in New Jersey's Bergen County, the white population doubled, but the African American population increased by only 709 blacks. Between 1880 and 1900, astounding increases were also witnessed in Los Angeles County, California. While the county's white population outside of the city of Los Angeles was three times larger by 1900, the county's black population increased over six times in the first decade, and nearly doubled in the next ten years.[8]

Nationally, there was a great shift toward the periphery by both blacks and whites. Yet, though masked by the larger numbers reflecting the growth of the white population, in many locations the black population was increasing at an even faster rate. By 1900, there were several suburbs, all on the east coast, that had over 1,000 black residents. However, in spite of the rapid rates of growth, estimates suggest that African Americans comprised less than two percent of the nation's suburban population.

At the turn of the century, the character of the black suburban population differed from region to region. Yet, with the exception of the South, it was possible to make several generalizations. After a significant number of blacks entered a suburban community, they began to form social institutions. One of the first priorities was the organization of a prayer group and the raising of funds to build a house of worship. During the formative period in the development of a black community, the church was always a visible presence. The majority of the first denominations introduced in a community were either Methodist Episcopal or Baptist. For example: African Americans established Grace Baptist Church (1888) and Greater Centennial A.M.E. Zion Church (1896) in Mount Vernon, New York; Union Baptist Church (1886) and St. Mark's Methodist Episcopal Church (1881) in Montclair, New Jersey; St. Catherine A.M.E. Zion Church (1841), Bethesda Baptist Church (1888) and Shiloh Baptist Church (1899) in New Rochelle, New York; Second Baptist Church (1870), Mt. Zion Baptist Church (1894) and Ebenezer A.M.E. Church (1882) in Evanston, Illinois; First A.M.E. Church (1887) and Friendship Baptist Church (1893) in Pasadena, California; and First A.M.E. By The Sea (1909) in Santa Monica, California. More often than not, these churches served not only as places of worship, but as meeting halls and community centers, and provided recreational facilities for youngsters.

To a large extent, the suburban African American population was always comprised of southerners who were lured to these communities by the promise of good employment. For example, although emancipated blacks had lived in Montclair, New Jersey since the 1830s, the increase in the community's black population after 1870 was promoted by the recruitment of blacks from the Carolinas to work in the estates of the town's more elite residents. This trait was apparent even in younger communities. The 1880 population of Santa Monica, California revealed that while eight of the town's 16 black residents had been born in California, five of the remaining eight came from the South. An older suburb like New Rochelle, New York, with a black community of 276, had 193 native New Yorkers and 65 southern-born residents.

Not surprisingly, due to their limited trade and educational opportunities, African American suburbanites, were overrepresented by service workers. A sampling of occupations in Englewood, New Jersey in 1900, revealed a minister, some skilled workers including a contractor and a mason, but far more service workers, including several janitors, 37 day laborers, 40 laundry workers and over 60 servants.

Only in several communities were there black residents of the more mobile classes. For example, Sandy Ground, a black enclave on New York's Staten Island, had several professionals before its demise in the early 1900s. The community produced a policeman, several teachers, two physicians and a dentist. Meanwhile, Evanston, Illinois hailed police, firefighters, a mail carrier, two physicians and a newspaper publisher between 1905 and 1910. Mount Vernon, New York had two physicians between 1900 and 1910, and two physicians and a lawyer five years later. Yet, in contrast, during the same period, Pasadena, California had several ministers, skilled and semiskilled individuals, but no black professionals.

The majority of these residents were not landowners, but renters, and they were distinguished from their white counterparts by income, occupation, level of education and place of residence. According to census figures in 1900, all but ten of Englewood's 386 blacks either rented or lived in someone's home, and none of the homes occupied by blacks in Harvey, Illinois were owned by blacks. On the west coast, only four of 23 households were owned by blacks in Santa Monica, while in Pasadena, only 36 of 100 black households were owned by them.

Apparently, African Americans were drawn to suburbia for various reasons. In part, encouraged by the pronouncements of black leaders and journalists, many southerners were inspired to believe that the North, and northern cities in particular, were a mecca from racial prejudice. Yet, the movement of blacks from the South to communities in the Midwest North and far West was perhaps a greater rejection of conditions in the South than the belief that these areas were the solution to a problem. Some came out of a sense of curiosity, others seeking a better life, but most came for the economic opportunities. From the 1890s through the post-World War One era, employment was available outside of the South. The magnetism of higher paying jobs pulled thousands of African Americans to the big cities. After arriving in the city, they found jobs as "scabs," factory workers, laborers, servants, service workers, and in the war industries.

The attractiveness of suburbia rested on a sense of comfort as well as employment. Many African Americans, particularly those of southern origin, felt ill at ease in the faster paced metropolis. The suburbs offered a lifestyle similar to their previous southern locales. Previous urban dwellers also saw an appeal associated with suburban living, but they too, came for employment, housing and better opportunities. However, the ultimate lure of suburbia came from unexpected sources. It was not from the whites who wanted to employ service workers, but from the black press, which focused on the timeless theme of land ownership using the words of a national leader to fuel this migration.

At the turn of the century, the most powerful voice in the African American community belonged to Booker T. Washington. This southern-based educator favored the politics of accommodation. He supported Jim Crow to appease whites, and preached a gospel of thrift and hard work to inspire the elevation of his people. Since he felt that whites would not give blacks respect until they respected themselves, his goal was to make blacks an economic force before they challenged the power structure for equality. In Washington's mind, this meant business and property acquisition before ballots and equality. This message left an impact on many Tuskegee graduates, including his own son. After relocating in Los Angeles, Booker T. Washington, Jr. quickly established himself as a key player among the area's black realtors.

The Washington thesis was not solely limited to Tuskegee students or southerners. While visiting northern cities, Washington advised his audiences to purchase land and homes. In response, many African American realtors used Washington's ideas to promote sales.[9] Shortly after his visit to the New York metropolitan area, this advertisement appeared in the *New York Age*:

> Dr. Booker T. Washington's advice to all industrious colored folks is 'Get A Home Of Your Own.' This advice was given in his recent speech at New Rochelle. Now is the time for you to start that home. We will help you build. We offer you choice home sites, $100 each, a few higher according to location, on terms of $5 down, $1 per week.[10]

This advertisement would not be uncommon, as over the next decade, the Washington thesis was constantly found in the black press. Even as Washington's power was waning, his words were still used to promote sales. As late as 1914, ironically the year before his death, an advertisement in the *California Eagle* stated; "Booker T. Washington says 'get land and get it quickly.'"[11]

Washington contributed to the suburban movement in several ways. By visiting suburbia, he gave support to the notion that blacks should leave the city and own their own homes. From 1896 until his death in 1915, he appeared in numerous northern, midwestern, and western suburbs during his fundraising speaking tours. However, despite his reception by whites and blacks alike, Washington did not use this opportunity to challenge the existence of racial residential segregation that he encountered in nearly every community he visited.

The African American press fueled Washington's words with editorials and advertisements lauding land ownership.

In New York, where black newspapers had been urging blacks to leave the city as early as the 1830s, the *New York Age* bombarded readers with the concept of suburban settlement. As early as 1905 there were prospective real estate offerings in many sections of the metropolitan area including Westchester County, Long Island and New Jersey. In each edition, the classified section was split between city and suburban homes and rentals. Meanwhile, in other parts of the nation, black papers were also stressing the need for blacks to purchase land. As early as 1892, Bernard F. Weber and Company used the *Chicago Eagle* while making a bid for black urban deconcentration. Their ad did not offer addresses, but rather mentioned the communities where they offered property. High Ridge, Ravenswood, Lake View and Evanston were listed as their specialties.[12] Thomas Tucker, the sole owner of the Suburban Realty Company, located in Harlem, used a different approach. He informed his clientele that he "sells homes in the city and suburbs and that he has quite a few nice homes in the suburbs."[13] While it appeared that he favored suburban homesites, he was covering both markets.

To make suburbia attractive to the masses, realtors used catchy phrases, slogans or storylines. An advertisement for Metropolitan Park, in Plainfield, New Jersey, stated that the location was "just 30 minutes from New York."[14] The hook, however, was the line that stated:

> Plainfield is a great residential center and thousands of Wall Street millionaires have located in this town, and their large retinue of servants makes it especially attractive to those seeking employment. . . . the town already has a fine public school system, six colored churches and full police, fire, telephone, telegraph, gas, and electric services.[15]

The Metropolitan Mercantile and Reality Company, who acted as agent for the property, sold vacant 25'x100' lots starting at $250 and would build rowhouses on the lots for an additional fee. On Wednesdays and Saturdays, customers were provided with free transportation to and from the train station and their site, and dinner at one of Plainfield's best restaurants. To sell another venture in Orange, New Jersey, the York and Jersey Mutual Real Estate Company offered blacks "another bargain which is unequaled. We have lots near New York, 30 minutes ride on the trolley. Lots measuring 25'x100' for $50."[16] In 1910, H. C. Conley and Company wrote: "Why Do You Pay Rent?" in order to convince blacks to buy homes on Chicago's South Side.[17] "Members of my race attention," was used by Milton Lewis, a Los Angeles area realtor, to inform patrons that he was a black agent. He was selling five acres of land in Sunland, near Burbank, for $200 an acre.[18]

In some respects, the message was open to interpretation. While blacks were persuaded to purchase homes, they did so both inside and outside of the city limits. The factors of good transportation, proximity to the workplace, population density, and the availability of decent homes were important ingredients in residential selection. A 1919 a *Chicago Defender* editorial entitled "Buying and Renting" advised blacks to buy property. However, while encouraging the acquisition of land, the editorial also seemed to tell blacks to vary their places of residence. The editorial said: "they are going out in the suburbs and not huddling like sheep in one particular section of the city. There is nothing that gives us a better standing in a community than to be owners of valuable property."[19] Blacks seemed to take this message to heart. In the New York, Los Angeles and Chicago metropolitan areas, blacks resided in several different suburban communities.

Unlike New York City, where Manhattan's density made housing available to only the very rich, Chicago and Los Angeles offered homesites both inside and outside of the city limits. Many of their earlier black suburbs were actually on the urban side of the border. For example, Chicago's blacks settled in Englewood, Hyde Park and Morgan Park, which were all within the city limits. In 1910, vacant lots along Chicago's State Street from 92nd through 95th Streets were described as future suburbs.[20] This property was depicted as "a 'suburb beautiful,' so splendidly situated, and with the richest and best drained soil in Cook

County as its foundation." The West Adams district in Los Angeles was one of the first areas considered by blacks leaving the Central Avenue ghetto. Watts and Venice, then suburbs, but soon to be annexed areas, were also very popular with the African American community.

However, although New York offered the greatest number of suburban communities outside of the city limits, here too, blacks found homes on the fringe just inside of the urban border. Several locations in the outer boroughs were hailed as suburban. To many African Americans, Queens—especially the neigborhood of Corona, Queensborough and Jamaica—represented the ideal suburb. A 1914 advertisement called "Jamaica: Queens' Borough Park." The Jamaica-based Queens Realty and Construction Company proclaimed: "rent money buys attractive modern home in New York's greatest suburb $100 and upward as a deposit ... the climate and other advantages can only be appreciated by a visit."[21] Weeks later, one- and two-family houses were offered in "Corona, Long Island." The properties were listed as a 22-minute ride and a five-cent fare from New York City.[22]

Between 1900 and 1910, the black suburban populations revealed modest signs of growth. Outer suburbs, like Harvey and Evanston, Illinois; Pasadena and Santa Monica, California; East Orange and Montclair, New Jersey; and Mount Vernon and New Rochelle, New York gained a strong black base. From 1890 to 1910, blacks established social and political institutions to ensure their futures. There were churches, social and fraternal organizations, black businesses, black newspapers, and usually a colored Republican's club to meet the needs of the community. Each suburb was served by a rail or trolley line that connected it with the larger metropolis. In such a manner, blacks were able to commute and not feel isolated from the urban center.

Santa Monica's small black population multiplied by more than three times, going from 60 to 191 people. Pasadena's black population also increased by 300 percent, from 218 to 744. The number of Harvey's African American citizens doubled from 83 to 215, while Evanston went from 737 to 1,160. However, New Jersey's communities revealed the largest numerical growth. During this decade East Orange increased from 1,420 to 1,907 persons and Montclair grew from 1,344 to 2,485 black citizens. Yet while each of the black populations increased faster than their corresponding white populations, the black presence was not significant enough to be considered a threat. Only in Montclair did the African American population approach ten percent of the total population.

Within each suburb, African Americans constructed their own societies. As black men continued their traditional fraternal and social organizations like the Elks and the Masons, black women broke new ground. They formed numerous social clubs, often just to bring people together. Once a week, usually on the servant's day off, African American women met to chat, play cards, or organize to help other blacks. Generally, the groups met in an assigned home or in local halls. Thursday was the meeting day in New Rochelle, and in this particular case, League Hall was reserved for this occasion. It was no surprise to local residents that "every major club or society of any note hold their meetings within this our own hall ... every Thursday evening for the year 1910 is taken."[23]

These groups were often geared to particular members of the black social classes, and the range of the organizations was quite diverse. In Evanston, Wednesdays and Thursdays were the domestics' days off; if a club met on another day, it was known to be for women of higher social classes. From their various names, the concerns of a particular group were usually obvious. For example, some of these were: the Monday Two Bridge Club, the Colored Working Women's Club, Pleasure Seekers Social Club, Phi Delta Kappa Sorority, Dolly Simple Sewing Club, Dunbar Women's Club, Silent Ace Bridge Club, Willing Workers Club, the Modern Cupidetts and the Harriet Tubman Republican Club. Virtually every suburb with a black community had at least five or more African American organizations. For the college educated, fraternities and sororities played a large role in establishing contacts. And for the older generations, the social orders were equally significant. In Chicago's suburbs, social organizations were even established for children: the Oriental Knights, formed in Phoenix; Evanston's Pierian Club for girls; and the *Defender* supported "Billikens," which organized chapters in Chicago and numerous area suburbs.

However, at the turn of the century, the development of the African American women's club movement heightened the social awareness of black women, who organized and began to demand their rights. Clearly, this movement also reached suburbia. While not all of the black women's clubs formed in suburbia were attached to this movement, the need for women to unify was significantly demonstrated. The formation of any type of women's group added a new dimension to the black suburban experience. If it achieved nothing else, perhaps it eased the sense of isolation and loneliness experienced by many African American women in suburbia.

It appears that making social contact was of even greater importance in the Los Angeles suburbs. Here, blacks attempted to establish numerous resort and social facilities. The *Eagle* always mentioned some new plan to construct a hotel or beachfront resort for the exclusive use of African Americans. One such resort, the Dunbar Tract, was to be developed in Venice. A 1914 account described the completed area to feature a hotel, lunch room and soda fountain for "colored" residents. Five years later, the La Bonita Apartments and Rooms on Belmar Place in Santa Monica advertised their facility as close to the beach and streetcar lines. "Spend your week-end or your vacation here at the water's edge. We rent bathing suits, thus making possible a daily plunge in the ocean."[24] As Santa Monica attempted to present itself as an entertainment site, blacks started planning amusement parks, music and dance halls, and beer gardens for members of their race. At the same time, one realtor promoted the creation of an African American community four blocks from the beach at Oceanside. He had 37 lots, all 50'x100' to sell to prospective parties. A few years later, Lincoln Beach Subdivision, containing beach lots one and half miles south of Venice and one half mile south of Playa Del Ray, was offered to blacks.

Further south in Huntington Beach, blacks attempted another venture. By 1926, the Pacific Beach Club was nearly a reality. Catering toward the more progressive members of the race, this development sold shares to interested parties. It was expected that the investors would earn a nice profit. Unfortunately, the project was the victim of racist protests and ultimately violence. Just weeks before it was to open, the entire facility was destroyed. Val Verde, a more exclusive resort for the upper classes, was constantly advertised after the demise of the Pacific Beach Club. However, this resort was not near the water but in the countryside.

Despite all of the positive accounts, early black suburban settlers did encounter acts of discrimination. Schools, for instance, were generally segregated, and most communities forced *all* black children to attend the same schools. Some school districts, like Evanston's, were not segregated by force but by the nature of the neighborhood. Here the predominantly black school developed in the area where the majority of African Americans resided. To avoid sending their children to school with blacks, Evanston's whites often sent their youngsters to private schools. Across the nation, African Americans were not hired as teachers in suburban districts until after 1940, and many of these school districts were not desegregated until the sixties. In most cases, particularly in the Northeast, court cases integrated the public schools.

Similarly, African Americans were not hired for most city positions; however, there were exceptions. Evanston was somewhat progressive in this area in many respects. They had several municipal workers, including police. By 1931, they elected Edwin B. Jourdain, Jr. as their councilman. Just before its annexation, Watts elected an African American trustee, but he complained that his colleagues ignored his presence. Although New Rochelle blacks were unsuccessful in early political campaigns, Chester Jones became the city's first black policeman in 1929. In contrast, Pasadena resisted hiring blacks for some time, and the first black hired was a street-sweeper. Over the ensuing years, Pasadena's earliest black workers were employed by the department of public works, but after 1940, they did hire two native sons, Ralph Riddle and Ray Bartlett, as policemen. Clarence Jones held the distinction of being the first black to run for a political office in Pasadena, but he was defeated by two other candidates in the 1929 primary. It would be over four decades until that city would have most of its "black firsts." While other communities would eventually see blacks in government and civil service positions, it would not be until the seventies that suburbia would see its first generation of black mayors.

While the black press covered all aspects of suburban life, before 1920 it often confronted racial issues indirectly. For example, the *Age*'s weekly New Rochelle column reported that although the city was beautifully decorated in honor of the fireman's parade, "It is the one social affair of our city that is entirely devoid of interest to colored people, and not one Negro will be seen in the line of parade."[25] On 12 March 1914, the *Age* reported that "Colored Americans are no longer segregated at the Montclair Theater, Montclair, New Jersey."[26] Five years later, while celebrating the election of Professor W. W. Fisher as president of the Evanston NAACP, the *Defender* noted that four blacks were "Jim Crowed" at an ice cream parlor at the intersection of Church and Benson Streets, and hoped the NAACP could prevent such problems.[27]

Yet it seemed that with each passing year, the patterns of discriminatory behavior increased. Between 1910 and 1930, Los Angeles area blacks encountered discrimination in several circles. While public policy reserved a pool for blacks within the heart of the city's developing black ghetto, whites tried to claim the oceanfront for themselves. Pasadena also segregated their public pool. The Brookside Plunge, that city's public facility, was reserved one day a week for use by African Americans. Later called "International Day," Wednesdays were open only to nonwhite swimmers. That evening, after the park was closed, it was reported that the pool was drained and fresh water pumped in for white swimmers. In 1914, African Americans formed the Negro Taxpayer's and Voter's Association of Pasadena. This group, organized specifically to deal with the Plunge, filed a protest with the city government. The Plunge remained segregated until 1945, when the NAACP won a court battle to end International Day. Yet, less than two years later, rather than allow interracial swimming, the city closed the pool.

In Manhattan Beach, blacks were arrested for violating a residency requirement at the beach. When it was learned that the victims were town residents and entitled to use the beach, they were then informed it was a private beach and not open to blacks. Their arrest and date in court resulted in a fine.[28] With the support of the NAACP, they were vindicated in an appeal. Santa Monica and Venice also imposed restrictions on the waterfront, allowing the formation of private beach clubs that excluded blacks. Prominent Santa Monica residents were responsible for the passage of a noise ordinance that closed several black music clubs, including the popular Caldwell's Garden. They also pushed for the exclusion of African American children in the town's previously mixed Boy Scout troop, and for blacks to be buried in a secluded part of the Woodlawn cemetery.[29]

Attorney Edward Burton Ceruti gained considerable fame representing blacks throughout Southern California.[30] Fair skinned and light enough to be considered white, Ceruti demonstrated that African Americans were often the victims of discrimination solely because of their race. Attending theaters posed levels of difficulty for African American patrons, and Ceruti increased his distinction by taking numerous theater discrimination suits. The case of *Mrs. J. Columbus v. La Petite Theater* in Santa Monica (1916) produced a cash settlement, although the smallest one possible, for Mrs. Columbus, who was denied her seats on the main floor of the auditorium. The following year, Ceruti gained another a victory in Pasadena where the

Crown Theatre charged two black women a 25 cent admission fee, while charging whites ten cents. However, despite these victories, such practices continued to be reported as late as 1930, when the *Eagle* announced that the Largo Theatre in Watts restricted a side row for black customers.

Suburban Chicago was another victim of the growing problem of suburban race relations. Between 1900 and 1920, Evanston's African American community had increased from 3.8 percent to 6.8 percent of the total population. Although blacks were generally respectable members of Evanston society, many whites favored restrictive policies. Years later, such antiblack sentiments and practices along Chicago's North Shore remained strong. In the twenties, a resident of lily-white Winnetka said of neighboring Glencoe, "It'd be terrible to have to live up in Glencoe—you know, they have a regular colony of negroes up there."[31] However, the speaker could have easily have said the same thing about Evanston! By 1930, Glencoe was 6.3 percent black, while Evanston was 7.8 percent black.

Despite the Illinois Public Accommodations Law of 1885, which prohibited discrimination based on race in public places, segregation quietly occurred throughout the city. Movie theaters and restaurants refused or separated blacks, street cars were "Jim Crowed," and rental housing was restricted. The Evanston Theater and the Vaudette Theater discriminated against their black patrons, and the Evanston Auditorium Hall was only available to blacks through rentals. In 1912, Mason Park was the sole playground open to black youth. Even an African American establishment, Jones' Restaurant, was closed to blacks. This eatery catered to whites, and therefore had to refuse black customers. Medical care was also restricted, as Evanston Hospital refused black patients and St. Francis Hospital only received a limited number of blacks. In 1914, husband and wife doctors Arthur Butler and Isabella Garnett Butler started the Evanston Sanitarium in their home. This facility, later known as Butler Sanitarium, was the only hospital that catered to blacks north of Chicago and south of Milwaukee, Wisconsin.

With the exception of the town's one high school, racial mixture was limited throughout the public education system. Yet despite its integrated structure, racial restrictions were quite visible in the high school. For example, in 1929 the Evanston Country Club prohibited black students from attending a school dance.

Northwestern University, the gem of the North Shore, historically relied upon racial separation. Although the university had African American students, there were signs of racial conflict as early as 1901. Sarah Ellis, the first black female student to live in a university dormitory, was given a single room in Chapin Hall. Her only contact with the other residents was at mealtime, but white reaction was instantly negative. Although she was not asked to leave the dormitory, her fellow students did request that she be served her meals in her room. By 1902, black women were denied access to campus dormitories, thus forced to seek private rooms. Virtually overnight, African American students found themselves excluded from numerous campus organizations, most athletic endeavors, and even physical education classes.

Town residents witnessed the rise of paternalistic society.[32] Whites encouraged blacks to build their own public facilities and to develop their own organizations. In fact, whites made generous financial contributions to the African American community to guarantee the development of separate lifestyles. By 1911, Evanston formed the nation's first all-black Boy Scout troop (troop seven), and in the following year the all-black Emerson Street department of the YMCA was born. And to add insult to injury, by 1914 this facility would be the site of Northwestern's black students' physical education classes. The waterfront also became restricted. Again, Northwestern supported the practice by refusing to admit its black students to the university's private beach. In 1936, with the assistance of the NAACP, William Bell, Jr. unsuccessfully challenged the system. He sued the university after he was able to buy a token but not enter the beach.

Attempts at homeownership also caused problems. In 1927, despite vocal objections of the community, A. T. Anderson, the senior partner of the Harlem-based A. T. Anderson and Company realty concern, bought a home in the exclusive white section of Mount Vernon. Mrs. Frances Swartzberg, who sold the property for $15,000, received a good deal of criticism from her former neighbors. Her reply to her critics was: "well, I'm not the first owner to sell to decent, respectable, prosperous colored people and you can rest assured I will not be the last."[33] Whites also responded negatively to black movement within communities. For instance, Doctors A. M. Williams and Errold Collymore purchased homes in the exclusive Highlands section of White Plains in 1930, touching off a local scandal. In light of their actions, the White Plains YMCA removed the doctors from their Committee of Management, and when Rev. Samuel Morsell, also black and the YMCA's Secretary, supported them by moving into Dr. Collymore's home, he was removed from his salaried post. A plot then developed to close down the private practices of the two men. When this failed, other measures were taken. First, a cross was burned on Dr. Collymore's lawn, and when that had no affect, the local residents put additional pressure on the YMCA. They told the YMCA that they would no longer receive community chest funds. Although the two doctors did not budge, Rev. Morsell relocated in New York City.

Two years later, the *Age* charged that throughout Westchester County, black domestics were being replaced by white foreigners, and that this action was creating a serious unemployment situation. In a related development, James Waite, a Mamaroneck tradesman, complained that whites tried to drive him out of business.[34] He claimed that his business has been destroyed three times since he settled in the county in 1922. Waite reported that he had received death threats and that once a woman tried to shoot him. Unfortunately, one of the attempts did lead to the deaths of two young girls, as a fire destroyed the house where his business was located.

Across the nation, as the problems lingered, the press was forced to pay greater attention to the needs of its readers. As a result, its actions produced more serious responses. When an election in Watts threatened the black residents, the *Eagle* attempted to rally blacks to vote as a solid block. This article spoke of the decency of Watts' black citizens, and the paper blasted candidates trying to deny blacks saloon licenses.[35] Continuing racial turmoil led *Eagle* editor, J. B. Bass, to become personally involved in the fight against the Klan. After publishing letters from worried Watts' residents, he visited G. W. Price, the reputed head of the Klan, in his Los Angeles workplace. After Bass traveled to Watts to denounce Price and the organization in a public forum, he was attacked on several fronts. Price responded with a libel lawsuit, and the Klan publicly supported the reelection of Mayor Cryer, while the NAACP and *Eagle* backed Judge Benjamin Bledsoe in 1925. The opposing sides battled to a stalemate. While the court dropped the charges against Bass, Mayor Cryer won in the primaries.

The following year, under the administration of Mayor Edwards, blacks could claim a bittersweet victory. While the community debated whether or not they should accept Los Angeles's annexation bid, the Klan took matters into their own hands. They stressed that annexation would drive up taxes, but also raised concerns about remaining a separate city with an increasing black population. The white population decided that joining Los Angeles offered much more than staying independent. Black voters supported the decision for two reasons. They believed that the racist policies could be brought to an end by joining the city, and as Los Angeles required its workers to live within the city limits, this would enable many blacks to keep their jobs. In the election, Watts' residents overwhelmingly approved the annexation.

During the same period, the *Eagle* denounced a Santa Monica paper called *The Interpreter*. It was believed that this paper was trying to spark racial unrest by supporting a town zoning proposition.[36] It was no surprise that the following year, the *Eagle* told Venice's black population not to vote for consolidation with Santa Monica "because Santa Monica hates them and Venice has always liked her Colored Citizens of whom she is proud for they have done well there."[37] The paper looked more favorably toward the suburb's annexation by Los Angeles in 1925.

An alleged 1923 attack of a white girl and her grandfather by an African American that sparked white mobs to attack the black community in Stowe Township, outside of Pittsburgh, is also significant. This time, several black papers carried accounts of this outbreak. Whites were described as storming and trying to destroy the homes of that area's 300 blacks. Similarly, the harassment of Mr. and Mrs. W. S. Kenner, the only black family in Gardena, California, received front page coverage.[38] The Kenners were visited by their white neighbors and encouraged to move out of town. When Kenner relied on a rifle to remove the protestors from his porch, he was subsequently arrested and thrown in jail.

Whether verified or not, racist acts were often depicted by the press as the work of the Klu Klux Klan. In order to chase blacks from a predominantly white domain, arsonists—allegedly Klan members—set fire to the Pacific Beach Club in 1926. Police never caught the suspects who fled from the scene. Other actions attributed to the Klu Klux Klan were reported in Manhattan Beach. In an attempt to chase that community's small black population out of town, suspicious ordinances directed toward blacks were raised in local meetings. When that effort failed, individual acts of harassment started. A few weeks later, a fire was set to the gas meter of Mr. and Mrs. James Slaughter, and a cross was burned across from their house.[39]

The name of the Klan was also mentioned when trying to chase Mr. and Mrs. St. Clair Edwards out of their newly purchased Jamaica, Long Island home. In this particular case, the Edwards family was informed by a Mr. Dougherty, the local democratic leader, that the "Klansmen of the neighborhood were determined no Negro should live in the neighborhood."[40] Dougherty reportedly told Edwards that he would see "Edwards and his family dead in hell before he would let them remain in their home."[41] Other community activists tried to put pressure on the former owners, attempted to purchase the home from the Edwards, tried to frighten the family by threatening to blow up the house, and held up a blackened hand in front of Mrs. Edwards.

While the suburban African American population steadily increased from 1880 to 1930, the period from 1920 to 1930 was the single decade of greatest growth. For example, in 1910 seven suburban communities had black populations of roughly ten percent. By 1920, this figure had been reached in 19 suburbs. A quarter of the total number of black YMCA and YWCA organizations were in suburbia, and a significant number of UNIA, NAACP, and Urban League chapters were also in these confines.

A sampling of suburbs in three metropolitan areas reveals patterns of African American settlement. In 1910, there were 777 blacks in Englewood, New Jersey, 744 in Pasadena, California, and 1,160 in Evanston, Illinois. Within ten years, Englewood had 1,138 blacks; Pasadena, 1,094; and Evanston, 2,522. Englewood and Pasadena increased at roughly the same rate, while Evanston's black population doubled. A decade later, each suburb roughly doubled their black populations with figures of 2,524; 3,015; and 4,938, respectively. African Americans represented 14.1 percent of Englewood's, 3.9 percent of Pasadena's, and 7.7 percent of Evanston's populations. This trait was not limited to these communities, as other suburbs within these metropolitan areas confirmed this trend. From 1920 to 1930, Harvey, Illinois increased from 171 black residents to 405; Santa Monica, California went from 282 to 740; and Mount Vernon, New York gained 2,263 blacks—from 1,345 to 3,608. These increases were comparable to the growth of African American communities in New York, Newark, Chicago and Los Angeles, all of which doubled during this same period. Yet, neither the total nor the white population of these urban centers or their suburbs grew as fast as the black populations.

Perhaps, then, it is not a coincidence that the backlash to black suburban settlement is exceptionally strong during this period. As in urban centers, suburbia came in contact with the Klan, limited acts of racial violence, the rise of neighborhood improvement associations, attempts to restrict or limit black residential settlement, and the segregation of public and private facilities.

During this era, the residential patterns of blacks in suburbia began to change. For example, before 1920 Evanston's African American population was generally unrestricted throughout the city. Blacks lived in many sections of the city, but most lived near the lake, which was then the most undesirable section of town. As this area became attractive to developers for commercial property, it was necessary to encourage the movement of blacks to other parts of the city. Thus, a segregated section developed on the city's west side. Physically this area was bounded by the sanitary district channel and the Chicago and Northwestern Railroad. The second and fifth wards arose as the home of Evanton's black community. Yet between the two wards, the fifth ward had the greatest concentration of African Americans. However, despite its congestion and pattern of growth, even in these wards the African American population did not exceed the white population.

Similarly, at first Pasadena's Afro-Americans lived in the downtown business district. Like Evanston's blacks, they were a minority in this neighborhood. However, over time, they too were forced to moved to this area and were encouraged to settle in the northwestern regions of Pasadena. When blacks first settled there, this section was not viewed as part of the city. It offered very little in terms of public utilities and was not considered very desirable. As a result, this land was offered at low prices considered affordable to most African Americans. Decades later, the northwestern corners of Pasadena and Evanston were labeled as the Negro sections of their respective communities.

In New Jersey, Englewood and Montclair also developed black sections. Prior to 1920, Englewood's blacks were scattered throughout the city, although the largest number of African Americans lived near Palisade Avenue. Eventually, blacks settled off of West Palisade Avenue in the vicinity of the railroad tracks, and on Forest Avenue, First and Second Streets in the southwestern end of the city. Over time, Englewood's southwestern ward grew into the black section of the city. In the vicinity of Montclair, blacks always scattered throughout the town, but more African Americans were concentrated near Glen Ridge and in the southern half of the town. However, around 1930, blacks started congregating in the areas south of Bloomfield Avenue. The South End arose as the "Negro colony," and the black community spilled over into adjacent Orange, producing a continuous African American neighborhood.

Quite often, black settlements were characterized by some type of physical barrier. The all-black suburb of Robbins, Illinois, established in 1918, was separated from virtually all-white Blue Island by a canal, and all-white Posen and predominantly white Harvey by the railroads. Evanston, Pasadena, Montclair, Englewood, New Rochelle and Mount Vernon were partitioned by train tracks. In each community, the black settlement was either near the tracks, or the white and black communities were separated by them. Prior to 1900, blacks lived on both sides of Mount Vernon, but eventually the largest concentration occurred south of the tracks. Before the establishment of the Winyah Avenue community, many of New Rochelle's blacks lived downtown in the vicinity of the tracks. Similarly, the largest concentration of blacks in Yonkers, New York was from the tracks to Wharburton Avenue. In Pasadena, the pattern was the same. Broken up by the main line of the Santa Fe and a spur of the Union Pacific Railroad, Pasadena's original black settlement was also characterized by old and frequently rundown frame houses.

Typically, the housing stock for most of these areas was

relatively poor. Yet in many cases, the housing stock was not very old. In California, the affordable bungalow was the staple for African Americans. In contrast to this one level development, midwestern and eastern suburbs had multi-storied housing. Evanston had some of the best. Its West Side featured late nineteenth century residences, virtually all of them built between 1845–1900. Yet throughout the country, many black homes lacked modern sanitary equipment. Included in this rank were "railroad shacks," often the only housing available to blacks. Whites gladly made these undesirable sites available for rental of sale to African American customers. Overall, most blacks preferred homeownership to renting. However, the number of black owners was low.

Whether owners or renters, many African Americans shared their living space to make ends meet. In many cases, large numbers of people resided in these households. Although they may not have been overcrowded, undoubtedly African American households were quite large. It was not uncommon for several families to live in the same house or household. Homes were divided or constructed to permit additional residents. Many had more than one entrance, frequently with blacks living in the rear. The census reveals numerous boarders living with black families. Sometimes these boarders were students, relatives, or friends of the family, but others were strangers. Boarders even had young children. A typical African American household could consist of the head and his immediate family, a member of his family and/or an in-law, and one or several boarders. There were even cases where grown children and their families could be found living with their parents.

As numerous communities tried to restrict black urban deconcentration, they attempted to publicize the absence of African Americans to discourage black settlement and ensure future white residents. In sending their message to African Americans, Lomita, California informed all by posting signs telling black to stay out. Gardena and Glendale, California confidently boasted that they had no blacks in their school systems; Cicero and Blue Island, Illinois stated that they had no black residents; and a local Santa Monica newspaper warned, "Negroes, we don't want you here; now and forever, this is to be a white man's town."[42]

Yet in order to maintain all-white suburbs, it was essential to contain blacks, regardless of class, in urban ghettos. This task relied in large measure, on cooperation from the urban centers. It was their role to confine blacks within the city limits. Suburban public policy, while able to restrict facilities and encourage realtors not to sell to blacks, could not impose laws to keep blacks out. No municipality was ever bold enough to pass a law *prohibiting* black settlement. Even attempts of harassment and violence were not completely effective. In each region there were several cases where blacks remained for years under extremely hostile conditions. Overall, African Americans knew the risks and decided which communities to avoid. Therefore, it seems obvious that assistance to limit migration clearly came from the cities.

Therefore, it was not a surprise that the growth of the African American population was not as strong a decade later. Outside of the social conflicts, the advent of the Depression had some impact on the growth of the black suburban population. Blacks were among the earliest victims of the nation's financial woes, and by the end of the twenties many blacks were strapped for cash. Numerous African American real estate concerns and enterprises were forced to either go out of business, face court proceedings or undergo reorganization. Throughout this difficult period, the African American press recorded the changes through articles of court battles and other business casualties, and finally in a decrease of real estate advertisements.

From 1930 to 1940 the suburban growth rate declined. While the black population increased in each city, the percentage of growth declined. For example, Englewood only increased from 2,524 to 2,999; Pasadena from 3,015 to 3,929; and Evanston from 4,938 to 6,026. However, a more significant figure was that blacks now comprised 15.8 percent of Englewood's, 4.7 percent of Pasadena's, and 9.2 percent of Evanston's total populations. A conscious effort had to be made to maintain the size of the black communities.

While similar figures were appearing throughout the nation, by 1930, in many New Jersey communities, blacks comprised over ten percent of the total suburban population. The metropolitan region showed Englewood, Orange, Montclair, Plainfield and Hackensack to be in this category, with East Orange not far behind. Westwood and Rahway also had the potential of reaching this plateau. On the New York side of the Hudson, Nyack was the only suburb where blacks made up ten percent of the population. Mount Vernon, New Rochelle, Ossining, Hempstead, White Plains, North Tarrytown, Rye and Bronxville all showed figures of five percent or better. In contrast, Monrovia had the largest percentage of Los Angeles County's blacks. Slightly more than four percent of its 10,890 residents were of African origin. With a figure just under ten percent, Evanston, followed by Glencoe, were the leaders for Chicago's suburbs.

Outside of Evanston, only in New York were there suburbs that were fast approaching the "tipping point." This figure, named by Chicago realtor Travis Dempsey, represented the magical number when whites felt outnumbered by the presence of blacks and began to flee. As this figure approached ten percent, white reactions conversely increased. The doubling of the black population from 1920 to 1930, combined with the increasing percentage of blacks in the community, forced a greater recognition of the African American suburbanite.

The impact of restrictive covenants was to limit suburban entry. They were especially effective in Los Angeles, as the covenants forced blacks to reside in undesirable areas. Here, the greatest role was played by the courts, which upheld the use of covenants within the city limits. The covenants restricted ownership and/or residency. Starting as early as 1919, with the case of *Los Angeles*

Investment Company vs. Alfred Gary, the state enforced these agreements. Perhaps the 1925 decision against the Long family was a critical blow to black mobility. Although blacks had lived in this Central Avenue area for 17 years, when the Longs lost their suit, others were filed against the remaining black residents.

When the Supreme Court addressed the issue in 1926, California's courts had already established a precedent. In failing to hear the case of *Corrigan vs. Buckley*, the Court yielded to the authority of the states. Their refusal was based on the premise that the rights of blacks were not violated and there was no state action. They viewed the covenants as an agreement made by citizens, therefore a legal contract.[43]

Further actions of the California Supreme Court in supporting covenants caused the removal of blacks from areas where they were currently residing. By 1928, the court had sealed the fate of the African American population. With 75-year and 99-year clauses, neighborhoods were strategically locked up for significant periods of time. Entire parts of Los Angeles were prohibited to black settlement. As the covenants were so successful within the city, it completely discouraged blacks from the suburban option. Blacks were given few choices. As the majority of Los Angeles was closed to them, those who wished to move progressed slowly southward along the Furlong Tract.

Chicago's suburban blacks were offered Evanston's west side or the southern suburbs of Robbins and Harvey. Since Robbins was all-black, there was no need for exclusion, but this was not the case in other two locations. Evanston tried to keep blacks on the west side, while Harvey attempted to fix its small black community. Within the city, property owners drew up restrictive agreements to institute additional neighborhood covenants. Hyde Park, Kenwood and Englewood also made plans to exclude blacks. Urban violence in Chicago warned blacks that there were only limited acceptable choices, and they would all have to be made within the black belt. Only in Morgan Park did a true black inner suburban community continue to exist.

Although New York was depicted as much more liberal area, its African American residents recognized that their rights were also limited. This area had covenants both within and outside of the city limits, but some were quietly ignored. However, in reality, most of the damage had been done.

African Americans were so widely dispersed throughout the metropolitan region that the covenants did not keep them out of towns that they had already reached, but rather kept them out of exclusive neighborhoods and communities with no existing black populations. The result was a patchwork of pockets that, to a large degree, still remain. Probably the greatest impact of these agreements has agreements has been seen in parts of Westchester County and on Long Island.

By the mid-thirties, suburban migration was effectively controlled. Through the use of covenants, citizen harassment and public policy, there were only a limited number of suburban communities open for African American settlement. These communities, of course, were ones with a previous history of black residents. There was no movement into new communities, and even the communities with blacks were reluctant about accepting additional citizens.

However, for the African American population, these settlements were already established. Suburbia was home. They had developed schools, churches and social institutions. It seemed unthinkable to consider leaving. Those who were there would have to make the effort to survive despite the circumstances. As individuals and as a collective body, blacks would have to work to improve their position, get along with one another and work together, and gain the support of their white counterparts. For better or for worse, African Americans had decided to stay. And, in their hearts, they knew that they had earned the right to be included in the suburban population.

Thus, for many African Americans, the desire to move to suburbia remained. Although there was now a shortage of employment, it was no longer necessary to live and work in suburbia. Unlike in the earlier stages of suburban development, African American residents became commuters. Modern improvements in transportation made commuting faster and less expensive, and therefore it was possible for African Americans to obtain employment in the cities. Whether in Mount Vernon, New Rochelle, Yonkers, Watts, Englewood, Santa Monica or Evanston, there were sufficient rail systems to move the masses. While the majority of suburban blacks still worked in their communities, there were exceptions. However, over time, this too would become commonplace. Three decades later, the majority of black suburbanites would no longer be service workers. Instead they would be members of the middle classes trying to enjoy the broader image of the suburban dream.

However, regardless of the location, the suburban legacy continued, just as it had begun. In various types of suburban communities, African Americans faced challenges from white society. They had to devise new strategies to remain a part of the suburban experience. Their search, as imagined by numerous realtors, outlined by Washington, and depicted by the black press in their columns and advertisements, was still the same. Although the chicken farm, railroad shack, small bungalow or servant's quarters would eventually be replaced by aspirations of a modern residence, the ultimate goal remained. It was a continuing search for opportunity, employment, equality, and most importantly, a place to call home. Amidst countless threats and hardships, African Americans still fought to make that dream a reality.

6

Middletown Reindustrializes
The Case of Muncie, Indiana

Dwight W. Hoover

Muncie, Indiana did not begin as an industrial town such as Gary. It was created as the county seat of Delaware County in 1827; the town then consisted of a few white citizens and a trading post run by Goldsmith Gilbert. Not until 27 years later was the town incorporated with a population of approximately 900.[1] As a county seat town providing legal and governmental services to the surrounding region and agricultural equipment to neighboring farmers, its growth was slow. Its early attempts to obtain transportation links to larger metropolitan areas failed when planned extensions of the Whitewater and Central canals did not materialize. Not until 1852 did Muncie gain such a link, the Indianapolis and Bellefountaine Railroad.[2] This did not stimulate growth as much as its promoters had hoped or claimed, however. Nor did succeeding connections prove to be much better.

By 1880, Muncie was still basically an agricultural village, dependent in large part on serving surrounding farms for its sustenance. The town's population was 5,219, and it contained 60 industries, most of which were one-person operations. The larger examples were partnerships between individuals with capital and those with skill. Representative industries were sawmills, grist and flour mills, brick and tile makers, and buggy and wagon manufacturers.[3] All catered to a local market; none aimed at a wider regional or national one.

Despite this fact, the basis for a larger industrial future had already been laid. As Alexander E. Bracken has said, "If Muncie had not yet developed an 'industrial culture' by 1880, it did possess an economic system based on manufacturing interests... Muncie was not yet a complete industrial city by 1880, but it was well on its way even before the tremendous expansion brought on by the gas boom five years later."[4]

The transformation to an industrial community that exported goods to a larger region began with the discovery of natural gas in the 1880s in the Trenton Field, which underlay parts of western Ohio and eastern Indiana. The supply seemed inexhaustible and attracted a number of industries to the area, the most prominent of which was glassmaking. Almost every small town in the region boasted at least one factory, and these factories made all kinds of glass articles, ranging from fruit jars to art glass. These articles were intended for a national market and were shipped to locations all over the United States. The rapid growth of glassmaking as a local specialty is well illustrated by succeeding censuses of manufacturing. In 1880, only four glass factories operated in Indiana; 20 years later there were 110.[5]

Muncie shared in the glass boom. It had no glass factories in 1881 but, by 1893, it had eight. Other industries also grew significantly. From two foundries in 1881, the number jumped to six by 1899, while the number of iron manufacturers grew from none to seven in the same period.[6] The town had exploded economically.

By 1900, Muncie's population had quadrupled from 1880, rising from 5,219 to 20,942. Its economic prosperity was reflected in changes in physical shape. It was during this period that a new stone courthouse was built, replacing the second brick one, and the downtown retail district became identifiable with the construction of many of the buildings that still line Walnut Street. New industries created their own suburbs as they came into town; Ball

Brothers, for example, built its factory in the Industry area several miles from downtown, while George McCulloch's foundry located in Whiteley, east of the center of town. In both cases, workers moved into nearby housing, causing the town to sprawl. To connect all these areas, a public transit system was developed in the 1890s, and to keep the peace a police force was created in the same era.

The pattern of rapid industrial and population growth ended abruptly in the early years of the twentieth century as the gas supply dwindled. The loss of cheap fuel resulted in a shrinkage of manufacturers as competitors from other regions proved too strong. By 1905, Muncie had lost two iron manufacturing and three glass plants (half of the number in town).[7] So severe was the loss that Muncie was only one of four towns in the state where the total value of manufactured products dropped in the five years from 1900 to 1905.[8] While the whole region also suffered (in the state as a whole, the number of glassmakers declined to 44), growth in other industries compensated for the loss. In Muncie, however, stagnation was the rule. No new industries entered the town in the years 1905 to 1910.[9] This stagnation was reflected in the slowing of population growth. The population of Muncie did increase slightly, from 20,942 to 24,005, during the decade from 1900 to 1910, but the population of the county actually decreased. All of this occurred in a period of national prosperity and population growth.

GROWTH AGAIN

Economic recovery characterized the next decade, however, as manufacturing output rose 34 percent and 19 new industries came to town, increasing the number 18 percent over 1910.[10] The reasons for the growth were twofold: World War I and the automobile. Both stimulated the production of machine tools and automotive parts, enough so that, by the 1920s, the production of the latter had outstripped, in total value, the products of the city's glass plants.[11] Because of economic vitality and annexation, Muncie's population had grown to over 35,000 people.[12]

Muncie did not have many automobiles in the gas boom era. The Lynds reported that a local tinkerer built a steam wagon that ran successfully in 1890, but the first real automobile appeared ten years later. By 1906, Muncie had approximately 200 automobiles,[13] none apparently built locally.

By that time, however, there were already industries in town that supplied parts for automobile makers in other cities. As was true everywhere in the early days of automobile manufacturing, parts makers originally engaged in other enterprises, ones that could easily be retooled into suppliers for automobile manufacturers. Two such early suppliers were the Muncie Wheel Company and Warner Gear. The first has long since disappeared, while the second persists as part of the Borg Warner Corporation and as an important base for Muncie's industrial superstructure. Both companies were founded by entrepreneurs who came to town during the gas boom.

Citizen's Enterprize Company, a group created to promote the growth of Muncie in the 1890s and a forerunner of the Chamber of Commerce, brought Muncie Wheel Company into the area in 1895.[14] The company first made wagon and carriage wheels; it later fabricated automobile wheels. It did not make that transition successfully, however, for by 1912, Muncie Wheel was out of business.

Much more successful was Warner Gear. Indeed, in addition to providing employment to thousands of Muncie residents for over 80 years, the company was the progenitor of the automobile industry in the town. The two brothers who founded the company can be said to be significantly responsible for the major role that industry played in Muncie's future development.

The Warner brothers—Thomas W. and John F.—were born in Shelbyville, Tennessee, where their father ran a general store. John, the older brother, left home at 16 to work on the Goodnight Ranch in Texas. After six years in the Lone Star State, he moved to Birmingham, Alabama, to work as an engineer in an electric light plant. In 1896, he went to Cincinnati and was employed in a bicycle factory; a few years later he took a similar position in Hamilton, Ohio. In 1902, he arrived in Muncie to join his younger brother, Thomas, and open a plant to make steering and transmission gears for automobiles.[15]

Thomas had gone to Cincinnati after leaving home and worked, as his brother had, in an electric light plant. In 1897, he moved to Muncie to organize the Warner Electric Plant, which, among other products, made automobile parts. In 1902, he and his brother began Warner Gear.[16] This company was successful and, in 1909, Thomas created still another company, the T. W. Warner Company. This company also built transmissions and steering gears, as well as control levers for cars. Its expansion, like the other companies, was rapid. It supplied equipment for such cars as the Moon, Norwalk, Davis, Kissel, Columbia, Willys Overland, Marion, Chandler, Haynes, Studebaker, Wescott, Stoddard-Dayton, American, Stutz and Cole. It later made transmissions and steering gears for Chevrolets and transmissions for General Motors trucks, and Oakland and Olds passenger cars.[17] Eventually, Thomas Warner opened a branch of T. W. Warner Company in Toledo to be close to automobile manufacturers in that area.

By 1914 there were seven automobile parts manufacturers in Muncie, including the Warners' three companies. They were Auto Parts Manufacturing, Moon Brothers, Muncie Clutch and Gear, and Muncie Gear Works.[18] As can be derived from the titles, the Muncie companies tended to specialize in gears, taking the lead from Warner Gear.

Five years earlier (1909) Muncie had witnessed the opening of three automobile manufacturing plants: the Riber-Lewis Motor Company of Anderson and Muncie, the C. H. Stratton Carriage Company and the Inter-State Automobile Company. The first two were ephemeral while the last was the foundation for General Motors. Stratton apparently made no cars after 1909, while River-Lewis ceased production in 1911.[19] The Inter-State lasted until 1919.

The genesis of the Inter-State Automobile Company came from the promotional efforts of the Commercial Club. During the period of stagnation following the exhaustion of natural gas, the Club had determined to bring an automobile manufacturer into the community. Its first effort in 1907 was to entice the Maxwell-Briscoe Company, which was looking for a site to build cars, into Muncie. The effort failed, however, as Maxwell chose the nearby town of New Castle, thus establishing a presence that later became a Chrysler one. Following this failure, the Commercial Club changed its tactics and decided to encourage local entrepreneurs to build instead of trying to bring in already established makers. The Club appointed a committee composed of George A. Ball, Joel M. Maring and Thomas Hart to begin the process. The committee bought land at West Willard Street and erected a two-building factory in 1908.[20]

All the committee members were industrialists who themselves had been induced to bring their glass business to Muncie in the early years of the gas boom and whose businesses had survived the depletion of gas. Ball was one of five brothers who had come to Muncie from Buffalo, New York, in 1887 to blow fruit jars, persuaded by incentives given by the town. Maring and Hart had transplanted their window glass firm from Bellaire, Ohio, a year later. James Boyce, Muncie's most prominent businessman, convinced them to settle in Boycetown, an industrial suburb platted by Boyce.[21] None had had experience in automaking, although the Balls were involved in Warner Electric. Most of the earlier direction, however, seems to have come from Hart.

In 1909, the first car came off the assembly line. It was a superior product but was expensive. It had a four-cylinder, L head, 4.7 liter engine and, by 1912, sported an electric starter, electric lights, and an electric fuel pump. The company eventually produced eight different models on three different chassis. Despite these advantages, the company was soon in trouble. By 1913, it was bankrupt and had filed for receivership.[22]

In 1914, Frank C. Ball, one of the five Ball Brothers and the leader of the group, took over management of the renamed Inter-State Motor Company because of the Ball interest and investment in the concern. Ball money helped the company on its feet again, just in time to take advantage of the economic stimulus of World War I. During that conflict, the company produced trucks, tractors and passenger automobiles for wartime use.[23] It still was not a prosperous company, however.

By war's end, local automobile and parts makers were ripe for takeover by larger interests. The town had a pool of skilled workers and the political climate was right. It was at this point that General Motors came to town.

The automobile industry had attracted a number of skilled persons into the community, persons who had wide experience in a variety of workplaces. One example will suffice. Clarence G. Wood was born in Bluff City, Kansas, but came to Indianapolis at the age of 14. He then moved to Muncie to work at Inter-State Automobile Company. He transferred to Warner Gear in 1909 and worked his way up to plant superintendent by 1915. He served in World War I, returning to become Vice President and Secretary of Hoosier Clutch.[24] Wood's career, while not typical, was not uncommon.

In addition, Muncie's mayor, Rollin C. "Doc" Bunch, dreamed of a larger, more prosperous Muncie and was a fervid booster of the town's industries. Though tainted by scandal and twice indicted on charges of corruption, Bunch had not yet been convicted of any crime and had won reelection in 1917 despite the combined efforts of the business elite, including the Balls, the unified Republican Party, and the Ministerial Association. He was determined to expand the city by annexing seven suburban areas; his purpose was to make Muncie a second class city. In order to do so, Bunch needed to increase the city's population from 25,000 to at least 30,000 people or to boost the taxable property to $20 million. Annexation would raise the population to nearly 40,000 and increase the property valuation considerably, although not enough to reach the $20 million mark.[25] This would enable the mayor to achieve a pet goal, to build a new city hall, one that was modern and befitting a city on the move. By 14 March 1919, the Board of Public Works had voted in favor of a new facility, and a campaigning Bunch had said that "Every other city in present need of a city building is erecting one" and that "none needs a city building worse than Muncie."[26] Annexation was eventually achieved and a new city hall was built, but not during Bunch's term.

ENTER GENERAL MOTORS

The sense that Muncie was on the move was heightened just a week after the Board of Public Works' action when the news broke that General Motors was coming to Muncie. The man making the announcement and most responsible for the move was Thomas W. Warner. T. W. Warner Company of Toledo, which Warner had founded, had become part of the rapidly growing Chevrolet Motor Company in 1916, and Warner, who had become a major stockholder and officer in General Motors, turned that division's eye on his hometown.

Warner had taken advantage of the meteoric rise of W. C. "Billy" Durant, who regained control of General Motors in the period from 1910 to 1918. Durant, who had lost control in 1910, used Chevrolet to win it back. Begun in 1909, Chevrolet grew rapidly under the guidance of Durant, who merged several automobile producers into one, the Chevrolet Motor Company of Delaware, in 1915. Durant then offered to bring that company in as a separate division of General Motors. The latter corporation refused, and Durant again expanded. Part of the expansion included the T. W. Warner Company, which gave Chevrolet much more capacity because of the supply of gears and transmissions. In 1918, Chevrolet had grown so rapidly that General Motors did agree to a merger, and the exchange of stock gave Durant control again.[27]

Durant, ever the expansionist, was in the process of acquiring new properties for General Motors in order to compete better with Ford. General Motors purchased the Inter-State Motor Company for $248,000 and assumed the company's debts and assets. The Inter-State Motor Company also collected $200,000 from the federal government to settle wartime contracts. General Motors then bought adjacent land for expansion for an additional $40,000.[28] Durant planned to use the old plant to produce a new model, the Sheridan, for General Motors. The Sheridan was introduced in 1920 and was one of the last of the new passenger car lines introduced during this period. It was not successful, however, and when the recession of 1921 occurred, causing General Motors to lose money for the first time in its history, the company ended its short life.[29]

Had this been the extent of General Motors' involvement, the impact on Muncie would have been minimal. This was not the case. On 9 September 1919, Thomas W. Warner, acting on behalf of General Motors, announced that the corporation would expand its facilities by building a new factory in Muncie for the Chevrolet Division. Using the T. W. Warner Company as its agent, General Motors planned to spend $4–$5 million over the following 18 months. Construction would start immediately, as would the hiring of 1,800 to 2,000 workers. Eventually, Warner predicted, a potential workforce of 6–8,000 would be employed. In order to house the new workers, according to Warner, Muncie needed 1,000 new housing units as soon as possible. He also projected a geometric population increase, saying Muncie would grow to a town of 100,000 in five years.[30]

Response to the announcement was immediate and enthusiastic. In an editorial entitled "Let's Rock the Boat," the *Muncie Evening Press* asked 500 homeowners to each build a new house and for holding companies and wealthy residents to supply the remaining 500 needed. The editor also recommended that the new building should be confined to a segment in the western part of the city and that the city leadership should take advantage of the growth to widen downtown streets to create a "real" uptown business district.[31]

On 15 September 1919, General Motors broke ground for the new facility. Four days later, the state of Indiana announced it would auction off the 500 lots given to it by Ball Brothers when the state assumed the assets and operations of Eastern Indiana Normal University. This auction would provide the land on which new homes for Chevrolet workers could be built. Again town boosters exalted, claiming the capital spent on building the 500 homes would amount to $500,000.[32]

The boom in Muncie was not without its darker side. Bunch had tried hard to keep a lid on prices during the war, in part to gain support from his populist supporters. Now prices were escalating. The demand for labor and materials escalated with the projected increases in construction and employment. Critics urged Bunch to postpone his plans for a new city hall, now possible because of annexation, because of skyrocketing costs. Bunch refused and, despite objections, the city council passed an ordinance to build and to float a $250,000 bond issue to pay for a new city hall.[33]

Nor was the new plant all that General Motors planned for Muncie. In August 1919, the corporation's directors had authorized the purchase of T. W. Warner Company for $5 million. The news was slow in reaching the town, not arriving until 4 October. Following the sale of the plant, Thomas W. Warner planned to join Durant to work at General Motors. The takeover was not accomplished immediately, though, as the Muncie facility was not then available. Instead, General Motors had to be content with a lease with an option to buy in 1923 for $902,000 in Liberty Bonds and 31,238 shares of debenture stock in the company.[34]

When General Motors assumed control of T. W. Warner Company and renamed it Muncie Products Division, it was no small enterprise. In 1924, the year after takeover, Muncie Products plant covered an area of eight acres and consisted of seven buildings with an overall square footage of 377,500. The workforce consisted of 2,200 people; the products for that year included 250,000 transmissions,

800,000 steering gears, 750,000 chassis parts sets and 500,000 sets of valves. Muncie Products was obviously a major producer of automobile parts, one that supplied not only the Chevrolet Division of General Motors but others as well. The plant remained in Muncie until the Depression. In August 1932, it closed and the equipment to fabricate parts was shipped to Detroit.[35]

During the 1920s Muncie was a major center of gear making. No sooner had one plant consolidated than another took its place. No sooner had G. M. announced its intention to buy out T. W. Warner Company, than John F. Warner created a new corporation, United Gear, also known as Warner Corporation. Formed in October 1919 and funded with a capital of $500,000, United Gear manufactured gears for the automobile industry at a location just west of Bell Brothers piano factory.[36]

Another automaker came to Muncie in the twenties, part of the continuing saga of Billy Durant. The recession of 1920, which hit General Motors hard, produced a number of casualties, some from the very top of the corporation. Among these was Durant, who had been speculating in the stock market—largely to support G. M. stock, according to his own testimony. When the price of G. M. stock dropped, Durant suffered severe losses, owing $20 million on margin calls. After much discussion, the Morgan and Du Pont interests agreed to pay the money owed to brokers, but only if Durant resigned as chief executive officer.[37]

Having lost control of General Motors again, Durant, undaunted, determined to recoup his losses by creating still another company. On 12 January 1921, he announced the formation of Durant Motors. During his settlement discussions with General Motors, he tried to buy three automobile assembly sites: the Sheridan Plant in Muncie, the Chevrolet Plant in Tarrytown and the Oakland Plant in Pontiac. His offer of 75 percent of book value was refused. A year later when General Motors had decided to terminate the Sheridan and declared the plant redundant, Durant purchased the Muncie facility to turn out Durant 6s and Stars.[38] The plant made cars until Durant

Motors went broke in the stock market crash of 1929. The plant then reverted to General Motors, which converted it for production of electrical equipment for automobiles. Delco-Remy, as it was renamed, continues in Muncie to this day.

Durant also bought John F. Warner's new corporation in September 1923. It, too, failed to survive the demise of Durant Motors. Only Warner Gear, Chevrolet and Delco-Remy remain solvent to remind Muncie citizens of the prosperous days of the twenties.

The extent to which automobiles captured Muncie in that day when it was a city of 38,000 is best shown by a census of vehicles conducted by the Lynds in 1924 of those registered in 1923. They found 6,221 listed, 30 times those owned in 1906. Included in the totals were 590 Chevrolets, 73 Interstates, 65 Durants, 62 Stars and 26 Sheridans.[39] In that day, Muncie residents could and did ride in automobiles partly or all made in their city. After the twenties, however, it was less possible.

What lessons can be learned from Muncie's experience in reindustrializing? The history of the growth of the automobile industry offers several. First, economic growth rarely occurs without substantial preparation and effort. A new industry does not appear full-blown overnight. It results from promotion by business leaders and by the cultivation of a network of individuals who use personal contacts to further their own and the community's interest. General Motors came to Muncie because of Warner who knew the community, who had built a thriving business there, and who realized that an opportunity existed to expand. That opportunity would not have been in Muncie to exploit if the Commercial Club had not instructed a committee composed of glassmakers to establish an automobile plant. Although the facility was not rousingly successful, it, along with the gear works, developed a pool of trained workers. Finally, a sympathetic political climate was provided by Mayor Bunch, who was determined to encourage economic growth and to expand the city. The automobile industry came to Muncie because the ground had been thoroughly prepared.

The second lesson concerns timing. Muncie attracted the automobile makers because it was in the forefront of development; it was on the ground floor. Warner Gear began making gears when the industry was in its infancy. Because it grew rapidly—rapidly enough to spawn other companies, including a branch in Toledo—Thomas W. Warner came to the attention of Durant. Thus Warner's interests paralleled those of Durant and enabled him to follow Durant into General Motors. Swept up by the rapid growth of Chevrolet from 1916 to 1919, General Motors was in an expansionist mood when Warner brokered the deal to bring the car manufacturer to the city. A year later and the recession in the auto industry would have prevented such a deal. Moreover, had the Balls allowed the Inter-State Automobile Company to go under in 1913 and written off their losses, there would have been no factory or other assets for General Motors to buy.

Finally, the automobile experience presaged the future of Muncie's other heavy industries. Begun and developed locally by independent entrepreneurs, the businesses were consolidated and merged into larger national corporations. The purchase of Inter-State by General Motors was an omen of future development. Others that followed were the purchase of Hemingray, a glass producer, by Owens-Illinois and of Indiana Steel and Wire by General Cable. The day of the family-owned business seemed over.

7

An Urban-Rural Dimension of the Scopes Trial

Burton W. Folsom

The Scopes trial of 1925 has long been viewed as a battle of city versus countryside. This trial did indeed seem to pit urban America—modern and scientific—against rural America—traditional and Bible believing. There was Clarence Darrow, the slick Chicago lawyer, promoting John Scopes's right to teach that evolution was a proven fact in the Dayton, Tennessee schools. Opposite Darrow was William Jennings Bryan, agrarian reformer, Christian activist, and three times the Democratic candidate for president of the United States. Bryan argued that local citizens should have the right to control what was taught in their own schools. If small-town folks wanted to teach the biblical view of human origin, they should be allowed to do so.

In this essay, I want to make three points. First, the intellectual community—especially the urban media—did indeed oppose Bryan strongly. Second, the real battle between creationists and evolutionists was fought at the grassroots level, in the state legislatures and in textbook committees, not on the editorial pages of a few urban newspapers and national magazines. In these battles, the urban-rural divisions do not seem to have been very sharp. Third, Bryan and his fundamentalist followers were not distinctly rural and not distinctly narrow in outlook; thus, they were more concerned with making textbooks neutral than with passing laws. When texts did change, these reformers were satisfied, and the uneasy truce between the creationist and evolutionist faiths lasted until about 1960.

If the national press had been the jury at Dayton, Scopes would have been acquitted and Bryan would have been convicted of reckless arguing and of debating while under the influence of bigotry. The headlines in magazines often tell the story. Bryan was cast as the villain in *Nation* ("Tennessee vs. Truth"), *New Republic* ("Tennessee vs. Civilization"), *School and Society* ("Thought: Free, or in Chains?"), *Forum* ("Inquisition in Tennessee") and *Literary Digest* ("Foreign Amazement in Tennessee") among others. Cartoonists also savaged Bryan as a bigot, an inquisitor and an idiot. Darrow was occasionally criticized, too, for his agnosticism and his method of interrogation. More often, though, Darrow was praised. The *Nation* called him "an enlightened man," the *New York Times* referred to his "rationalism, his utterances, and his courage," and the *New York Sun* called him "the champion of the cause of youth."[1]

H. L. Mencken, a strong critic of rural America, led the way in the flailing of Bryan. As editor of the *American Mercury*, Mencken's opinions set trends for intellectuals in general and many journalists in particular. Two of his articles about the trial have been widely reprinted and discussed since they were written. The first, "Hills of Zion," ridiculed some eccentric Christian worshippers outside of Dayton. The second, "In Memorium: W. J. B.," denounced Bryan as a demogogue and an imbecile.

> Bryan . . . was, in fact, a charlatan, a mountebank, a zany without sense or dignity. . . . It was hard to believe, watching him at Dayton, that he had traveled, that he had been received in civilized societies, that he had been a high officer of state. He seemed only a poor clod like those around him, deluded by a childish theology, full of an almost pathological hatred of learning, all human dignity, all beauty, all fine and noble things. He was a peasant come home to the barnyard. . . . What moved him at bottom, was simply hatred of the city men who had laughed at him so long. . . . He lusted for revenge upon them. He yearned to lead the anthropoid rabble against them, to punish them for their execution upon him by attacking the very vitals

of their civilization. He went far beyond the bounds of any merely religious frenzy, however inordinate.... By the end of the week [of the trial] he was simply a walking fever. Hour by hour he grew more bitter. What the Christian scientists call malicious animal magnetism seemed to radiate from him like heat from a stove. From my place in the courtroom, standing upon a table, I looked directly down upon him, sweating horribly and pumping his palm-leaf fan. His eyes fascinated me; I watched them all day long. They were blazing points of hatred. They glittered like occult and sinister gems.... Thus, he fought his last fight, thirsting savagely for blood. All sense departed from him. He bit right and left, like a dog with rabies. He descended to demagogy so dreadful that his very associates at the trial table blushed. His one yearning was to keep his yokels heated up—to lead his forlorn mob of imbeciles against the foe.[2]

Mencken, although unique, was not alone in castigating Bryan. In fact, some of the harshest criticisms came from urban Southern intellectuals. Dixon Merritt, a Tennessee journalist, wrote in *The Outlook* that Bryan was "no longer the boy orator of the Platte, but the chronic scold of the Suwanee." Even George F. Milton, editor of the Chattanooga *News* and a friend of Bryan's, said in *World's Work* that the antievolution law was "an assault upon the freedom of thought and opinion." Joseph Wood Krutch, a 31-year-old Knoxville native, flayed Bryan for being a "fraud," Dayton for being a "stronghold of ignorance and bigotry," and the South for its "inflexible obstinancy [that] give[s] utterance to the blackest prejudices." To Krutch, the people in his home state were "an ignorant population," the state's leaders had "failed," and to "nine-tenths of Tennessee the only world it knows is with it and Bryan." Bryan, in this view, suffered from "obvious intellectual incompetence" and "mental backwardness" which Krutch unmasked each week during the trial for the New York-based *Nation* magazine.[3]

Some popular novels of the twenties created in fiction what reporters said was fact. For example, *Elmer Gantry* (by Sinclair Lewis) and *Teeftallow* (by T. S. Stribling) portrayed evangelists and antievolutionists as corrupted and ignorant.[4]

The only source of support for Bryan among intellectuals was indirect and after-the-fact. It came from a group of young Southern writers who took the title, "Agrarians," hardly an urban-oriented name. In 1930, they issued a book called *I'll Take My Stand*, which defended Southern history and culture. Donald Davidson, a Tennessean and a leader of the group, defended Bryan on such narrow grounds that it may have done him more harm than good. Davidson said that Southerners had the right to be cut off from the rest of the nation if they so desired. Since the group of Yankees who came to Dayton to defend Scopes merely wanted to impose their agnostic and industrial values on the South, Bryan and the Tennesseans were right to prefer instead local control over what they could teach. Davidson himself was not much interested in religion but thought that it was useful in preserving a strong agrarian society. His defense was more a defense of the Old South than of anything else.[5]

Mencken immediately challenged Davidson. "The opinion of New York, like that of any other cultural capital, is always immensely tolerant," said Mencken. Furthermore, "the naughtiest atheism is measurably more consonant with civilization than the demonology prevailing in rural Tennessee." Mencken was astounded that Davidson could

> believe in all seriousness that the Bryan obscenity at Dayton was a private matter, on which the rest of the country had no right to an opinion. What he overlooks is that it was made an indubitably and even vociferously public matter by the deliberate (if idiotic) act of the very "believers in God" he now defends, and that before it came to an end the whole world was looking on. Having been invited to the show, the world pronounced a verdict upon it, and what that verdict was he may discover by going to Capetown, or Samarkand, or Bogota, and telling the first literate man he meets that he is from Tennessee.

Mencken concluded that Davidson showed "a poor hand at the dialectic to expose one's self to such obvious ripostes."[6]

Darrow and the Scopes trial scientists scored with the media, but they were a minority and had trouble making headway at the grassroots level. A larger group of Bible-believing Christians, or fundamentalists, did not buy the arguments presented for evolution. Bryan had been their leader, but others continued his work to promote a more neutral discussion of evolution in schools across the country. The fundamentalists tried to use political muscle to offset the pro-evolutionists' media muscle.[7]

Among the fundamentalists, there was occasional disagreement on tactics. The Bryanites, like their dead hero, wanted only to restrict the teaching of evolution as a fact. After his death, however, some fundamentalists tried to purge evolutionary thinking entirely. Some school boards would not hire any science teacher who believed in evolution. A few teachers were fired primarily for teaching evolution as a theory. These problems flared in city and countryside alike. During 1925, for example, in the District of Columbia, antievolutionists organized to stop paying those teachers who taught the theory of evolution. Portland, Oregon, refused to permit its teachers to discuss either evolution or creation in class. In Paducah, Kentucky—the hometown of John Scopes—Scopes's sister and two other teachers were fired for their evolutionist views. Even in schools in New York City and Atlanta, teachers explained the theory of evolution in class at some peril to their jobs.

Sometimes extremists discredited themselves by their hyperbole. Mordecai R. Ham, for example, the minister of the First Baptist Church of Oklahoma City, attacked Dr. William Bizzell, president of the University of Oklahoma, saying:

> I do not say that Dr. Bizzell is a willing tool of the bolsheviks. I do say that he, along with the rest of the college presidents of the United States who permit the so-called scientific teaching of Darwinism in their schools are dupes of a great system born in Russia.

Such tactics do not seem to have been effective. The antievolution bill that the Reverend Mr. Ham supported was defeated.[8]

Many different types of antievolution bills were introduced. During the twenties, 20 states in the nation considered some type of antievolution law. The results were mixed. They were most successful in the South, where Mississippi (1926) and Arkansas (1928), after the Scopes trial, joined Oklahoma, Florida and Tennessee. In Louisiana and Texas, antievolution bills passed the House but were blocked in the Senate.[9] The Arkansas campaign is worth a close look, because it was the only state ever to hold a referendum on the teaching of evolution. An analysis of the campaign and of the election results reveals something about the sources of antievolutionism.

Bryan's influence can be seen in the Arkansas campaign. The proposed law prohibited "the teaching that man descended or ascended from a lower order of animals." But as the Arkansas *Democrat* in Little Rock pointed out, the wording would permit "the discussion or presentation [of evolution] as theory." At least, "that is our interpretation of the campaign propaganda sent out by the proponents of the measure." The antievolutionists were not objecting "to referring to 'theory of evolution' but they do resent the declaration that man's kinship to a lower order has been proven."[10]

Bryan had spoken in Arkansas on antievolutionism in 1924, and during the campaign four years later the antievolutionists used many of Bryan's arguments. What was more interesting was the campaign of those who opposed the amendment. They rarely used scientific evidence; instead they used fear of ridicule. The national press's ridicule of Bryan and Tennessee had made inroads into Arkansas. The Arkansas *Gazette*, also published in Little Rock, ran an article headlined, "Shall Arkansas Make Itself a Laughing Stock?" The article referred to Tennessee's poor public image as a result of the Scopes trial. Earlier the editor had argued that the proposed law would "unfortunately advertise abroad a state that has suffered sorely from being unfortunately advertised." The Arkansas *Democrat* (Little Rock) concurred. Its editor asked, "Why tell the world that the state of Arkansas denies that which 99 percent of the scientists declare is true? Why court ridicule?" The newspaper later concluded that "Act No. 1 can do nothing other than retard the state's progress by making it ridiculous in the eyes of the world."

At the University of Arkansas, various leaders of student organizations were pragmatic about their opposition to the amendment. "We do not want to be laughed at, as are the graduates of the University of Tennessee, and practically boycotted by larger universities and medical schools when we seek to pursue our education further."[11] Despite this fear of ridicule, however, the antievolution law passed with a 63 percent vote.

Who comprised this majority? We can check the county vote, then look at each county's literacy rate and population to see if antievolution laws especially attracted illiterates and rural people. Virginia Gray did such a study and found that many rural areas were indeed antievolution strongholds. But contrary to Darrow's stereotype, illiteracy is statistically connected (+ .43) with pro-evolution voters. In other words, the illiterates of Arkansas wanted evolution to be taught in their schools much more than did the literate folk. Some of this Gray explained by the African American vote; this group tended to be illiterate and pro-evolution. However, this also suggests that those Christians who believed in the literal interpretation of the Bible were not, as a group, any less educated or less intelligent than those who did not. Many educated people rejected evolution and accepted Bryan's argument about its harmful consequences when taught as true. That may explain why Fayetteville, the home of the University of Arkansas, voted over two to one for the antievolution law.[12]

Data from other states also suggest that antievolutionists were not necessarily less educated or even more rural than those who favored evolution. After Bryan's death, the major antievolution leaders were all urban preachers with large urban congregations. They included John R. Straton of New York City, Aimee Semple McPherson of Los Angeles, William Bell Riley of Minneapolis, and J. Frank Norris of Fort Worth. The North Carolina legislature voted on an antievolution law in 1925, and about half of those antievolution lawmakers who favored it had a college education—a proportion apparently close to that among the pro-evolution voters. All four of the physicians in the House voted for the antievolution bill. In Kentucky in 1922, the House defeated an antievolution bill, 42 to 41. Without strong help from west Kentucky, the state's most rural region, the pro-evolution forces would have lost. The nine legislators from the state's most western counties voted seven to two for teaching evolution.[13] Such evidence is not conclusive, but it does suggest that the media image of the antievolutionist as rural and uneducated may be Darrow hyperbole and not statistical fact.

Passing laws was not the antievolutionists' only goal; in fact, this was a last resort. What Bryan and his followers really wanted was for science textbooks to give a more neutral treatment of creation and evolution theories. Bryan had long criticized science textbooks and had lobbied with different publishers, asking them for neutral treatment of evolution in the schoolbooks they printed.[14]

From about 1924 to 1960, the major biology textbooks used in high schools across America, in both rural and urban areas, did become more neutral in their discussion of evolution. This was the conclusion of Judith Grabiner and Peter D. Miller, who completed a thorough study of the changes made in the major high school biology text-books during and after the twenties. According to Grabiner and Miller, the writers of the three new biology texts published from 1914–1921 were forceful promoters of evolution as the truth. In fact, Truman Moon's *Biology for Beginners* placed a picture of Darwin on the frontispiece and this statement in the text: "both man and apes are descended from a common ancestor from which both lines have developed."[15]

In 1924 and 1925, four new biology texts came out. By this time, Bryan had written to several publishers, and

Florida and Oklahoma had passed antievolution laws. The four new textbooks reflected Bryan's criticisms and were much more neutral on the subject of evolution. Three hardly mentioned evolution, and the fourth did not apply it to the origins of the human being. Grabiner and Miller concluded that

> the publication of such books at precisely the time when some legislatures had passed, and others were considering, antievolution laws was no coincidence. Events following the Scopes trial clearly show that the changes in the textbooks were responses to the antievolution movement.[16]

After the Scopes trial, the authors of the three older biology textbooks got the message. They did some revising and made their treatment of evolution more neutral. The metamorphosis of George Hunter's Civic Biology is especially interesting because this was the book Tennessee had adopted and Bryan had held up for criticism at the Scopes trial. Hunter's book came out in 1914 before the antievolution fervor, and he promoted Darwin as a "great ... scientist" and evolution as a solid "doctrine." Hunter pictured an "evolutionary tree," which tried to connect simple forms of life with more complex forms. Students were told to "copy this diagram in your notebook." In a section on the "evolution of man," Hunter adopted a racist argument. He described five races: the "negro type," the "brown race," the "American Indian," the "yellow race," "and finally, the highest type of all the Caucasians, represented by the civilized white inhabitants of Europe and America."[17]

During the Scopes trial, Bryan attacked Hunter in general for presenting evolution as a fact, and in particular for his picture of the evolutionary tree. "Here we have Mr. Hunter," Bryan said at the trial as he held up the book. "This is the man who wrote the book Mr. Scopes was teaching. And here we have the diagram ... He tells children to ... copy this diagram and take it home in their notebooks.... Shall [children] be detached from the throne of God and be compelled to link their ancestors with the jungle?" Bryan denounced Hunter more than Scopes, who was merely accused of teaching what Hunter had written. Because Hunter ignored creation and presented evolution as true, he had, Bryan believed, forced Tennessee to secure neutrality through the law.[18]

When Hunter heard these attacks, he feared that "the Scopes trial publicity would drive his book out of the classroom." He was eager to make changes. After the trial, he hastily brought out a second edition and retitled it *New Civil Biology*. Most of what was new, however, was his improved neutrality on evolution. The section on evolution was now called "development" and was much shorter. Gone was the evolutionary tree that so offended Bryan, and with it Darwin and even the mention of the word "evolution." No longer did Hunter say life formed "millions of years ago." Now he began his section on human beings by saying, "Man is the only creature that has moral and religious instincts." Finally, the section on race was no longer racist. Even from the grave, Bryan's influence was felt.[19]

As more and more textbooks took a neutral stance on evolution, fundamentalists had less and less need for antievolution laws. Indeed, because the antievolutionists were not distinctively rural, their campaign to change textbooks had not been rural, either—it was wide-ranging and somewhat sophisticated in strategy. Maynard Shipley, president of the Science League of America, watched the fundamentalists switch their focus from antievolution laws to textbooks. He concluded that "so much antievolution feeling was created that the textbooks are being altered to meet the views of the fundamentalists." Other scientists saw this trend, too. The *Quarterly Journal of Biology* reviewed two new biology texts in 1929 and concluded: "They have been written with the statutes of Tennessee, [Mississippi] and Arkansas in mind."[20]

These new, more neutral textbooks set the tone for the next 35 years. Most authors probably believed in evolution, but they did not impose their views on their high school readers. Instead, they described evolution in guarded terms that left open the possibility of creation. College texts in science, three of which were written by Scopes trial scientists, still presented evolution as a proven fact. Since less than ten percent of college age people went to college in the twenties and thirties, Bryan's antievolution campaign did make a difference—not so much in new laws, but in new textbooks that did not threaten the faith of Christian students.[21]

The success of Bryan's campaign was still noticeable in 1950. In that year, Estelle Laba and Eugene W. Gross published a study that surveyed eight high school biology textbooks used in highly urbanized New Jersey. They concluded that "New Jersey has never legislated against . . . teaching [evolution]. Yet even without legal assault, many textbooks used here are . . . evasive in their treatment of organic evolution." The authors further discovered that almost 40 percent of the high school biology teachers in their sample avoided discussing the evolution of man in their classes."[22]

As late as 1960, the antievolutionists' goal of neutrality on the teaching of evolution was still being fulfilled. Tennessee, Arkansas and Mississippi still had their antievolution laws, but these were no longer needed or enforced. No legal case was ever initiated in those states against any teacher for teaching evolution, even when it was taught as a fact. As long as the textbooks were reasonably even handed on evolution, the antievolutionists were satisfied.[23]

Given the state of scientific research, neutrality also seemed to make sense. By the sixties, evolution was being more openly criticized, even by a growing minority of scientists. The truths of the twenties were often the discarded theories of the Sixties. Blood serum tests, vestigial organs and embryos were all discredited by the sixties. So was much of the fossil evidence. Other anthropologists were busily trying to find substitutes. Such confusion was bound to have consequences and in the sixties, a group of scientists formed the Creation Research Society and began promoting faith in creation instead of faith in evolution.

This group, which by the eighties included over 600 trained scientists, put out a quarterly journal and a variety of books criticizing evolution.[24]

Other scientists pushed harder than ever for evolution. In 1959, during the centennial celebration of the publishing of Darwin's *Origins of the Species.* Hermann J. Muller, a genetics professor at Indiana University, gave a speech entitled "100 Years Without Darwinism Is Enough." He urged high school teachers and others to reimpose the teaching of evolution as a fact. George Gaylord Simpson of Columbia University also promoted this cause in speeches and in print. For nine years Simpson had worked under evolutionist Henry Fairfield Osborn and eventually has succeeded him as curator at the American Museum of Natural History.[25] Simpson used the Scopes trial to make his pitch for teaching evolution as "the most fundamental and general principle" of biology. "The fact is," Simpson said, "that [today] there are innumerable towns and whole cities that are just as opposed as Dayton, Tennessee, was to the teaching of evolution. And they are more successful in preventing it." Simpson explained why he thought this problem existed: Scopes had to "[submit] the question of the truth of evolution to the court and jury," instead of to the scientists. Therefore, Scopes lost because "a majority doubt, disbelieve, or . . . oppose" evolution. To reverse this result, Simpson argued that "legislatures, judges, and juries cannot decide the correctness of a scientific theory or the results of any scientific investigation. That can only be decided by future research in the self-correcting style of science." Simpson, then, wanted to take the authority for selecting textbooks out of the hands of "incompetent" textbook commissions and put it into the hands of the scientists.[26]

Like Osborn, Simpson wanted to use evolution to re-make society. He dreamed "of developing the enlightened citizenry" and believed that "everyone should enter the world into which Darwin led us." In fact, to Simpson, "the main reason why teaching evolution is important lies in its implications for mankind." Simpson became a crusader and campaigned among high school teachers and others to promote his dream of everyone following Darwin. But two obstacles emerged. First, when Simpson talked to teachers, "not . . . all [were] willing to learn. As regards my subject, evolution, a significant minority of them simply do not believe a word of it. . . ." Second, many of those who did believe Simpson were hamstrung by "antiintellectual control of science education by incompetent agencies." These agencies, or textbook commissions, denied that evolution was "the fundamental fact of life"; they wanted a neutral treatment of evolution. "Some biology textbooks," Simpson lamented, "omit evolution. Most of them relegate evolution to a single section, preferably at the back of the book, which need not be assigned."[27]

What the evolutionists could not achieve by argument, the federal government could achieve by edict. Simpson and his followers lobbied for help from the federal government to counter the antievolutionist strength. With federal support, the American Institute of Biological Sciences sponsored the writing of the Biological Sciences Curriculum Study (BSCS) textbooks. As Grabiner and Miller have noted, the BSCS books "completely transformed the profile of high school biology texts." According to the *Biology Teachers' Handbook*, which accompanied the BSCS books, "It is no longer possible to give a complete or even a coherent account of living things without the story of evolution." In the *BSCS Newsletter*, E. E. Lee wrote that "evolution is not only one of the major themes, but is, in fact, central among other themes; they're interrelated, and each is particularly related to evolution." Evolution was so heavily promoted it was "identified and accepted by a large group of distinguished scientists, science teachers, and other educators."[28]

Naturally, many creationists tried to stop this trend. But as Grabiner and Miller point out, "1964 was not 1926; this time the texts were adopted, unexpurgated. Scientists participated in the hearings. The prestige, power, and financial support of the federal government were behind the scientists and the new textbooks."[29]

One step the creationists could have taken would have been to pass and enforce Bryan's antievolution laws. This option was soon closed by the Supreme Court in *Epperson v. Arkansas* (1968), in which antievolution laws were ruled a violation of free speech.[30]

After the Epperson decision, those who have wanted neutrality on the teaching of evolution in the classroom have again worked through state legislatures: this time to pass laws to secure a "balanced treatment" or "equal time" for creation in any classroom discussions of human origins. Tennessee, Arkansas and Louisiana passed such laws. The American Civil Liberties Union (ACLU) has taken these laws to court, arguing that they are an "establishment of religion" and therefore a violation of the First Amendment. In *McLean v. Arkansas* (1982) and *Edwards v. Aguillard* (1987), the ACLU won its cases. These rulings helped lead the creationists to another approach: to go through the courts to have the teaching of evolution as a fact struct down as a similar "establishment of religion," the religion of secular humanism. Evolution, like religion, makes assumptions about God and the universe that are often acts of faith. Therefore, creationists argue, teaching evolution is as much a violation of the First Amendment as teaching creation is.[31]

The effectiveness of the earlier textbook campaign, as well as subsequent efforts by antievolutionists, is more comprehensible in light of our understanding that this group has had a broad base; antievolutionists were not (and are not) just "country folks," as some scholars have asserted. The highly partisan *urban* press played a significant role following the Scopes trial, certainly, but this is only one point to be considered. The battles at the grassroots level after the trial do not seem to have followed clear urban-rural patterns. Bryan and his followers, both urban and rural, wanted changes in textbooks, and when those changes were accomplished, the antievolution crusade became dormant until the sixties.

8

Mistaken Identity

Putting the John Reber Plan for the
San Francisco Bay Area into Historical
Context

David R. Long

James D. Hart's encyclopedic *A Companion to California*
includes one of the more exhaustive treatments of the
Reber Plan and its author:

> Reber, John (1887–1960), Ohio-born, self-taught engineer
> who conceived of the so-called Reber Plan to divide San
> Francisco Bay by earthwork dams (topped by highways
> and railways) to form a salt-water bay and two fresh-water
> lakes. The plan was seriously considered for some time.[1]

Today, most Californians who remember John Reber echo
Hart's themes. In March 1988, I asked San Franciscans if
they recalled anything about Reber. Those who did invariably responded: "He wanted to dam the bay, didn't
he?" Although more thoughtful in their reaction, historians
have treated Reber in a similar fashion. Turrentine Jackson
and Alan Patterson's *The Sacramento-San Joaquin Delta*
offers the most thorough historical analysis of the plan. It
devotes a chapter to Reber and couches his project in the
context of California water policy history.[2] Thus, from
Market Street to the halls of higher learning, the Reber
legacy is remarkably consistent. Most observers remember
him as an engineer and his plan as a failed dam.

John Reber had considerable support from the

engineering community, but he never claimed to be part of that guild. Rather, he was very adamant that he *was* a *planner*. As he saw it, his job was to envision a regional design that would comprehensively treat the Bay Area's needs. Engineers could then determine the project's feasibility. Thus, while his plan included two dams, it also dealt with an impressive range of regional urban issues, including: transportation, harbor development, water, defense, residential expansion, reclamation, recreation and wildlife conservation.

Despite his emphasis on typical planning issues, Reber was a maverick relative to mainstream practitioners in the American city and regional planning field. As Reber conceptualized his project from 1907 to 1931, the field's most influential leaders were Daniel Hudson Burnham and Thomas Adams, who spearheaded the City Beautiful and the City Functional movements, respectively.[3] Reber's work, however, owed nothing to the trends of the day. Rather, his massive, diverse and integrated project came from his observations of the Bay Area's geography and from the expressed wishes of the region's people. As a consequence, his plan was more geographically specific than those of his contemporaries. Ironically, it was also more in step with the thoughts of many planning intellectuals and it foreshadowed methodologies that were years away from the field's mainstream. Reber was also a Bay Area prophet. He raised planning issues that would concern the region for decades to come and offered the area its first comprehensive regional plan.

THE ORIGINS OF THE PLAN

John Reber began work on his planning venture shortly after migrating to the Bay Area in 1907. It is hardly surprising that Reber envisioned a new structure for the convalescing region. The great 1906 earthquake still left its ashen mark on San Francisco and many other area communities. For years, Reber had traveled throughout the

country as a theater producer and actor. He never explained what drew him to the Bay Area during the trau-
matic times of this postquake period. As a native Ohioan,
however, he was simply one of many in a massive
midwestern migration to the Golden State that had begun
in the later part of the nineteenth century.

John Reber continued to travel, albeit primarily within
the confines of his adopted region. During a few laborious
ferry crossings from San Francisco to Oakland, Reber began
thinking about the region's bays. He realized that the
waters linked area municipalities to an extent, but they
were ultimately more divisive than unifying. Reber's
impatience with these slow boat-rides sparked his plan.
While his design has long been remembered as a dam,
Reber originally conceived it as an earthen bridge and a
faster way across the bay.

After initiating an independent study of the Bay Area,
Reber added additional features to his fundamental bridge
concept. For the next 20 years, visitors to the University
of California's libraries could see John Reber's balding
head as it peeked over a stack of books at some overburdened table. As often as he was in the library, however,
Reber was out surveying the shores of his new home,
attempting to situate the individual fixtures of his emerging design. Yet the planner's most important research
came as a byproduct of his professional theater work. In
his working hours, Reber employed and was employed by
people from a variety of social classes and professions; he
used these contacts to gauge public opinion concerning
Bay Area planning needs. His cross section of acquaint-
ances included farm and labor leaders, local and national
politicians, industrialists and real estate developers, as
well as common laborers and performers. Although Reber
spent many hours in quiet contemplation, he still adapted
well to social settings. He had a natural ability to find
common ground between himself and the members of his
hybrid social circle. Reber's gift was so great that California statesman Hiram Johnson once told him: "You undoubtedly know more Californians well than any other

person."[4] In the same spirit, the *California Farmer* later referred to the campaign to implement the Reber Plan as a "people's movement."[5]

THE PLAN AND ITS GOALS

Despite the human influences that impacted the project, Reber's plan had a heart of earth and stone. Twin barriers or "moles" formed its core. The design called for the structures to connect San Francisco with the Oakland Estuary and Marin County with the City of Richmond. A hydraulic fill paralleling the Oakland-Alameda shoreline would have created a river linking the barrier's reservoirs.[6] Thus, Reber proposed a giant "horseshoe" to envelop the Golden Gate, resulting in two fresh water lakes and a central salt water harbor.[7] At the center of the fill, Reber sited a series of six ship locks to allow vessels to pass through his barrier configuration as they sailed inland or out to the Pacific.

As for the original focus of the Reber Plan, land-based transportation, the size of the two barriers would have accommodated a combination of automobile, rail and trolley routes. Both moles were four miles long, the northern one measuring 600 feet across and the southern 2,000. Thus there was ample room to experiment with a variety of crossing schemes.[8] When Reber arrived in the area, ferrys provided the only means for traversing San Francisco Bay and its sister bays, San Pablo and Suisin. In addition to being slow, these ferrys were often overburdened. In later years, some travelers went to great lengths to secure a space on the morning crossing. They would wait overnight by the docks, cramped in the backseats of their cars.

There were, in addition, other plans to rationalize regional urban traffic. On the San Francisco Peninsula, Reber planned to create four separate eight lane roads as "feeders" for his mole system.[9] Around the horseshoe he designed new dock facilities that, as he said, "would create 50 miles of new deep harbor frontage within the bay . . .

making the harbor ten times bigger than it is."[10] Wealth derived from these new facilities would have been spread throughout the region, from Sunnyvale to San Jose, Newark and Antioch.

Anchoring the entire regional transportation system was the most integrated grand central station in planning history. Originally, as with most central terminals in the early twentieth century, his station was to link the area's major railroad lines (the Western, Northwestern, Southern Pacific and Santa Fe), which terminated in different locations. The Northwestern even deposited its passengers at San Rafael, while freight went on to Petaluma or Ignacia.[11] In its final form, Reber's station integrated Bay Area transport in a single building that housed facilities for all forms of rail, automobile, sea and air traffic.[12] In addition to comprehensively coordinating the region's transportation facilities, Reber's transportation scheme was farsighted in two respects. He avoided problems of finding a site for the terminal on the already congested waterfront by placing it on new land to be created by reclamation. His project also addressed air transport needs before it was customary to do so. Even the volumes of *The Regional Plan for New York,* the touchstone of the City Functional Era, which appeared as Reber first publicly displayed his work, only tentatively accommodated budding aircraft technology.

No matter how daunting the prospect of rationalizing the existing system of Bay Area transportation, supplying the region with water was an even more ominous and insoluble problem. Reber took the words of the *San Francisco Downtowner* to heart: "Water is wealth in California, indeed it is the staff of life itself."[13] By this criterion, however, the Bay Area was nearing its deathbed. Even with the completion of both the Hetch Hetchy and East Bay "MUD" systems by the mid-thirties, the area's water supply could not cover even modest estimates of future regional needs. The product of existing water systems also cost much as four times that of comparable urban areas, such as Los Angeles and Seattle.

Ironically, the San Francisco Bay served as the mouth

SAN FRANCISCO BAY PROJECT—THE REBER PLAN

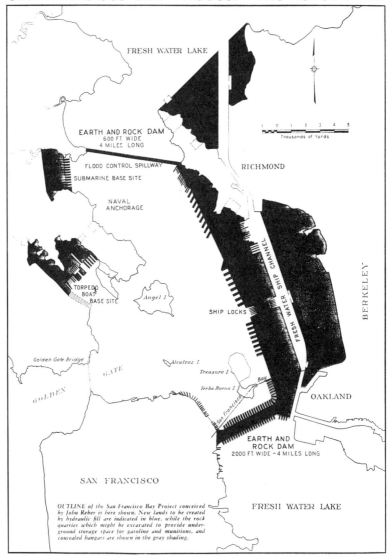

FRESH WATER LAKE

EARTH AND ROCK DAM
600 FT. WIDE
4 MILES LONG

FLOOD CONTROL SPILLWAY

SUBMARINE BASE SITE

NAVAL
ANCHORAGE

RICHMOND

TORPEDO
BOAT
BASE SITE

Angel I.

SHIP LOCKS

BERKELEY

FRESH WATER SHIP CHANNEL

Golden Gate Bridge

GATE

Alcatraz I.

Treasure I.

GOLDEN

Yerba Buena I.

Bay

OAKLAND

San Francisco

EARTH AND
ROCK DAM
2000 FT. WIDE – 4 MILES LONG

SAN FRANCISCO

OUTLINE of the San Francisco Bay Project conceived
by John Reber is here shown. New lands to be created
by hydraulic fill are indicated in blue, while the rock
quarries which might be excavated to provide underground storage space for gasoline and munitions, and
concealed hangars are shown in the gray shading.

FRESH WATER LAKE

1. From the Reber Papers, San Francisco Bay Delta Hydraulic Model
(SFBDHM). (Unless otherwise indicated, all following illustrations are
from Reber Papers). Reprinted by permission.

2. From Charles Wollenburg, *Golden Gate Metropolis, 1985*. Reprinted
by permission.

and the only Pacific outlet of California's mightiest
watershed, the confluence formed by the Sacramento and
San Joaquin Rivers.[14] When fresh water entered the bay,
however, salty Pacific tides contaminated it. According to
estimates from the late twenties, 33 million acre/feet of
water was lost annually to the Golden Gate, a volume
equal to twice the Colorado River's flow through seven
states.[15] Reber hoped to separate the fresh and salt water
with his barriers, resulting in two reservoirs that would
have held ten million acre/feet of water. The state's mighty
Shasta dam, California's largest in the forties, held less
than half that amount.[16] With so much water at his disposal, Reber believed that the storage capacity of his lakes

would be able to satisfy the needs of the 12 Bay Area counties as well as those of six neighboring counties.[17] In a later design, entitled "Streamlining California," he also advocated channeling some of this water south to Los Angeles and surrounding communities.[18] As engineer L. H. Nishkian put it, the new supplies would have meant that "area municipalities could have all the fresh water they wanted to use for industry for nothing—just the cost of pumping."[19]

The Bay Area also needed space to accommodate new industry and growth. John Reber's massive reclamation project would have created new industrial areas, residential sites and parklands along the natural boundaries of the bays. In all, he proposed to salvage 20,000 acres of new land, an area equal to two-thirds the size of San Francisco.[20]

In addition to new transportation systems and irrigation water, the Reber Plan promised salinity and flood control. Farmers in the Delta Region (east of Suisin Bay) suffered enormously due to the interplay of the Sacramento–San Joaquin River Basin and Pacific Ocean. When plentiful, fresh water naturally prevented sea water from encroaching upon area farms. During droughts, however, ebbing rivers allowed ocean water to pass up the Sacramento River, contaminating farms and wells along the way. At times briney water came within ten miles of the state capital.[21] By 1940 California authorities annually released 2.4 million acre/feet of water from their mountain reservoirs to keep the ocean at bay. Reber's earth and stone barriers were an alternative to this massive "wall of water" that is still employed today. Unusually high river levels also caused problems for the Delta, as destructive floods periodically washed through the area. Reber designed siphon spillways along his barriers that would keep his lakes at a constant level and abate the flood problem. The spillways would channel excess river flows through the moles and into the central harbor.[22] In all, Reber hoped his barrier design would increase productivity in the Delta by 600,000 acres.

During the World War II and Cold War years, John

Reber emphasized his provisions for national defense. He argued that his water and transportation systems were as solid as the plan's moles. Reber believed his crossings could withstand anything short of a series of direct bomb hits. Yet, if the barriers did give way, they could be easily repaired with earth and rock. (Reber used similar reasoning the illustrate his plan's earthquake precautions). The existing area water systems and suspension bridges, however, were not as secure. A single pipeline served San Francisco's Hetch Hetchy water system. The Golden Gate and Bay Bridges, according to some estimates, could be destroyed with 150 dollars worth of explosives.[23] Additionally, repairs to the Hetch Hetchy pipeline or the suspension bridges would be very time-consuming and would require materials such as iron and steel, which were usually difficult to obtain during a war. Reber also stressed the advantages of his new transportation system over existing bay bridges in the event of wartime mobilization or evacuation, especially during atomic attack. He believed his scheme was less apt to gridlock. In the fifties, local and national political leaders signed on to Reber's thinking. "Federal authorities," commented San Francisco Supervisor Pat McMurray, "have recognized the need for an earthfill crossing to aid in the evacuation of people in the event of an atomic attack."[24]

While Reber intended to create indestructible access routes and a source of plentiful, inexpensive water for existing military posts and bases, he also wanted to see to new martial facilities constructed throughout the area. He sited installations around the gigantic horseshoe created by the project's moles and hydraulic fill. Additionally, Marin County received two naval bases; one submarine base was just north of Sausalito, and a torpedo boat facility was south of the barrier that terminated at Point San Quentin. Airbases and a naval site would be built on the fill along the East Bay shoreline. The most novel facility, however, was a mammoth underground storage area that the planner hoped would result from quarrying for the barriers' rock beneath area hills.[25]

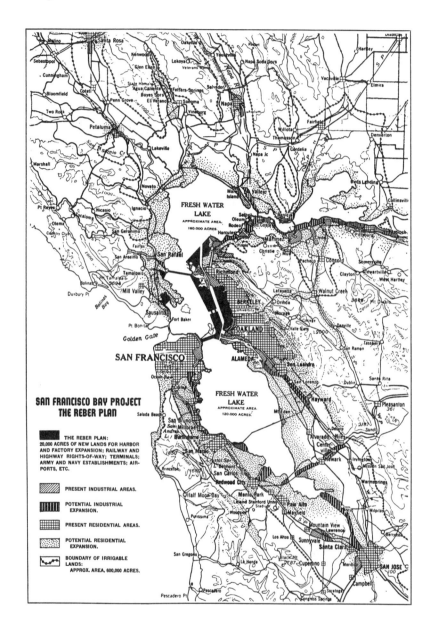

3. From the Reber Papers, SFBDHM.

4. From the Reber Papers, SFBDHM.

As Reber frequently hinted, defense and urban development were often symbiotic, especially in the American West. Military facilities normally created an increase in the demand for goods and services in local economics, a fact well understood by urban leaders who often waged their most bitter intercity battles to procure such installations. Thus, if the creation of these new Bay Area bases remotely followed the typical pattern, the Reber Plan promised new jobs for Marin and Alameda Counties.[26]

Reber's plans for both industrial and residential expansion also paralleled his liberal distribution of harbor and military facilities. Here again, the planner attempted to share the wealth. In particular, he hoped his design would spur growth in areas often bypassed for the San Francisco Peninsula and Contra Costa and Alameda Counties. Reber's plan reached north, south and east of this traditional urban center. While smaller cities such as Napa and Petaluma received industrial sites, it was the pattern of residential growth that particularly departed from the norm. The traditional corridor, which ran east from San Francisco to Oakland and then north to Richmond, received far less attention than the more outlying portions of the Bay Area.

The Reber Plan also included area-wide recreation, conservation and preservation measures. Noting the glaring disparity between tourism revenues for the Bay Area and Los Angeles, Reber designed facilities that he hoped would allow his region to catch up. For the shores of his reclamation project, he planned public beaches, fishing piers, gardens and parks.[27] His wildlife conservation measures also addressed the tourism problem. By stocking his lakes with a variety of trout, perch and bass, he hoped to create "the greatest fishing hole in the world."[28] In designing a series of fish ladders for the area's salmon and shad, which traveled the Sacramento and San Joaquin Rivers via the San Francisco Bay, Reber hoped to preserve the area's migratory fish as well. Even his ship locks did their part, serving as conduits for the migratory beasts.

Although such wildlife-centered measures added to the price of the San Francisco Bay Project, supporters believed it would be money well spent. Reber asserted that the sale of reclaimed land alone would pay construction costs.[29] While the salvage project involved over 20,000 acres of property, it also created prime innercity and beachfront real estate. Reber promised a return on investment from a number of sources. In the Delta, 600,000 additional acres of farmland could be cultivated with the combination of the plan's irrigation projects and its salinity and flood control features. Attracted by improved transportation coupled with cheap land and water, new industries would locate to the region. Likewise, the military installations could have charged new growth. In all, advocates estimated the Reber Plan's worth to be ten times its cost of construction, making it one of the few truly self-financing plans in history.

Finally, to secure his plan's construction and guide future development, Reber lobbied to create a regional planning authority. He believed the area needed an organization with even more executive power than the California Toll Bridge Authority, which oversaw the construction of bay crossings. The new organization, however, would have to address a much wider range of planning issues.

REBER'S PROJECT AND PLANNING ORTHODOXY

As a testament to Reber's imagination, his was perhaps the largest project in two eras of great plans. The earliest of these, the City Beautiful, signaled the emergence of the field in the United States. As its name implies, the movement emphasized the physical beautification of urban areas. Its proponents hoped that by restructuring America's cities they could "elevate the masses" and create political, social and economic well-being. The second era, the City Functional, was far less poetic than its predecessor. In it, statistical analysis replaced artistic sensibilities, and more staid suggestions replaced bold proposals. Both the Cities Beautiful and Functional sought to address roughly the same needs, but the latter focused more heavily on economic issues. Reber did share a kindred spirit with both movements. He collected data and focused on scientific analysis in a manner reminiscent of the City Functional. At no time, however, did he abandon his unparalleled vision. In this sense, John Reber also allied himself with members of the earliest planning movement.

Ultimately, however, Reber was a maverick, and his distance from methods employed by the field's practitioners allowed him to create a design that was geographically specific. Ironically, in doing so he intuitively aligned himself with the thoughts of many planning intellectuals, and his work foreshadowed future methodologies.

The "White City" of the 1893 Columbian Exposition has traditionally been credited with helping to professionalize the planning field by launching the City Beautiful. A team of architects, coordinated by Daniel Hudson Burnham, created a utopian city that set a new standard for American architecture and also introduced fair-goers to the concept and promise of comprehensive planning.[30] Along the shores of Lake Michigan, Burnham and his fellow architects created a plaster facade of a stately and orderly city that represented an artful combination of Greek, Roman and European styles. Certainly the City Beautiful movement also had many antecedents to the White City. Additionally, some earlier civic leaders had been involved with fairly comprehensive urban designing.[31] Yet, 21.5 million people, a sizable portion of the U.S. public, flocked to the White City.[32] In the end, the display and the interest it generated came to define an American planning ideal as it coalesced ideas that had been evolving for many years.

The White City influenced American municipalities on many levels. Individual examples of its architectural style colored the construction of civic centers, college campuses and boulevards. On a grander scale, however, the display helped create the notion of the City Beautiful and its orthodox application. The movement inspired bold city and regional plans across the country, from Memphis to New York to San Francisco. The display along Lake Michigan also secured Daniel Burnham's position as the leader of this American planning movement. It was his 1909 *Plan of Chicago* that became the most expansive expression of the City Beautiful.

The complete Chicago design called for a highway and park system spreading over 4,000 square miles. Within this fundamental web, the plan had six primary features designed to rationalize, beautify and decongest the region. Burnham relocated and consolidated freight and passenger rail terminals, advocated a new port scheme to separate through and local water-borne freight, and introduced a new pattern of diagonal roads within the city to link different sections of the community to the commercial center. The planner also envisioned a new fashionable business district north of the Chicago River, linked to the old business area by a novel double-decked bridge with a level for cars and one for trucks; and he suggested a series of beaches, parks and off-shore islands for the Lake Michigan frontage. Finally, Burnham focused his inspirational energies on two classically inspired community facilities, Grant Park and a Civic Center.

While often noted for his aesthetic achievements, Daniel Hudson Burnham obviously treated the Chicago region in ways that can only be deemed "functional." Yet, Burnham was a passionate man, and aesthetics were his love. He believed that beauty had more value than any other consideration.[33] There was an economic side to this argument (a beautified Chicago would attract wealthy residents and tourist dollars), but the social and political implications of his planning were more profound. He believed that his creations would serve as a type of municipal flag that would inspire good citizenship and benefit the whole of society. When citizens are lifted above the "usual life" of their thoughts and feelings, he asserted, "the state of which [they are] part is benefitted thereby."[34]

In pursuit of his planning goals, Daniel Burnham left himself open to some stinging criticism. His *Plan of Chicago* suggests the construction of European-like buildings, complete with uniform cornice heights. These structures would serve as a backdrop for the gondolas crowding the plan's imaginary lagoons. In short, as Christine Boyer and Mel Scott have noted, Burnham and City Beautiful proponents often spent too much time suggesting what the "American city should look like."[35] Many observers believed the pretensions of these designs were very un-American in political and structural terms. Louis Sullivan saw quasi-feudalism in the White City. More contemporary writers called the City Beautiful "imperial."[36] Mel Scott believed these Old World architectural styles were inappropriate to a democratic society. The White City's amalgam of borrowed designs certainly enthralled Columbian exposition visitors, but the display was, as Scott puts it, "as improbable in the Midwest as a gleaming iceberg would be in the Gulf of Mexico."[37]

While Reber and City Beautiful practitioners like Daniel Burnham suggested substantial alterations to existing urban environments, Reber's planning style was more geographically specific than his contemporaries. City Beautiful designers addressed specific canons. Most of these designs, for instance, included diagonal roadways (as a logical reaction to the traditional grid system). Burnham included them in plans for Washington, D.C., Cleveland, San Francisco and even Manila. An unfulfilled City Beautiful design for New York, completed without Burnham's help, did the same. In the end, these mainstream works were similar regardless of their location. They usually included massive classically and European-inspired buildings, uplifting parks, civic centers and an architectural unity of both design and scale.

The *Regional Plan of New York*, the touchstone design of the City Functional, was also theory-driven. While Burnham had scaled soulful peaks with his suggestions, Thomas Adams and this new breed of planner concerned themselves with mortality and shipping rates rather than with civic inspiration. The City Functional evolved as a reaction to criticisms launched at the aesthetic and visionary components of the Burnham-lead movement.[38] It was a "practical" planning approach in methodological and political terms. These mainstream planners wanted scientific analyses to shape their decisions, and they pursued ideas that they believed could survive politically (unlike Burnham's lagoons).

Both early planning groups did share a fundamental aim, however, the decongestion of America's cities. Essentially, *The Regional Plan of New York* can be summarized with three points that build on this idea. First the design suggested the "diffused recentralization of industry" to lessen congestion in existing centers and to create new ones. Second, it advocated the "diffusion of residence" to coincide with new industrial centers and reduce the distance from home to workplace. Third, the proposal included designs for the "sub-centralization of business" for greater consumer convenience.[39] Points one through three were to be attained primarily by a massive highway and park system.[40]

In the end, while Burnham was criticized for suggesting too much, commentators harpooned Adams and his committees for not advocating enough. While City Beautiful practitioners dreamed of new urban utopias, the planners of New York called only for minor changes in the existing pattern of development—"noncontroversial public controls to curb the market's worst abuses."[41] As the regional plan committee saw to the publication of its project's many volumes, Lewis Mumford pointedly criticized Thomas Adams's lack of vision. In later years, some historians would view the plan's conservatism as a ploy to protect existing elite capital investments.[42]

Whatever the value or impetus of the plans of Chicago and New York, the fact remains that they were much more theory-driven than the Reber Plan.[43] Mr. Reber certainly exhibited the strength of vision that characterized the City Beautiful and concern for practical needs that drove the City Functional, but he did not approach his planning of the San Francisco Bay Area with a predetermined framework. He did not promote his version of beauty and, although industrial and residential dispersal were implicit in his plan, Reber was not particularly committed to the idea of diffusion. Instead, he allowed the Bay Area's geography, his personal experience and that of the region's citizens, to fire his imagination. His plan was therefore more geographically specific than most in his day.

Although John Reber operated without regard to the theories that drove the Cities Beautiful and Functional, by focusing specifically on the Bay Area and needs of its people, his efforts clearly echoed ideas espoused by many planning thinkers. "Urban planning is not something which can be learned in one place and imitated in another," wrote late nineteenth century planning forerunner Sir Patrick Geddes. "It is the development of a local life . . . in its own way and upon its own foundations."[44] The profile of a good planner, Russell Black noted in 1938, consisted primarily of "common sense and good judgment," qualities that he found many times more important than a professional education (or theoretical training).[45] Shortly after Reber's death in the sixties, Alan Altshuler claimed that a planner needed to do two things: understand a community in question; and gauge the effect of a plan upon individuals and their area.[46] Following his own "common sense," Reber did this.

Although, like most of the *Regional Plan for New York* and much of the *Plan of Chicago*, the Reber Plan remains unrealized, the author's grasp of the needs of the Bay Area was remarkable. A U.S. Army Corps of Engineers 1963 study, the result of many years and several million dollars of effort, listed six areas the region needed to address: water conservation, additional bay crossings, rapid transit, navigation improvements, land reclamation and the establishment of a Bay Area planning authority.[47] Reber, of course, had been advocating such measures since the early thirties. The plan's political life also indicates that it represented many of the Bay Area's needs. It was an active issue from the thirties to the sixties. Such a shelf-life is unusual for a specific regional plan, and Reber's project, as a whole, was certainly considered over a longer period than were the pinnacle designs of both the City Beautiful and City Functional eras.

Structurally, the Reber Plan was also quite different

from its contemporaries. In terms of its size, John Reber's San Francisco Bay Project was arguably the largest of the two early planning eras, which were marked by massive plans. His design directly affected an area more than 80 miles in diameter. His complementary "Streamlining California" plan called for a canal and highway system that would connect Southern California to the Reber Plan and thus expand its effect by several hundred miles.[48] Reber's broad strokes and vision allowed him to address emerging concerns not present in the Chicago and New York designs: air transport, water conservation, agricultural development, national defense and wildlife. Additionally Reber's proposed physical unification of the Bay Area emphasized structural integration to a degree beyond that advocated in the two better known designs. The linking of all area transportation systems in his grand central station provides one striking example, but his proposal to literally bond the region's eastern and western peninsulas truly underscored his notions of unity and integration.

Granted, the Reber Plan's barriers fostered much of the project's diversity and created its high degree of integration. Such a structure was impossible in Chicago and New York. The fact that Reber created such a novel structure and one that was considered for so long, however, indicates that his nontraditional planning style allowed him to design beyond orthodox boundaries. More than his contemporaries, he specifically tailored his ideas to a unique urban environment.

JOHN REBER AS PROPHET AND ACTIVIST

Reber's specific focus on the Bay Area and the needs of its people had another unintended and prophetic result: it foreshadowed future planning methodologies. In creating his design, Reber actively consulted a cross section of the region's citizenry. This practice was unusual for the times. Burnham and Adams consulted almost exclusively with professionals or elites. Reber's pluralistic efforts were a layman's "client analysis," a methodological approach that was decades away from the planning mainstream.[49] The extent to which the general public was involved in the construction of Reber's design (and later with its promotion) also foreshadowed a participatory planning style that was on an even more remote horizon.

Reber served a prophet-like function for the Bay Area as well. Many renowned urban designers had targeted the region in their work, from Daniel Burnham himself, to Charles Mulford Robinson and Frederick Law Olmsted. Until Reber unveiled his project, however, none had offered a truly regional plan for the Bay Area. As Mel Scott put it, "The very existence of a plan for the entire bay was tonic, for it promised to evoke other plans and it turned the spotlight on the future."[50]

CONCLUSION

Thus, John Reber was a planner with a massive, diverse and integrated urban design, not strictly an engineer advocating a pair of dams. He was a maverick relative to the practicing regional planners of his day, and yet his actions were intuitively in step with much of the field's intellectual discussion. Not theory, but the San Francisco Region's geography and people fired his imagination. Prophetically, he approximated planning methodologies that were years away from the mainstream and, with the completion of the Bay Area's first comprehensive urban design, John Reber highlighted planning issues of the region's future.

9

Preparing for Armageddon
The Role of the City in Civil Defense Planning During World War II

Robert Earnest Miller

During World War II, many American cities and towns developed elaborate air raid precautions modeled after the British response during the blitz. The heavy bombing of British cities served as a justification for American civilian defense planners and municipal officials in formulating air raid precautions of their own, and it stimulated popular interest in civilian defense. Big city mayors like Fiorello H. LaGuardia of New York played a key role in soliciting support from the federal government for civilian defense planning. Unlike most of the other belligerent powers, however, the United States escaped many of the hardships of total warfare. Aside from enemy submarine activity along the Pacific and Atlantic coasts early in the war, and the Japanese balloon bombs that caused relatively few casualties during the final months of the war, the United States was spared the wholesale destruction visited upon many other countries.[1]

As a result, civilian protection plans were never fully implemented in America. Nevertheless, more than ten million Americans volunteered for some type of civilian defense work before and during the war. This essay will examine how state and municipal civilian defense planning evolved even before the Japanese attack on Pearl Harbor, and how the Office of Civilian Defense (OCD), a federal agency, coordinated those plans during World War

II. When Allied forces launched counterattacks in the Pacific and North Africa in 1942, the danger of enemy attacks diminished in America. For the duration of the war, OCD engaged its volunteers in a variety of homefront chores designed to maintain morale and combat complacency.

PREPARING FOR THE WORST, 1940–1941

In 1940 few Americans felt threatened by the early Nazi advances in Europe and Scandinavia. War Department officials had warned President Franklin D. Roosevelt that sporadic "hit-and-run" air raids by the enemy were possible, but little attention was given to civilian defense planning. The American defense effort focused, instead, on converting the nation's economic resources to the production of armaments, ammunition and supplies for the Allies. Even after the fall of France, in June 1940, War Secretary Harry H. Woodring warned Roosevelt that a general call by the federal government for state and local civilian defense organization would "needlessly alarm our people...."[2]

When the German Luftwaffe intensified its bombing missions on British cities, however, many Americans wondered if they were equally vulnerable to enemy attack. While the danger of any actual enemy attack of North America was marginal at best, many Canadian and American municipal officials felt compelled to take some precautionary measures to protect potential civilian and industrial targets.[3] Veterans' organizations like the Veterans of Foreign Wars (VFW) and the American Legion also pressed the federal government to develop a civilian defense program and offered to train interested volunteers in methods of gas and air raid defense. In some Atlantic Coast states, the War Department built up a Ground Observation Corps staffed by civilian volunteers to monitor and record all air traffic. Veterans' groups provided the nucleus for many of these units. Roosevelt offered only lukewarm encouragement to these private and independent efforts. Civilian defense, the president believed, should stem from the police powers of the states and cities.[4]

Accordingly, in August 1940 President Roosevelt encouraged governors to form state and local defense councils and to develop civilian protection plans. At the same time, he established the Division of State and Local Cooperation (DSLC), a subordinate unit of the National Defense Advisory Commission (NDAC), to coordinate and standardize state and local defense initiatives, including civilian protection. Within a few weeks, 25 states established officially sanctioned defense councils. The War Department provided educational equipment and training materials to the state councils for distribution to their local defense councils in the cities.[5]

At first, the DSLC worked mainly with communities that had been affected by the war boom. The DSLC forged a strong relationship with business leaders who had a big stake in the defense effort. Since defense plants represented obvious potential targets for the enemy, corporate leaders were encouraged to assist municipal officials with civilian defense plans.[6] Despite calls for greater preparedness, the DSLC, like the Roosevelt administration, generally advised against mass participation in civilian defense. The DSLC was concerned that a general "call to arms" would induce panic. Instead, the federal government stressed the need for civilian defense "planning." The *National Municipal Review* endorsed the administration's position. The editors conceded that "the sudden conquest of other countries had given rise to a desire in the United States that 'we do something' and do it fast." However, they advised against any "hasty, ill-conceived plans, . . . at this stage, it is very much a job for experts."[7]

In November 1940 the DSLC formed an Advisory Committee on Fire Safety to study the effects of incendiary bombs dropped on British cities. The committee concluded that the spread of fire, especially in densely populated areas, posed the greatest danger should an enemy air raid occur. The DSLC encouraged local defense councils to take inventories of public and privately owned firefighting equipment. The committee also stressed the need for mutual aid plans among neighboring fire departments in larger cities. At the same time, some organizations conducted independent studies; the American Legion, the American Women's Voluntary Services, and the New York City Fire Department sent fact-finding missions to London to observe firefighting techniques and civilian defense organization.[8]

The British experience also influenced state and local civilian defense planning. In New York, for example, the Governor's Council on Evacuation studied the need for removing children from metropolitan areas to less populated regions, as Great Britain did. Likewise, Stanley M. Isaacs, president of the Manhattan Borough, informed Mayor LaGuardia that a partially constructed, five-story parking garage could be converted to an air raid shelter should the need arise.[9] Other Americans responded to the plight of the British people as depicted in newsreels and films during the blitz.[10]

Municipal officials who saw the need for elaborate air raid precautions began to look to the federal government for financial support and leadership. In January 1941, LaGuardia submitted a report on civilian defense organization and administration in the United States to the United States Conference of Mayors (USCM), a national organization over which he presided. LaGuardia drew on the findings of the fire officials he had sent to England in November 1940. The mayor declared:

> Modern aerial warfare has placed a tremendous responsibility on the cities and their civilian population. On the shoulders of the local authorities has fallen the whole burden of 'passive' or civil defense—fire protection, medical and hospital services, restriction of lighting, protection of transport, armament-producing plants and utilities, evacuation and housing, clearance of debris, and other noncombatant tasks.[11]

According to LaGuardia and other big city mayors, civilian protection was essentially an urban concern. They felt that a federal civilian defense agency (other than the DSLC) could better serve the interests of state and local defense councils. The mayors' dissatisfaction with the DSLC stemmed largely from its tendency to work through state rather than municipal authorities. Many mayors argued that direct links were needed between the federal government and the coastal cities most vulnerable to enemy attack. As head of the USCM and mayor of the nation's largest city, LaGuardia found himself in a unique position to demand a greater federal role in civilian defense planning. Appealing personally to Roosevelt in January 1941, LaGuardia contended:

> The whole experience of England indicates that national policies are essential in such fields as financing the cost of [air raid] shelters, warning systems, communications control, [and] mutual aid plans. . . . Other countries have learned that the responsibility of civil defense and the loss of a city is not local but involves and injures the entire country.[12]

In February 1941, at the USCM regional meeting in St. Louis, mayors from cities between the Allegheny and Rocky mountains requested that the War Department set up an Advisory Committee for Civilian Defense of the Cities. President Roosevelt responded slowly to the mayors' requests to create a federal civilian defense agency. The president worried about provoking isolationist critics. Daniel W. Hoan, assistant director of the DSLC, echoed Roosevelt's concerns at the February USCM meeting when he warned mayors that any attempts to mobilize broad-based support for civilian defense could "spread hysteria and retard the whole program." Roosevelt realized, at the same time, that the administration's inaction might alienate some of his most ardent supporters.[13]

The president instructed Bureau of the Budget director Harold D. Smith, former ambassador to France William Bullitt, and presidential assistant Wayne Coy to formulate a plan for the federal government's role in civilian defense. In April 1941, the three advisers recommended that the president create an Office of Home Defense by executive order. Smith, Bullitt and Coy envisioned a federal agency that would coordinate the efforts of the 44 states and over

1,000 local defense councils in the event of air raids or other emergencies. At the same time, morale would be boosted through the encouragement of volunteer activities designed to give people a sense of partnership in the defense effort.[14]

Roosevelt and his advisers conducted a search for the "right man" to head the civilian defense agency. After several weeks of deliberating, the president determined that Fiorello LaGuardia would be perfect for the job. The president wanted the new agency to be led by a "big name," a nationally known personality who could attract attention to civilian defense. On 20 May 1941, Roosevelt signed Executive Order 8757, which created the Office of Civilian Defense (OCD). LaGuardia agreed to head the new agency on a part-time basis without pay. The new agency varied only slightly from the original home defense plan.[15]

Essentially, Executive Order 8757 divided the OCD into two general divisions, both chaired nominally by LaGuardia. The Board for Civilian Protection was comprised of representatives from the Departments of War, Navy, Justice, and the Federal Security Agency, as well as civilian representatives from the United States Conference of Mayors, the American Municipal Association, and the Council of State Governments. According to the Executive Order, the board would "advise and assist in the formulation of civil defense programs and measures . . . designed to afford adequate protection of life and property in the event of an emergency." On the other hand, the Volunteer Participation Committee, which was composed of 45 members appointed at large by the president, would "serve as an advisory and planning body in considering and developing programs designed to sustain the national morale and to provide constructive civilian participation in the defense effort."[16]

Despite the OCD's broad mandate, LaGuardia made it clear from the start that civilian protection would be given priority over other programs. Just after his appointment to the OCD, LaGuardia stated: "An auxiliary fire department, and an auxiliary police department, and an auxiliary medical department—that is all there is to civilian defense." The Volunteer Participation Committee began to take shape and coordinate substantive programs in September 1941 only after LaGuardia appointed Eleanor Roosevelt to develop volunteer programs in recreation, nutrition, child care and consumer information. LaGuardia publicly supported her initiatives, but privately he dismissed her work as "sissy stuff." The First Lady recalled later that "every activity which Mayor LaGuardia did not want in his part of the program was thrust into my division."[17]

The OCD was strictly an advisory and informational agency. The ultimate responsibility for civilian protection fell upon state and local authorities. In order to coordinate the activities of the state and local defense councils, LaGuardia set up nine regional offices congruent with the Army Corps Areas. The War Department assigned one reserve colonel and one Air Corps officer to each regional office. Likewise, state and local defense councils, whenever possible, reserved a place for army and naval reserve officers. Defense councils seldom attracted the "best and brightest" that the military had to offer. Nonetheless, the presence of uniformed officers and their approval of civilian protection plans helped legitimize the authority of the state and local defense councils.[18]

In July 1941, LaGuardia encouraged police and fire officials from more than 100 Atlantic Coast cities to attend the War Department's Chemical Warfare Service training at Aberdeen, Maryland. At the same time, he sent delegations of police, fire and public health officials to England to observe virtually every aspect of civilian defense.[19]

Based on his knowledge of Great Britain's civilian defense effort, LaGuardia agreed with earlier reports arguing that fires started by incendiary bombs posed the greatest danger to American cities. After one air raid in London, 530 fires burned simultaneously. Therefore, LaGuardia encouraged municipal fire departments in "target cities" in America to enlarge their permanent firefighting forces three to five times by recruiting auxiliary firefighters. These cities would also require additional firefighting equipment, such as portable pumpers, firehoses, steel helmets and gas masks, which should be placed in strategic locations around the city to assist the auxiliary forces. LaGuardia reminded municipal fire officials that "every city is now a legitimate target." The OCD head continued:

> This means that the civilian population is exposed to attack. The entire technique of warfare has changed, for now there is no isolated zone of war. Rights of those not in the uniformed service no longer exist.[20]

LaGuardia hoped to stir American municipal officials into action with his gloomy predictions. The OCD had the unenviable task of motivating state and city officials to prepare for the unimaginable. During the summer of 1941 LaGuardia delivered up to 50 speeches per month. His constant references to the British experience during the blitz served as unpleasant reminders to a largely complacent audience, who still felt relatively safe. Historian Thomas Kessner conceded: "Even when he [LaGuardia] did have an idea worth trumpeting, his shrill voice had become so common that few paid it much heed." On the other hand, the OCD had to temper some of its doomsday predictions in order to dissuade overzealous preparedness schemes. In spite of those formidable obstacles, many cities developed civilian protection plans and began to offer training courses for aircraft spotters, air raid wardens, fire watchers, and auxiliary firefighters and police. Air raid precautions and evacuation plans, like those in England, were often adopted by local defense councils in the United States.[21]

In June 1941 some of the earliest blackout tests were conducted in Seattle, East St. Louis and Pittsburgh with the cooperation of army officials. Many municipal leaders assumed that their own cities represented the most logical target for enemy-directed sabotage or enemy bombers. In Los Angeles, auxiliary police patrolled municipal water and power lines, protecting against potential sabotage. An enterprising local defense council in Bridgeport, Connecticut

constructed a "bomb taxi"—a steel-reinforced vehicle—
that could assist in the removal of unexploded bombs.
Harvard Law School Dean James M. Landis, the regional
OCD director for New England, applauded the efforts of
Connecticut defense officials. Landis warned:

> We have yet to sense fully the implications of events
> abroad, to realize . . . that our situation is one of deadly
> peril. . . . We in New England stand at the most accessible
> point of attack, and with its increasing defense industry,
> New England remains the ideal target for enemy action.[22]

Even in inland cities, which were presumably less vulnerable to enemy air raids, civilian protection plans were
enacted. In Cincinnati, Ohio, nearly 500 miles from the
Atlantic seaboard, civilian defense planners asserted:

> the citizens of every community have a right to assume that
> their representative officials have considered every possible
> provision for their protection and safety against sabotage
> or any act of war.[23]

By late November 1941, every state and nearly 6,000
cities had formed defense councils. Over 750,000 men and
women had volunteered for some type of civilian defense
work, and nearly 200,000 first aid certificates had been
issued since the OCD was created. Texas, the largest state
in the Union, had 890 local defense councils, while West
Virginia had only its state defense council. Coastal regions
were presumably the most vulnerable to enemy attack.
New England states claimed more than 1,200 local organizations, but the Pacific Coast lagged behind with 612.
Midwestern states with large industrial bases belied the
OCD's assumption that civilian defense was strictly a
concern of coastal regions. Ohio and Illinois had 150 and
148 local defense councils, respectively.[24]

The OCD, however, had been fighting an uphill battle
promoting civilian protection plans to state and municipal
leaders and to the public. In early December 1941, American attitudes about U.S. involvement in the war still remained sharply divided: there were those who supported

the interventionist strategy of economic and military aid to the Allies, and there were those opposed to it who wanted to remain isolated from the sordid events in Europe. Isolationists also opposed the OCD's preparedness efforts. The *Chicago Tribune*, a major isolationist newspaper, lambasted the OCD, characterizing it as an agency created by "a war minded administration to whip up war fever." The *Tribune's* editors charged:

> The United States is not at war, and if the citizens of the middlewest <sic> have their way it won't be. There are no invaders beyond yonder tree. . . . The nonsensical program of the OCD, inviting busybodies to do some 250 useless things that can only add to the confusion of the defense program . . . can only be classified as defense boon-doggling. . . ."[25]

The attack on Pearl Harbor, of course, changed everything. For a brief moment, political and social differences that had hindered the defense effort vanished. Suddenly, groups and individuals that had expressed little interest in civilian defense, openly avowed support for all necessary measures to protect the homefront. According to LaGuardia:

> Civilian protection not only became one of the immediate objectives of an aroused people, but one of the most important means of unifying the noncombatant population by giving it an opportunity for effective, united action.

Moreover, the attack on Pearl Harbor seemed to make relevant the OCD's frequent comparison of the British and American civilian defense programs.[26]

THE UNITED STATES GOES TO WAR, 1942

At 8:40 A.M., 7 December 1941, during the midst of the attack on Pearl Harbor, a radio announcer in Hawaii shouted into his microphone: "This is no maneuver . . . this is the real McCoy!" On the island of Wahiawa, volunteer civilian defense workers had already responded to the enemy attack. Auxiliary firefighters aided by a "brigade" of Boy Scouts helped extinguish a fire set by a fallen enemy planes. By the night of 8 December, OCD officials, in cooperation with the territorial government, had put a blackout into effect. "That raid," noted LaGuardia, "demonstrated again that we live in a new kind of war. The customs and rules of civilized belligerents are ignored, and civilian populations no longer enjoy any immunity whatsoever."[27]

Just after Pearl Harbor, many West Coast communities worried that their cities would be the next targets of Japanese bombers. In retrospect, it is easy to see that enemy air raids on the North American continent were extremely remote. Historian Roger Daniels has pointed out that during most of December 1941 the nearest enemy bombers were more than 500 miles west of San Francisco. Nevertheless, in an atmosphere clouded by wartime hysteria, anything seemed possible.[28]

Civilian and military authorities adopted a siege mentality. During blackout tests along the Pacific Coast, sirens wailed in the few cities that possessed them, only adding to the confusion. In San Francisco, residents mixed up air raid signals, not certain whether a warning or an "all clear" signal had sounded. An unruly mob of more than 1,000 men and women roamed the streets of downtown Seattle, "enforcing" the blackout. As police officers stood by idly, the crowd hurled objects at one blue neon light that still burned. A young female participant explained the crowd's reckless enthusiasm. "This is war," she declared, ". . . one light in the city might betray us."[29]

After he learned about the attack on Pearl Harbor, LaGuardia contributed to the melee when he drove though the streets of New York in a car equipped with a loud speaker shouting: "Calm! Calm! Calm!" He left immediately for the West Coast, accompanied by Eleanor Roosevelt, to examine the state and local defense councils' level of preparedness. Much to his chagrin, the OCD head discovered that many local defense councils were still mired in the earliest stages of planning. At meetings in several West Coast cities, he and the First Lady emphasized the need for uniform procedures in blackouts and air raid drills and encouraged state and municipal leaders to assume financial responsibility for civilian defense.[30]

Elsewhere, cities and towns across the nation mobilized their civilian defense volunteers. Many local dense councils felt overwhelmed by the popular interest exhibited suddenly in civilian defense. In rural New Hampshire, three weeks before Pearl Harbor, Thorsten V. Kalijarvi, the head of the air raid wardens service, could attract only 85 people to a civilian defense meeting. Just one week after Pearl Harbor, however, more than 1,500 residents turned out for that meeting. On 8 December, the overburdened staff of a Civilian Defense Volunteer Office in New York closed its doors at 5 P.M., promising to train additional interviewers so that it could remain open on a 24-hour basis. Over 40,000 men and women, working four-hour shifts, attempted to operate more than 1,300 aircraft observation posts on the Atlantic seaboard. In Massachusetts, thousands of auxiliary police helped state troopers guard railroads and public utilities, deemed the most likely targets of saboteurs. On 11 December, the civilian defense coordinator in Norfolk warned residents that the city "may be attacked by German airplanes any night . . . We are taking full preparations to defend your homes and your lives as far as possible from the effects of airplane bombing." In coastal as well as inland areas, from New York to Cincinnati, civilian defense workers guarded bridges, tunnels and defense plants. City Manager C. O. Sherrill even investigated the idea of converting Cincinnati's partially constructed subway system into an air raid shelter. The underground passages, however, were too shallow.[31]

With the cooperation of the army, blackout tests were conducted in large and small cities alike. Typically, these first tests were less than successful. Without fully trained air raid wardens, curious residents often remained outside during blackouts to see the darkened skyline. Some cities, like Cincinnati, were unable to turn off their lights easily; gas street lights had to be extinguished individually. A civilian defense official in Cincinnati conceded that he had "no idea how far progress has gone in congested areas of the City, where fire... could sweep and cover many blocks, while trouble in the suburbs would be unlikely to spread...." Only a few cities possessed sirens large and loud enough to be heard. David Brinkley, then a young reporter in Washington, D.C., recalled that city's first air raid drill as a major disappointment. "Everyone was ready and waiting, a little excited... as they hid under their beds," said Brinkley. The one functioning civilian defense siren, a holdover from World War I, could scarcely be heard. The OCD encouraged the use of church bells and factory whistles until sirens could be obtained.[32]

In coastal areas where the possibility of an enemy attack loomed largest, many volunteers scrambled to protect the homefront. In February 1942, a Japanese submarine surfaced briefly and shelled the coastal town of Santa Barbara. The incident caused little actual damage, but it raised tensions of already jittery Californians and army officials. Then, on 23 February, at 2:25 A.M., throughout Los Angeles air raid sirens blared and antiaircraft guns blazed. Army officials explained after the event that enemy planes had been spotted, though there was no substantial evidence that any planes were in the area. A Los Angeles policeman, Tom Bradley, who later became mayor, recalled the confusion during the "Battle of Los Angeles":

> ... there was bedlam. Sirens going off, [anti]aircraft guns firing. It was panic. Here we are in the middle of the night, there was no enemy in sight.... They were shooting at random.... It was panic that simply overwhelmed us.[33]

In hopes of avoiding any further debacles, the OCD printed and distributed over 57 million copies of *What To Do In An Air Raid*, a tersely worded eight-page pamphlet that schooled many Americans unfamiliar with the responsibilities of total war. Cartoonist Milton Caniff, the creator of "Terry and the Pirates," provided seven illustrations of stern-looking, resolute Americans to reinforce the underlying theme of the pamphlet: "You can help lick the enemy with your bare hands, if you will do a few simple things."

Families were encouraged to prepare a "refuge room" in the safest part of the house, and to stock it with non-perishable food, drinking water, mattresses, chairs, a table and toilet facilities.[34]

The air raid warden became the principal link between the local defense council and the average American. Ideally, the OCD envisioned each community recruiting and training its volunteers. A fully trained air raid warden, one on each block, would be knowledgeable of his neighbors' needs and abilities. Moreover, in the event of an emergency the warden could take charge of the neighborhood and assist local fire, police and emergency rescue workers. Civilian defense plans could only succeed, however, with everyone's full cooperation. The OCD implored:

> When the air raid warden comes to your home, do what he tells you. He is for your protection. He is your friend. He will help you whip the enemy.[35]

The OCD's frequent references to Great Britain's civilian defense program led many Americans to believe that similar protective measures would be enacted in the United States. Indeed, concerned and well-intentioned individuals wondered why state and local defense councils had not taken more drastic measures in defense of the homefront. For example, many parents worried about the safety of their children, especially when they were away from home. Yet only a few states had seriously considered implementing England's plan to evacuate children from large metropolitan areas to the countryside. LaGuardia conceded that it would be relatively simple to evacuate up to 25,000 families from New York City, but if hundreds of thousands of people wanted to leave, the city could not finance such a move nor provide the logistical support. In January 1942, Eleanor Roosevelt addressed the matter of evacuation in a radio address on "Family and Home Defense." She told listeners that the safest place for children was at home. She encouraged parents to read aloud to their children or to play board games with them during air raid drills to reduce anxiety. If civilian protection drills occurred during the day, she assured listeners, school officials were well versed in safety procedures, and children should remain at school.[36]

Others expected vast networks of public bomb shelters to be constructed. However, in February 1942, army officials informed the OCD that "the possibility of sustained bombing attacks on American cities is so remote as to make inadvisable any widespread program for the construction of bomb shelters." The army had estimated that it would cost nearly $1.5 million to provide an adequate number of shelters. Even if the funds were available to construct the shelters, the materials certainly were not. Total war had come to America; there was no dispute about that. However, since no bombs fell on American cities, civilian defense would never be the all-out effort that it was in England.[37]

Paradoxically, the OCD and the Roosevelt administration continued to make ample use of the rhetoric of total war in 1942 by exaggerating the danger of attack. The OCD estimated that 52 million Americans lived in "target areas," based on each city's vulnerability to attack and its importance to national defense. Concerned Americans were aware of the German and Japanese submarine activity off the Atlantic and Pacific coasts and worried about further enemy air raids. Roosevelt aggravated these concerns at a February press conference by stating that the enemy "can come in and shell New York tomorrow night, under certain conditions. They can probably drop bombs on Detroit tomorrow night . . . under certain conditions."[38]

By February 1942, both Fiorello LaGuardia and Eleanor Roosevelt had resigned from their OCD posts. LaGuardia had been criticized within administration circles for overextending himself. Likewise, his constituents at home felt that the war required the services of a full-time mayor.[39] The First Lady encountered political problems of her own. Her five-month tenure as assistant director in charge of volunteer activities, even shorter than LaGuardia's, raised the ire of Congress on more than one occasion. Many felt that she advocated programs that were superfluous to the war effort. Others bristled at her appointments of friends and proteges, including a young dancer, Mayris Chaney, to coordinate a program in "rhythmic dancing" for children. *Time* magazine dubbed Chaney and other loyalists of the president's wife as "Eleanor's Playmates." Chaney first met Eleanor Roosevelt during FDR's 1936 reelection campaign. In 1938 Chaney invented a new dance called the "Eleanor Glide" in honor of her friend. It was clear to the editors of *Time* that the dancer's presence at the OCD was based solely on her friendship with the First Lady rather than on her expertise in children's recreational activities.[40]

Despite some determined opposition to the OCD in Washington, popular support for volunteer defense work surged. By February 1942, more than five million Americans had enlisted for some type of civilian defense work in more than 8,500 state and local defense councils. Most of these volunteers received training in first aid, incendiary and gas defenses, and blackout procedures.[41] Ironically, just as these volunteers completed their training in the summer and fall of 1942, the Allies racked up impressive victories against the Imperial Japanese Navy in the Pacific and the Germans in North Africa. As the Allies improved their military position, whatever threat of enemy invasion that had existed in the United States began to diminish.[42]

PRACTICAL APPLICATIONS OF CIVILIAN DEFENSE
TRAINING ON THE HOMEFRONT, 1942–1943

Even though American cities were never bombed as anticipated, civilian defense training was applied to other homefront problems. In 1942 hospital administrators mobilized nurses' aides to care for the wounded when Boston's Coconut Grove nightclub burned to the ground, killing more than 500 people. Other civilian defense workers in the District of Columbia, Virginia and Maryland assisted stricken families when the Potomac flooded. General U. S. Grant III, the head of OCD's civilian protection branch, was encouraged by the response of air raid wardens and other emergency personnel. "This type of organization and devotion to duty," noted Grant, "will serve any community well in the event of a bombing by our enemies." Later in the war, local defense councils in Ohio, West Virginia, Pennsylvania and Illinois performed proficiently in assisting in flood relief and firefighting. During the aftermath of the Harlem race riot in August 1943, auxiliary policemen and emergency medical personnel helped restore order and transport wounded to nearby hospitals.[43]

Despite these brave deeds, several advisers close to President Roosevelt felt the OCD should be disbanded. But the president worried that such an action would cripple the civilian defense workers' morale. As a result, the OCD remained intact, but it began to stress the need for community mobilization rather than civilian protection. Air raid drills and blackout tests were conducted sporadically until November 1943, when the War Department placed local protective forces on a standby basis.[44]

The OCD encouraged volunteer participation in other types of morale-building activities. For example, in Seattle, Detroit, Cincinnati, Buffalo, New York and many other large cities, local defense councils helped develop and staff child care centers for working mothers. At its peak, the nationwide child care program served over 130,000 children in over 3,000 centers.[45]

Civilian defense volunteers engaged in several other nonprotective programs that focused on the needs of the community, including: victory gardens, nutrition and consumer information, recreation, and race relations. By 1943 more than ten million Americans had volunteered for some type of civilian defense work; more than 45 percent of these volunteers engaged in nonprotective, community service activities. These volunteers typically assisted overworked and underpaid social welfare officials in their community. These services never commanded the widespread media attention that civilian protection had mustered in nearly every community. Still, it could be argued that child care workers and recreation assistants provided services that ultimately benefited the homefront more than the efforts of air raid wardens and fire watchers.[46]

Analogies to the British civilian defense program had helped stir Americans to action prior to Pearl Harbor. However, once the threat of further attacks diminished, by 1943, that analogy no longer applied. OCD officials constructed an alternate analogy for its volunteers. Everyday homefront chores like rationing, purchasing war bonds and collecting salvage were compared to the responsibilities and sacrifices of soldiers on the fighting front. For the duration of the war, complacency, rather than incendiary bombs, posed the greatest danger to the American homefront. As a result, the Roosevelt administration maintained its civilian defense program long after the threat of enemy attack had subsided in order to maintain the national morale and to give the millions who had volunteered their time and effort a real sense of partnership in the American war effort.

FROM "TOTAL" WAR TO COLD WAR: CIVILIAN DEFENSE PLANNING IN POST-WORLD WAR II AMERICA

As early as 1943, after the Allies had gone on the offensive, some federal officials, including OCD head James Landis, debated whether that agency had fulfilled its purpose and should now be terminated. Conversely, others envisioned a need for civilian defense in postwar America. For example, John B. Blandford, Jr., a contemporary analyst of urban affairs, felt that the war had helped reinvigorate community activism. He noted that

> the war in defense of democracy has renewed the interest of and rededicated the American People to the preservation and improvement of their democratic institutions, as shown by increasing citizen participation in government process through working with selective service boards, price control and rationing boards, civilian defense, . . . and other war service and community activities.[47]

Some New Deal liberals like sociologist Louis Wirth, the chairman of the Illinois Defense Council, hoped to sustain the sense of voluntarism that had blossomed during the war. Wirth wanted to direct the efforts of local defense councils toward the social and economic problems inherent in postwar planning. He informed his colleagues at the University of Chicago:

> If we are able to salvage even a part of the war-born capacity for concerted community action for the peace to come, the cities may thereby find the strength and the means whereby to deal with some of their most serious problems which have . . . defied solution.[48]

The kind of widespread public voluntarism to which Blandford and Wirth referred had enabled "the experts"— city managers, mayors, fire, police and public health officials, among others—to attend to the more pressing postwar problems facing most American cities and towns. During the early months of the war, the threat of an enemy invasion had sidetracked them temporarily from their normal responsibilities. Many cities and towns had devoted time, energy and money to local civilian defense programs; mayors, city managers and other municipal officials, moreover, had coordinated the efforts of local defense councils. By 1944, however, civilian defense plans were no longer a pressing concern. According to *The Municipal Year Book*, "next to war production, city planning was the most popular homefront activity . . ." among municipal officials.[49]

Civilian defense activities were gradually suspended in the more than 11,000 local defense councils. These wartime organizations had never been intended to take over services traditionally provided by states and cities. On 30 June 1945, President Harry S. Truman signed Executive Order 9562, which officially terminated the operations of the Office of Civilian Defense.[50]

In less than two months the war was over. The atomic bombs dropped on Hiroshima and Nagasaki in August 1945 punctuated the Allies' victory over Japan and ushered in the Atomic Age. While much of Europe, Africa and Asia was devastated by the war, the United States emerged from the war with fewer scars. In the new world order that was emerging, civilian defense planning appeared to be anachronistic. But almost before the dust had settled on the battlefields, relations between the United States and the Soviet Union had deteriorated, and the optimistic hope for "One World" vanished.

In the aftermath of Hiroshima, in 1948, the United States Conference of Mayors reflected on the human costs of the decision to drop the bomb. They concluded that the greatest demand on municipal officials was "to play their part as community leaders towards the strengthening of the United Nations and the building of a world in which atomic energy will be used solely for the welfare of mankind." At the same time, municipal leaders urged the federal government to provide material assistance for civilian defense problems. In March and April 1950, scores of concerned Americans—including mayors, American Legion commanders and directors of local civilian defense organizations—paraded before the Joint Congressional Committee on Atomic Energy and expressed the need for comprehensive civilian defense planning.[51]

Just as Roosevelt responded to the demands of municipal officials in the early forties when he created the OCD, Truman, likewise, created the Federal Civil Defense Administration (FCDA), on 1 December 1950, by executive order. The new agency was headed by former governor of Florida Milliard F. Caldwell, Jr. Urban officials were disappointed, however, with the FCDA's limited role in civilian defense planning. The FCDA, like the OCD during World War II, operated on a small budget and was strictly an advisory and informational agency. In the early fifties, the FCDA distributed pamphlets and films to schools and community organizations to educate and train people in methods of civilian defense. Some of the earliest FCDA pamphlets, like *This Is Civil Defense,* tried to stir its readers out of complacency:

> Modern civil defense is nothing like civil defense in pre-
> vious wars. Where once our danger was from fire bombs
> and high explosives, now it is from the atom bomb. The
> wide oceans that used to protect us have given way to the
> global bomber. Today we face more kinds of danger than
> ever before, and our danger is much greater.[52]

The FCDA grimly calculated the damage an atomic bomb could inflict: thousands of people would be killed, and buildings would be reduced to rubble. "Without civil defense," the FCDA warned, "a nation is helpless. With it, cities can get up off the floor and fight back after an attack." FCDA-sponsored films, like *Our Cities Must Fight* (1953), offered the same kinds of ominous warnings. The federal government was willing to admit that the atom bomb had raised the stakes considerably. American cities faced grave dangers. Yet, the civil defense program of the fifties was modeled on the same kinds of assumptions that shaped the civilian defense program of the forties. In each case, federal officials suggested that communities could survive an enemy attack if, and only if, they were organized.[53]

To the chagrin of state and local officials, federal support for a broad-based, permanent civilian defense program remained limited. In 1951, Congress failed to pass a $600 million appropriation for the construction of air raid shelters, the stockpiling of medical supplies, and for training, education, research and administrative costs. The United States Conference of Mayors declared that "our cities can come to but one conclusion—that we should not take this program too seriously."[54]

In the past 40 years, most cities have gone beyond the federal government's narrow concept of civilian defense to plan for natural as well as enemy-induced disasters. Paradoxically, even though the spectre of atomic warfare posed a greater threat to national security than Nazi bombers armed with incendiary bombs ever had, the postwar civilian defense program—which still exists today—never achieved the same proportions as it had during World War II.

10

A Clash of Priorities

The Federal Government and Dallas Airport Development, 1917–1964

Robert B. Fairbanks

Recently a growing number of urban historians have focused on the complex relationship between the city and the federal government since the Great Depression. Studies of housing, highways, suburbs and relief programs are just some of the topics used to exam how this new partnership has shaped the city's politics, molded its morphology, and affected its economic and social well-being.[1] One area of great importance to modern urban development—airports—has received little attention from urban scholars in this context. Mark Gelfand's massive study of urban-federal relations, *A Nation of Cities*, provides no references to the federal government's role in municipal airport development. The neglect of airport development in this book and others is particularly strange since airports have had an important impact in shaping both the economic and spatial development of modern cities.[2] Airport development also provides an opportunity to explore the developing tension between cities and the federal government as the latter became more involved in a host of urban issues. This history of Dallas Love Field explores how federal aviation strategies sometimes clashed with local priorities in airport development.

Dallas, Texas, in the first third of the twentieth century, grew into a medium-sized city with big city aspirations. This retailing, wholesaling and financial center looked northward and desperately wanted to become the "New York of the Southwest." Led by a business elite that became even more dominant during the thirties, Dallas reflected the urban ethos of growth and order that Blaine Brownell found in his study of southern cities during the twenties.[3]

ESTABLISHING LOVE FIELD

Dallas's early contact with the federal government with regard to aviation was most always positive. Civic leaders convinced the Army Air Corps to establish a military training center in their city in 1917 by turning over 600 acres of pasture land to the Corps for an airfield. The following year, after the Army had declared the field surplus, 15 local businessmen purchased Love Field. That field remained little more than a stage for daredevil stunt fliers until the United States Post Office in 1925 started letting airmail contracts to civilian aviators. The first such airmail flight from Dallas occurred on 12 May 1926. Two years later, the Army designated Love Field as the headquarters for the 8th Army Reserve Air Corps.[4]

Despite the important role the Post Office and the military played in promoting aviation, civic leaders and the city government funded Dallas's early airport development. Indeed, on 15 December 1927, Dallas voters approved a $400,000 bond issue designated for the city's purchase of Love Field. The decision of the city to buy and improve Love Field came only after the Dallas Chamber of Commerce had failed to persuade nearby Fort Worth to develop a joint airport to serve both cities and defray expenses.[5]

The Chamber of Commerce supported a municipal airport because it envisioned a great future in aviation for the city but feared that private investors could not bear the expense of continued expansion, demanded by the rapid improvements occurring in aviation. The Ulrickson Committee, charged with developing a long-term bond program for the city, agreed that Dallas should buy Love Field and recommended the bond issue. "In view of the growing importance of Dallas as a distribution center," the Committee observed, "and in view of the possibilities of commercial aviation, we believe it to be an entirely justifiable investment for the city to acquire a suitable air port and to develop same."[6] In response to criticism that the airline companies should own and operate the local airport, Dallas Postmaster John W. Philp argued that since cities had long acquired city seaports, the new technology demanded the same control of air facilities for landlocked Dallas. Finally, the Postmaster warned, Dallas needed a municipal airport since "most Texas cities have either already secured or are now negotiating for municipal fields."[7]

Dallas's commitment to municipal airport ownership appears to be part of a national trend characteristic of the late 1920s. Encouraged by Charles Lindburgh's successful flight across the Atlantic in 1927—which, among other things, helped demonstrate the airplane's potential— municipalities throughout the nation turned to airport ownership.[8] Dallas refused to stop with ownership, however. In 1931, Dallas voters passed a $300,000 aviation bond to improve the airfield. By 1934, the city manager was able to report that Love Field had been transformed "from an unfenced weed-covered field into a modern airport, fully equipped with the most modern apparatus for control of air traffic and given its highest rating . . . by the United States Department of Commerce."[9] The city also purchased another airfield southwest of the city specifically for the use of the military reserve. The Dallas experience during these years was not unique. Throughout the nation at this time, cities, rather than the federal government, financed airport development. Prior to 1933, less than one percent of airport expenditures came from federal funds.[10]

As in most other areas of municipal development, the Great Depression changed all of that. Because local funds disappeared for all public works programs, and relief demands increased, municipalities turned to the federal government for help. President Franklin D. Roosevelt responded with a variety of relief programs, which included airport development. By 1939, the Civil Works Administration, the Federal Emergency Relief Administration, and the Works Progress Administration (WPA) poured more than $139 million into airport construction.[11] Although most of that money went into the development of smaller airports, Dallas did secure a $35,000 WPA grant. This paid the labor for an aggressive program of city-sponsored improvements in 1938 to help Love Field meet the federal government's new and more rigorous standards for first class airports.[12]

The effort to improve the field was led by the newly established Dallas Citizens Council, formed in 1937 by the city's elite banking and businessmen to provide united and energetic leadership for the city. Working with the Chamber of Commerce, it successfully secured voter approval of a $300,000 general obligation bond for airport improvement in 1938.[13] Federal legislation that same year would increase the federal government's involvement in airport development. United States participation in World War II three years later would have an even greater impact on municipal airport development.

The Civil Aeronautics Act of 1938 not only proved an important milestone in the history of aviation in this country, but also would greatly impact the relationship between cities and their federal government. Under the Act, Congress called for a six-year program of improvements for the nation's airports. And for the first time in its history, Congress agreed to provide money specifically for airport development. Strong support for the Civil Aeronautics Administration's role in airport construction and control came from the United States Conference of Mayors in 1939.[14] The federal government also expanded its regulatory powers under the Civil Aeronautics Act of 1938. Under the act, the Civil Aeronautics Authority (CAA) would only grant new routes for an airline after it proved the public convenience and necessity of such a route. This licensing power would have a definite impact on municipal airport development.[15]

URBAN RIVALS TRY A JOINT REGIONAL AIRPORT VENTURE

The new availability of federal financial assistance as well as the rapidly changing aviation demands persuaded Dallas officials to request federal money soon after it became available. After the newly formed Civil Aeronautics Administration (CAA) received requests from Forth Worth, too—a city less than 30 miles from Dallas—it encouraged both cities to investigate the possibility of developing a joint regional airport. The newly formed Texas State Aeronautics Advisory Committee held a meeting on the matter, 1 October 1940. Dallas officials welcomed the idea, particularly when they thought the federal government would provide huge sums of financial help. Fort Worth, however, feared that any joint airport would be in reality a Dallas airport, and refused to support joint ownership. That city argued that the 26 miles separating the two cities warranted separate airports.[16] Shortly after the meeting, Dallas lost some of its enthusiasm for a midway airport when it learned that the CAA would not immediately produce $1.8 million for the proposed regional field.[17]

Despite the cool reception to the idea, the CAA's regional office in Fort Worth continued to press officials in both cities to support a joint airport. To gain their attention, it refused to honor either city's request for federal funds for airport improvement. Airlines serving both Dallas and Fort Worth, American and Braniff, endorsed the CAA's proposal for a joint airport since operating larger aircraft between the two cities proved costly and inefficient.[18]

Unhappy with its failure to secure a commitment from Dallas and Fort Worth, the CAA took another approach. That agency invited officials of Arlington, located between Dallas and Fort Worth, to sponsor the proposed regional airport. American and Braniff airlines agreed to purchase the necessary land and turn it over to Arlington. The CAA would then construct an airfield with runways between 3,400 and 4,500 feet in length on that land. The proposed development of a regional airport without their involvement proved too much for leaders in both Dallas and Fort

Worth and forced them back into the regional airport picture. In October 1941, Dallas, Fort Worth and Arlington signed a tri-city pact to establish Midway Airport. According to the agreement, the airlines would purchase 1,000 acres of land and deed it to the three cities who, in turn, would form a corporation to construct hangers, repair shops and a terminal. The federal government promised to provide money to construct the actual runways and control tower.[19]

Despite this agreement, the cooperative venture never took place. Personality conflicts arose between Dallas Mayor J. Woodall Rodgers and Fort Worth's leading citizen, newspaper publisher Amon Carter (a major stockholder in American Airlines), over the final location of the administration building. When plans for the building were altered from the preliminary site to one more advantageous to Fort Worth in the final plans, Rodgers exploded.[20] He charged the relocation had been made to placate Carter and warned that this was the beginning of a "progressive steal" of the airport by Fort Worth. He angrily called off negotiations and rebuked the change of plans as "a monumental insult" to Dallas.[21] Although some Dallas civic leaders thought the controversy over the administration building's location should not interfere with the development of a regional airport, the city's leading newspaper believed otherwise. According to the *Dallas Morning News*, "this [was] not a situation to be laughed off as being too childish to squabble over."[22]

Dallas withdrew from the airport agreement, but the CAA proceeded to build its runways for the army under the Landing Areas for National Defense Program and turned the field over to Arlington. Meanwhile, army officials poured money into Love Field, an action that would have a major bearing on the city's postwar airport plans.[23]

PLANNING FOR FUTURE AIRPORT DEVELOPMENT

Despite the breakdown in the Midway Airport talks, Dallas leaders realized that their own Love Field would soon be an inadequate airport for the larger planes coming into service. Wedged in between Bachman Lake on the north and neighborhoods and business areas on the south, east and west, Love Field's position as the area's leading airport seemed doomed. And when the city hired Harland Bartholomew of St. Louis in 1943 to develop a master plan for the entire city, he strongly recommended that the city build a new airport. Unhappy that the federal government's proposed regional airport was nearly 19 miles from downtown Dallas, Bartholomew found an airport site just eight miles from the central business district in southwest Dallas.[24] However, at the very time Bartholomew was preparing his report, the U.S. Army reached an agreement with the city of Dallas to greatly expand Love Field.

The U.S. Army Air Force Ferrying Command's decision to make Love Field a major base of operations had a profound impact on that airport's future. On 21 December 1943, the army offered to spend more than $6 million over the next three years to improve the airport if the city agreed to secure the necessary land. Shortly after that agreement, one Dallas newspaper reported that "Municipal government's sentiment is centering more and more on Love Field expansion and development and less . . . [on] the development of the proposed Lake June airport." Although the city agreed to buy land for the proposed Lake June Airport site in southwest Dallas for the time when 10,000-foot runways would be necessary, that airport's development, according to the *Morning News*, "was well in the future."[25]

Federal government involvement in Dallas's airport development in the 1940s was real, then but somewhat confusing. The CAA had promoted a regional airport midway between Dallas and Fort Worth and had worked hard to secure an agreement with these two cities. Even after the agency's original proposal fell through, Secretary of Commerce Jesse Jones intervened and reopened the Midway Airport case in 1943, only to fail again. Meanwhile, the U.S. Army expanded Love Field so it would be able to handle four-engine aircraft. The expansion sparked renewed enthusiasm and support for Love Field to be the city's "superairport" after the war and permitted a way to assure that. Voters supported the reemphasis on Love Field by approving a $1 million bond issue on 8 December 1945, for the airport's development.[26]

FORT WORTH AND MIDWAY AIRPORT

Fort Worth responded to its postwar air needs differently. Aware that its current airport, Meacham Field, would be unable to handle four-engine airplanes, it undertook a search for a new airport site. The city found some available land six miles south of downtown and selected it as the site for its new airport. But it appears that the CAA convinced Fort Worth officials to purchase Midway Airport from Arlington and develop it as a commercial field. That transaction took place on 28 October 1947, after the CAA assured Fort Worth that it would immediately appropriate $340,000 for improvements at the airfield.[27]

Although Dallas leaders at first reacted cautiously to Fort Worth's decision, they became infuriated when the CAA released its National Airport Plan for 1948. As part of the Federal Airport Act of 1946, Congress required the CAA to develop a National Airport Plan to promote an efficient public airport system. The 1948 plan proposed that Midway be developed to serve the Dallas-Fort Worth area as the primary airport and reduced both Love Field and Meacham Field to secondary status.[28] To see its hated rival, Fort Worth, gain the support of the federal government was too much for some Dallas leaders. They attempted through their congressman, J. Frank Wilson, to kill the CAA's appropriation for the Midway Airport. Wilson told his colleagues that the CAA attempted to "kick Dallas in the teeth" by making Midway the de facto regional airport.

Despite Dallas's efforts to defeat the Midway Airport

line in the general CAA appropriations bill (including a full-page ad in the *Washington Post*), Congress approved Fort Worth's money.[29] Dallas also lost its appeal to the CAA. After hearing the evidence, one CAA examiner concluded "that the Dallas protest was nothing more than one city's rapacious desire to deprive its neighbor of its inalienable right to prosper." The CAA's examiner also chided the city, noting that much of Dallas's air commerce had been built up more by federal expenditures at Love Field than by Dallas "initiative, forethought and financing." Midway Airport would be developed, according to one CCA official, because that agency wanted the airfield "for defense purposes." Efforts to overturn the appropriations in the federal court system proved just as futile.[30]

Dallas leaders also bristled at American and Delta Airlines, strong supporters of the Midway Airport scheme. Dallas Mayor Rodgers accused the airlines of a "vicious stroke of ingratitude. Like the old cattle rustling instinct," Rodgers continued, "they want to drag passengers across the county line and put Fort Worth's brand on 'em."[31] Fort Worth denied that the expanded Midway Airport, to be renamed the Greater Fort Worth International Airport-Carter Field, was anything but strictly a Fort Worth Field. Dallas leaders thought otherwise, since the airport's 19-mile distance from downtown Fort Worth was about the same distance as from downtown Dallas. Dallas leaders also remembered how the CAA had been promoting a regional airport for the Dallas-Fort Worth area since 1940. And in 1948, the Assistant Secretary of Commerce confirmed Dallas leaders suspicions when he urged the city to join in Carter Field's development. As a result of this threat to Love Field, Dallas officials mapped out a new strategy for expanding and improving Love Field.[32]

Despite these plans, some Dallas civic leader discussed the possibility of joining Fort Worth in developing Carter Field as a true regional airport. For instance, the powerful Dallas Citizens Council met in April 1951 and voted to investigate just such a possibility. After Amon Carter personally offered Dallas an opportunity to join in the development of the Fort Worth airport, one Dallas newspaper reported that "It is no secret that some of the city's most influential businessmen have changed their thinking about the 19 mile airport [Carter Field] and are ready to negotiate with Fort Worth on any basis."[33]

John W. Carpenter, member of the Dallas Citizens Council and president of the Dallas Chamber of Commerce, appeared to be the most vocal supporter of joint development of Carter Field. "If you disregard personalities and disregard politics," Carpenter advised, "after careful analysis you cannot fail to see that Dallas should support the Midway Airport as it originally did." Others, however, disagreed. The day after Carpenter's comment, the *Dallas Times Herald* rebuked the Chamber president in a front page editorial. According to the *Times Herald*, Carpenter's statements were "a serious embarrassment to the overwhelming majority of Dallas citizens who desire to expand the facilities of their home-owned airport."[34]

Civic leader Stanley Marcus, president of the elegant Nieman-Marcus Department Store, also had reservations about the future of Love Field. He reluctantly agreed to chair a Chamber of Commerce committee on that future only after the Chamber convinced city council to engage an outside airport consultant to evaluate Love Field's future.[35]

THE BUCKLEY REPORTS

Council's employment of James C. Buckley on 21 November 1951 proved an important turning point in the history of Love Field. Buckley, a terminal and transportation consultant from New York City, had been director of airport development for the Port Authority of New York. In that position, he had served as the chief architect of regional airport development for Greater New York. In Dallas, his main charge was to evaluate the future of Love Field with the opening of Carter Field only a year away. His thorough study not only argued Love Field's continued importance due to its convenient location to downtown fliers, but for the first time provided a well-documented overview of the tremendous economic value of Love Field. Not only did Love Field provide more than 3,600 jobs and a payroll of over $74.5 million, but its passenger and freight cargo service played a critical role in promoting the broader economic development of the city. The potential for Love Field was great, but Buckley warned that substantial and expensive development was a must if Love Field were to achieve that potential.[36]

Although he recommended cooperating with Fort Worth to plan a long-term program of regional airport development, his report gave a ringing endorsement to Love Field and would shape Dallas's airport policy for the next ten years. Buckley believed that the convenience of Love Field would continue to make to it an important airport. As a result, he recommended that Love Field should remain the city's primary airport. He also proposed that the city should oppose any schedule pattern filed by the airlines for the Dallas-Fort Worth area that failed to provide that all regional trunkline airline schedules should serve Love Field. Finally, he concluded that at a minimum, Love Field could expect to maintain 65 percent of the area's traffic.[37]

The same month that Buckley gave his completed report to council, he initiated another study for the Dallas Chamber of Commerce. It reviewed the city's present and prospective air service and identified significant gaps in that service. The final report, submitted to the Chamber on 15 October 1952, recommended that the city attempt to secure new or improved service to 75 communities.[38]

The Buckley reports created a new enthusiasm among the city's leadership for maintaining and improving Love Field. A $10 million airport bond proposal for airport improvement in Dallas proved one of the first manifestations of this renewed commitment to Love Field. The January 1953 bond issue, if approved, would provide money to expand Love Field's runway from 6,200 to 8,500 feet and build a parallel runway at a similar size. The money would also be used to develop a larger terminal building and to create a new, general aviation airport in Oak Cliff.[39]

Supporters of the bond issue poured more than $50,000 in the campaign and argued it was one of the most important issues the public had ever voted on. Banker Robert L. Thornton, possibly the most influential man in Dallas, warned that Dallas was at the crossroads. "We must go forward," he cautioned, "or be like some of the towns that the railroads passed up. If we don't follow the word of the experts who say we must expand Love Field, what word are we to follow?" Disparate groups such as the Dallas Building Trades Council, the Negro Chamber of Commerce, the Dallas Home Builders Association and the Oak Cliff Chamber of Commerce supported the bond.[40]

Others in Dallas, however, opposed the expansion of Love Field. More than 700 blacks who lived in nearby Elm Thicket jammed the North Temple Baptist Church on 19 January and urged the defeat of the bond. Wondering where so many displaced African Americans would live in a city with an already severe black housing shortage, black optometrist J. O. Chisum warned that additional airport expansion would push them into "unfriendly [white] communities."[41]

Another group more concerned about the safety hazards posed by Love Field for the congested urban area, argued that Dallas needed a new airport built further away from urban congestion. The Air Safety Committee, as it was called, warned that runway expansion posed a direct threat to nearby schools. Both groups cited the recently completed federal study on air safety, popularly known as the Doolittle Report, to attack Love Field expansion. That airport would be unable to provide the necessary safe zones and runway lengths recommended by the report. They also repeated Doolittle's warning that future airport development should take place on the city's fringes, far away from densely populated areas. Despite the opposition of these two groups, more than 19,000 Dallas voters agreed with the economic arguments and passed the bond by a 4,000 vote margin.[42]

Eleven days after the bond election, consultant James Buckley completed a detailed master plan for Love Field's future development. Planning for Love Field into the 1970s, Buckley called for an ultimate runway expansion of 8,500 feet. He also recommended a new terminal building to meet the demands of the rapidly expanding airline traffic.[43] The successful bond issue and the completed plan did not guarantee Love Field's regional dominance, however. The growing involvement of the federal government in aviation matters would ultimately decide the fate of Love Field.

FIGHTING FOR LOVE FIELD

After Carter Field opened on 24 April 1953, Fort Worth leaders undertook an aggressive campaign to secure more commercial air traffic. American Airlines moved six of its flights from Love Field to the new Fort Worth Airport, much to the joy of its largest stockholder, Amon Carter. Tom Braniff, owner of Dallas based Braniff airlines, was also courted by Fort Worth but decided to stay in Dallas after being named Dallas man of the year.[44] Fort Worth constantly intervened in the attempts of Dallas officials to secure new flights for Love Field. Whenever an airline applied for new routes into the North Texas region, Fort Worth pushed the CAB to make Carter Field the terminus for the entire region. Fort Worth's first success in this regard sent shock waves through Dallas. When Central Airlines requested permission to fly into the Dallas-Fort Worth area from Oklahoma, Fort Worth requested that its airport be used as the sole terminus for the flight. When the CAB, still interested in promoting a regional airport for the area, agreed to the request on 13 July 1953, Dallas's worst fears were realized. For civic leaders grasped that the CAB's power to designate airline travel to a single airport in a region could thwart any future development of Love Field traffic and make Carter Field, without Dallas input, the regional field of that area.[45]

For the next several months following the CAB edict, Dallas leaders worked to have the decision reversed. Three of the city's business leaders flew to Washington to discuss the ruling and other matters with CAB Vice Chairman Harmar Denny. The Dallas delegation emphasized how growing Dallas deserved additional aviation service. But Denny and his fellow CAB member Joseph Adams explained that the CAB had to look at the "national transportation picture, including efforts to reduce subsidies." Unable to get redress from the CAB, Dallas turned to Congress. Mayor Robert L. Thornton and Chamber of Commerce President Ben H. Wooten requested that Senator John S. Cooper, chair of a review committee of the CAB, investigate that agency's treatment of Dallas. The civic leaders thought the CAB had been negligent in not granting Dallas competitive air service to both coasts. The *Times-Herald* summarized their feelings when it editorialized that "the federal government is proving so strict in its policy that it is virtually ruling out competition. Through the CAB and other agencies it is not permitting Dallas to go after air service as it once obtained railroads."[46]

When discussions with the CAB and Congress failed, Dallas appealed the CAB decision to the U.S. Court of Appeals, claiming that "there is not any such point as Dallas-Fort Worth." Shortly after the Court turned down the appeal, an embittered chair of the Chamber's aviation committee, Angus Wynne, Jr., complained that "no board sitting in Washington should be able to dictate to Dallas which airport they [sic] should use.[47]

When the CAB ruled against Dallas several months later in another air service case, the *Dallas Times Herald* ran a headline that read, "Chamber Says New CAB Edit Violates City Rights of Dallas." In the article that followed, businessmen and Chamber of Commerce president W. W. Overton concluded that the CAB decision was "a scandalous disregard of the board's obligation" to build a sound air transportation system to serve Dallas traffic.[48]

Although Dallas leaders were able to secure some additional routes for Love Field before the year ended, new controversy soon appeared. Under the prodding of CAB chair Char Guerney, on 14 November 1954 Fort Worth offered to sell half interest in Carter Field to Dallas. Angered at Guerney's actions, Dallas Chamber of Commerce President Jerome K. Crossman, attacked the idea and charged Guerney with injecting himself "extra-legally into the affairs of [the] community."[49] Consultant James Buckley also advised the city to turn down the offer because moving airline operations to Fort Worth's Carter Field would have an adverse impact on employment and payroll in the Love Field area of Dallas. After consulting with the council, Mayor Rodgers formally rejected the offer despite threats from the Assistant Secretary of Commerce, John R. Allison, that he would push Carter Field as the transcontinental route terminal for both Dallas and Fort Worth.[50] Dallas's unwillingness to cooperate with Fort Worth led the new CAB Chair, Joseph J. O'Connell, Jr.—who also favored a regional airport—to announce that he would approve any airlines request to move from Love Field to Carter Field.[51]

Dallas, which had earlier tolerated federal intervention in the airport business, now bristled at action that seemingly favored its rival and posed an economic threat to the city's welfare. The conflicting goals of federal policy—which emphasized an efficient, safe and cost effective national air system—and Dallas policy—which stressed economic development for the city and dominance over the region—created an era of federal government baiting by the city's leadership that was probably unprecedented in the city's history.

Just when the conflict seemed at crisis level, the federal government appeared to back down. Not only did the CAB start granting Love Field more flights, but in 1956 the CAA even allocated $375,000 to Love for its airport expansion program. That same year saw the CAA reclassify Love Field from continental to intercontinental status. The softening of the federal government's campaign to force Dallas into a regional airport agreement may have had something to do with the failure of the Willow Run regional airport developed for Greater Detroit. That airport, more than 30 miles from Detroit's downtown, had been abandoned by the airlines in 1954. Baltimore's Friendship Airport, midway between that city and Washington, also had not been very successful. Fort Worth's Carter Field seemed destined for the same fate as its number of passengers and planes steadily declined during the mid-fifties.[52] These developments, as well as the dedication of Love Field's $7.5 million terminal in 1957, led the *Morning News* to celebrate Love Field's apparently secure status in an editorial entitled "Love Field Triumphs After Long Struggle."[53]

The emergence of commercial jet travel in the late fifties, however, made conjested Love Field vulnerable once again and gave new life to the regional airport concept.[54] Not only did jets intensify the noise problem for surrounding neighborhoods, but they needed longer runways. Indeed, the FAA's Airport Plan for 1959 called for Love Field to develop parallel runways of 9,200 feet. In response to this plan and to the growing congestion at the busy airport, Dallas leaders initiated a $9 million expansion program in 1959. In November of that year, plans met a snag when the FAA rejected a local request for $838,000. The FAA turned down the request, in part, because the Love Field plans had not provided an adequate clear zone (safety zone at the end of the runway) nor was the proposed 8,000-foot runway long enough to satisfy the FAA.[55]

Fearful that Fort Worth and the federal government were about to mount another offensive to force Dallas to join in operating Carter Field, the city accelerated its airport program even without federal aid. However, a lawsuit was filed by 43 Love Field homeowners, attempting to halt the expansion plans. This delayed construction for nearly two years and helped to refocus attention on the area's need for a larger, more regionally based airport.[56]

The early sixties again proved difficult for Dallas as the FAA refused to funnel additional funds into Love Field while at the same time granting federal dollars to Carter Field. Even more disconcerting for Dallas leaders was a joint FAA/CAB policy in 1961 that supported the development of regional airports.[57]

Matters only worsened when Najeeb E. Halaby, head of the FAA and a native of Dallas, testified before a Senate subcommittee the next year that the FAA would "not put another nickel in Love Field." Claiming that the field was simply too congested and unable to meet the demands of future aircraft, the FAA chief warned that new appropriations for Love would be a waste of money. He chastised the city for not developing a regional airport with Fort Worth and called Dallas's commitment to Love Field nothing more than a "pure, unadulterated case of childish civic pride."[58] Twelve days later the CAB ordered an investigation to determine if there should be a regional airport in the Dallas-Fort Worth area. Halaby's remarks and the CAB's actions created a new uproar in Dallas.[59]

To city leaders who were justifiably proud of their airport, built mostly with Dallas money, the remarks seemed a declaration of war. While other southern cities were fighting ferociously with the federal government to maintain segregation of blacks, Dallas leaders were battling to save their airport in which the city had invested $32 million, and to keep its $35 million payroll in the corporate limits. The federal government's actions struck them as unfair since local tax money had played such a major role in the airport's development. According to one estimate, Fort Worth had received $4.70 in federal airport aid for each passenger using Carter, while Dallas received about 43 cents per passenger in federal aid. As a result, much of Love Field had been developed with general revenue bonds to be paid back from income derived from airport landing, rental and parking fees. Dallas leaders feared the removal of commercial air traffic from Love Field, then, would eliminate much of the projected revenue and add an additional tax burden to Dallas residents. These concerns help explain why local officials stubbornly fought the regional airport idea.[60]

Moreover, Dallas was already feeling the economic impact of the suburban migration of people and businesses, and suspected that a truly regional airport located beyond the corporate limits would further encourage the suburban trend. This context helps explain why Earle Cabell, the conservative mayor of Dallas, promised to fight the federal government "with every weapon at my command." Chamber of Commerce Aviation Committee chair, H. L. Nichols, also protested the "deliberate and massive attack upon Dallas and its airport . . . by two agencies of the federal government." Nichols charged that such action "marked a misuse of Federal Power in an effort to dictate to Dallas a course of action contrary to Dallas's own interests."[61]

Although FAA officials continually pled with Fort Worth and Dallas to come up with long range plans for a regional airport, Dallas officials ignored the advice and stubbornly supported Love Field. Not only local self-interest, but the city's heated rivalry with Fort Worth helps explain Dallas inaction. According to one resident, "To sit down and talk to people from Fort Worth is just like President Kennedy sitting down to talk with the Russians. The only way any progress (?) can be achieved is complete surrender."[62]

The CAB hearing over whether Dallas-Fort Worth should have a regional airport (and if it would be Greater Southwest or Love Field) started on 7 July 1963. Examiner Ross Newman began the hearing in Arlington, Texas, midway between the rival cities, and finished it on 20 September in Washington.[63] During those weeks, FAA officials testified against Love Field, emphasizing the noise problem at the Dallas airport. Even more telling were the accusations that Love Field had neither adequate runways nor the capability for instrumentation to safeguard flights as Carter Field did. One FAA official listed seven factors that would keep Love from being an acceptable regional airport.[64]

Dallas spokesmen countered that their airport met FAA safety requirements. They also emphasized how Love Field's convenience saved Dallas travelers time and money. Moreover, they reminded Newman that Love Field was a cornerstone in the city's economy. Finally, consultant James Buckley testified that Dallas and Fort Worth were "separate and different types of communities and economically incompatible in their service air requirements." As a result, he saw no justification "for the use of the federal government to deprive one of the nation's major air traffic generating centers of conveniently, available, scheduled air service at its own airport."[65]

Love Field proponents also questioned Fort Worth's ability to finance the improvements needed to give that airport true regional status, if it were chosen to serve that purpose. According to Dallas figures, Fort Worth voters would have to approve a $49.7 million airport bond issue to meet the proposed improvements for Carter Field. This would raise the city's bonded indebtedness by 55 percent.[66]

Even a more compelling argument against making Carter Field the area's regional airport was Dallas's absolute refusal to participate in that airport's development. According to Mayor Cabell, Dallas would go out of the airport business if the CAB made Carter Field the area's regional airport. Not only would it close Love Field, but it would refuse to bail out Fort Worth by cooperating in any matter with Fort Worth. The Dallas position placed the CAB in an awkward position since it seemed highly probable that Carter Field could gain regional status even without Dallas's help.[67]

Indeed, the Dallas position probably helps explain examiner Ross I. Newman's ruling on 7 April 1964. His simple sentence verdict read: "It would not be in the public interest to designate either Greater Southwest or Love Field as a regional airport to serve the Dallas-Fort Worth area."[68]

The Dallas victory was short lived, however. On 12 June 1964, the CAB announced it would review Newman's decision. After that review on 30 September 1964, the CAB ruled that both cities must be served by a single facility. That decision gave the cities 180 days to find a location. If they failed to agree on a site, the CAB threatened that it would locate one. That ruling doomed Love Field as the area's dominant airport.[69]

Although the decision outraged some Dallas leaders, others, weary from battling with the federal government, tired of negative publicity and concerned that Houston might capture Dallas's long lead in aviation if something was not done, acceded to the pronouncement and started negotiations that eventually led to the highly successful Dallas-Fort Worth International Airport, located just north of the old Carter Field.[70] City officials did not abandon Love Field as they had once threatened, however. Instead, they converted it into a successful general aviation facility that also retained some short range commercial flights. The past few years have seen a push both within and outside of Dallas to allow more commercial flights to use this field because of its convenience to both downtown and north Dallas businesses.

CONCLUSION

The Love Field airport controversy underscores some of the problems posed for cities by an expanding federal government after the Great Depression. For although that government provided much assistance for urban needs, it also produced growing regulations and increased control. Sometimes, as in airport development, the federal government pursued one set of goals—the promotion of a safe and efficient national airway system—while the city pursued a different set of goals—the promotion of an economically prosperous city. Both sides sought the help of "experts" who adopted their clients' perspectives.

As the federal government intervened and threatened Love Field's future, while at the same time promoting Fort Worth's Carter Field, responsible Dallas government and civic leaders unleashed a vicious and well-publicized attack on the federal government's motives and purposes. Whether this helps to explain the city's extremely conservative political posture during these years, or is merely a symptom of this conservatism, is hard to ascertain. However, the airport controversy certainly gave citizens of this "can do" city good reason to be wary of the growing involvement of the federal government in the fabric of urban life. Indeed, the negative experiences many growth-oriented Sunbelt cities had with federal regulations and bureaucracies in the fifties and sixties, due to their sometimes conflicting agendas, may help to explain the continued political conservatism of those cities to this day.

11

Erastus Corning, 2nd and Democratic Politics in Albany, New York, 1942–1983

Ivan D. Steen

On 28 May 1983, the citizens of Albany, New York learned that their mayor, Erastus Corning, 2nd, had died in a Boston hospital. To many of the city's residents the news seemed almost unbelievable, even though the mayor had been hospitalized for some months. Corning had been at the head of Albany's government for so long—nearly 41 years—that the man and the title had become nearly inseparable: some Albanians—so the story goes—thought that "Mayor" was his first name! A substantial portion of them had never known another chief executive in their city. Erastus Corning, 2nd, was first sworn in as mayor of the city of Albany on 1 January 1942. As far as is known, he held his office longer than any mayor in American history. Moreover, the political organization he represented had been in solid control of New York's capital city since the early twenties.

How can we explain this incredible longevity of both a city's political organization and its principal officeholder? The task is not a simple one, and a thorough analysis cannot be accomplished in a brief paper. But my ongoing study of this era—based on a variety of printed and manuscript sources and extensive oral history interviews—

has begun to provide some explanations that we might consider.[1]

ALBANY POLITICS BEFORE CORNING

For the first two decades of the twentieth century, the city of Albany was dominated by a Republican political machine headed by William F. Barnes, Jr. The Albany Democrats, under the leadership of Patrick McCabe, were weak and factionalized. But Barnes began to lose interest in city politics, and his subordinates lacked the skill to deal with overconfidence and greed. Scandals came to light that provided opportunities for the opposition. And that opposition began to organize, as new leadership emerged in the Democratic party. The O'Connell brothers, Edward and Daniel—of Irish working-class background—teamed up with the Corning brothers, Edwin and Parker—scions of one of Albany's patrician families—to take control from "Packy" McCabe. It was an excellent alliance: Ed O'Connell, an attorney, was a fine political strategist; Dan, whose political savvy was second to none, was a true man of the people; the Cornings provided money and influence. Portraying themselves as reformers who wanted to rid the city's government of the corrupt Republican rascals, they succeeded in having Dan O'Connell elected to the Board of Assessors in 1919; and in 1921 their candidate for mayor, William S. Hackett, was victorious.

Hackett was a very popular mayor, and the new regime seemed to be providing reasonably honest and effective government. In 1926, while on a visit to Cuba, Mayor Hackett was killed in an automobile accident. The Democrats replaced him with John Boyd Thacher II, who also proved to be a popular mayor. Thacher served in that office until 1940, when he was elected Children's Court Judge. It was during his term of office that Albany gained national attention, in 1933, as a consequence of the bizarre kidnapping of Dan and Ed O'Connell's nephew, John J. O'Connell, Jr.—an event that provided the backdrop for William Kennedy's novel, *Billy Phelan's Greatest Game*. It was also during these years that Dan O'Connell emerged as the sole leader of the Democratic machine: Edwin Corning died in 1934, Parker Corning bowed out of politics in 1937 (he died in 1943), and Ed O'Connell died in 1939. The O'Connell machine was well entrenched, and most Albanians seemed satisfied with their city's government. The machine was well organized and made skillful use of patronage to help ensure a loyal following. Also, as its predecessors—both Democratic and Republican— had done, it manipulated property assessments for political purposes. Although charges of corruption were made that sometimes led to state-sponsored investigations, the organization weathered these with scarcely a scar.

When Mayor Thacher left office in 1940, a year of his term still remained. The president of the Common Council, Frank Harris, was in line to succeed him, but this would have required Harris to resign from his state job. Instead, Harris resigned from his city post, and an obscure alderman, Herman Hoogkamp, was elevated to the council presidency, and from there to the office of mayor. Hoogkamp obviously was just a fill-in. The Democratic candidate for mayor in the 1941 election was Erastus Corning, 2nd: there was little doubt that he would win that election.

THE CORNING FAMILY

Most citizens of Albany probably did not know very much about their new mayor in 1941, but they certainly were familiar with his family. The Corning family had moved from Connecticut to Chatham, New York, in 1805. In 1814, the first Erastus Corning, then 19 years old, moved to Albany. Within a few years he became the owner of his own hardware business, and he soon became a successful and wealthy businessman. In addition to being a hardware merchant, he was an iron manufacturer, railroad developer, land speculator and banker. He is best known as the founder and first president of the New York Central Railroad. Erastus Corning was also a prominent politician:

he served as mayor, state senator and congressman, and he was a major figure in the Democratic party. His son, Erastus Corning, Jr., continued the family involvement in business and politics, but he was less successful and less prominent than his father. In fact, much of the family fortune had disappeared by the time he died.[2]

Having more or less skipped a generation, the Corning financial and political skills showed up again in Erastus Jr.'s sons, Parker and Edwin. Parker, a Yale graduate, was a founder of the Albany Felt company (now Albany International) and served as chairman of its board until his death in 1943. Edwin, a graduate of both Groton and Yale, worked with his older brother to revitalize the old family iron interests, establishing Ludlum Steel in neighboring Watervliet, New York. Edwin was the company's president and Parker its vice president. Both brothers also served as bank directors and trustees. Ludlum Steel prospered, but the family's finances were dealt a serious blow by the Great Depression. In 1932, Gurnett and Company, a brokerage house in which the brothers were partners, suspended business and was forced to liquidate many of the stocks in which it had a substantial interest— among them Ludlum Steel.

Parker and Edwin Corning were both very active in Democratic politics as well. We have already seen that they worked with the O'Connell brothers to oust the Barnes machine and establish Democratic hegemony in Albany. In 1922, Parker was elected to the U.S. House of Representatives, where he served seven terms until his discomfort with some New Deal philosophies and legislation prompted him to step down. Edwin headed the Albany County Democratic organization, formed a close relationship with Al Smith, and, with support from Smith, became chairman of the New York State Democratic Committee in 1926. That same year, he became the Democratic candidate for lieutenant governor, and served in that post under Smith for two years, simultaneously retaining his chairmanship of the state Democratic committee. When Smith made his unsuccessful run for the presidency in 1928, Edwin Corning was believed to be a leading contender to succeed Smith as governor. But Edwin, who was only 45 years old, had recently suffered a stroke. He withdrew his name from consideration, resigned his state party chairmanship, and after finishing his term as lieutenant governor, completely bowed out of politics. This cleared the path for Franklin D. Roosevelt's nomination as the Democratic candidate for governor of New York State.[3]

THE EDUCATION OF ERASTUS CORNING, 2ND

Erastus Corning, 2nd, son of Edwin and nephew of Parker, had politics in his blood. He recalled few topics other than politics being discussed in his home during his childhood. His first formal education was at the Albany Academy, but when he was 12 years old he was sent off to Groton, his father's old school, to be properly educated under the aegis of Endicott Peabody. Groton strove to train gentlemen leaders for America, and an extraordinary number of its graduates became prominent in public service. Franklin Roosevelt was a Grotonian, but while his career at Groton was not outstanding, Erastus Corning's was. He led his class in academics nearly every year, receiving serious competition only from his good friend and classmate, Joseph Alsop. Erastus was business editor of the school publication, *The Grotonian*, and, as was expected of all the boys, he participated in athletics, debates and other activities.[4]

The teenage Erastus, although immersed in academic and extracurricular activities at Groton, was interested in Albany and New York State politics. His father wrote to him about political matters from time to time, and he occasionally asked his mother to send him news of local politics. His father's nomination and election as lieutenant governor especially thrilled him, and during the campaign he asked his mother to send him "a lot of those Smith-Corning buttons say 40 or 50. Lots of boys will wear them if I can get the buttons."[5]

In 1928, following graduation from Groton, Erastus

vacationed in Europe, and that fall he was off to Yale. There was never any doubt that he would attend Yale, his father's *alma mater*; Erastus's son would follow the same pattern. Not only was attending the father's schools a common custom for the sons of America's elite families, but most Grotonians went to either Harvard or Yale. At Yale, he was a good, but less enthusiastic, student, and he was elected to Phi Beta Kappa in his senior year.

Upon returning to Albany in 1932, Erastus founded an insurance company, and he retained that business throughout his life. With the ailing Edwin Corning spending most of his time in Northeast Harbor, Maine, Erastus took care of many of his father's obligations and kept him posted on events in Albany. On one occasion, Erastus represented his father at a Ludlum Steel outing in 1934. This event was planned by the employees and paid for by the company. After attending the picnic, Erastus sent his father a copy of the program "and your badge, which I felt very proud to wear as your representative. It was a great picnic," he reported. Erastus genuinely seemed to have enjoyed himself. He described some of the activities:

> I got into a dancing contest with Mrs. Leo Cherney against Mr. & Mrs. Garacino and with John Cherney as judge our team was declared the winner. Somehow I had to make a short speech in the ballroom, and just said that I knew how much you would have liked to have been at the party. It really was grand and I never thought I could set myself up as a beer drinker, but after Saturday I am not so sure.[6]

His father's death in 1934 was a great blow to Erastus, but it seemed to propel him to move into politics. That year he served as a delegate to the Democratic state convention, and the next year he successfully ran for a seat in the New York State Assembly.

The events of 1936 provide an illustration of the manner in which the O'Connell organization dealt with the careers of party officeholders. That was the year that Parker Corning announced that he would not seek reelection to Congress. To replace him as a candidate, the Albany County Democratic Committee named William T. Byrne, who had been serving in the New York State Senate since 1923, and Erastus Corning was named as the candidate to replace Byrne. Corning won easily, and his new job gave him political experience and public exposure. By 1941, with six years in public office behind him, that experience, his family background and his closeness to Daniel O'Connell made him a logical candidate to run for the mayor's office. And at age 32, he became the youngest mayor in Albany's history.

THE CORNING YEARS

The city Erastus Corning had been elected to serve as chief executive was among the nation's oldest. First settled by the Dutch in 1624, it officially became a city under the English when Governor Thomas Dongan of New York signed its charter in 1686. Located on one of the major routes of transportation to the West, Albany served as an important trading center, and most of the principal foreign-born groups who migrated to the United States were represented in the city's population. Of all the peoples who settled in Albany, none left a more significant stamp on the city than did the Irish. While primarily a commercial center, a variety of manufacturing enterprises also contributed substantially to Albany's economy. But as the twentieth century progressed, a growing number of Albany's citizens were employed by a burgeoning state government. Albany's position as New York State's capital city has had a major impact on all phases of its existence. When Erastus Corning assumed the office of Albany's mayor, he presided over a city in which the most recent federal census (1940) had counted 130,577 residents. Although at the present time Albany's population is less than 100,000, that decline can not be ascribed to the city's political leadership; rather, it is symptomatic of a national trend affecting America's older cities, especially those located in northern climes.

It would be impossible, of course, to discuss the events

of Erastus Corning's 40 plus years in office in any detail, but we might focus, if only all too briefly, on a few of considerable significance.

Probably the most dramatic of these began in 1943, Thomas E. Dewey's first year as governor of New York State. One of Dewey's campaign pledges had been to clean up what he claimed were corrupt practices in Albany City and County, and to break the O'Connell organization. To do this, he launched what was probably the most extensive state investigation ever made of a local political organization. Corning and Dan O'Connell anticipated the probe, and they surely had no love for New York's new Republican governor. On 31 December 1942, Corning wrote to John J. O'Connell: "We are welcoming today our little mustachio carpet-bagger from Michigan, and look forward to having a nice time with him in the next few months."[7] And the following September, with the investigation already underway, he wrote to his brother:

> The Governor has started an inquiry into our method of taxing real estate here in Albany, with all the appurtenances of a full fledged investigation, though the fellows on "the hill" deny very vehemently that it has any political significance. This kind of an investigation is just like one we went through eight or nine years ago, and we firmly anticipate nothing too startling will turn up. As a matter of fact, we have some pretty choice and juicy ideas of our own in connection with the general picture that may make our little friend feel that he's got hold of a wild cat by the tail.[8]

And in December, he wrote to a friend:

> We are busy and have been so for the past three months fending off the attacks of the little Governor in his war against Albany. The little fellow is attacking with the utmost fury from all sides and is, to my mind, a mental case, with the one great obsession that the city of Albany is the enemy of all the world, and he is the knight in shining armor who must exert his every effort to slay this horrible dragon, Albany, N.Y. We are giving him back everything

we can [and] it really is quite a battle. It is amusing to think that this little lad aspires to the presidency. . . .[9]

And battle it was! What were the "juicy ideas" that the Albany Democrats had in mind? One of them was to have the county district attorney launch a probe of the Republican controlled state legislature. Also, it was difficult for the state to secure a grand jury that would return indictments, since the O'Connell organization controlled the jury rolls. In any event, Dewey finally had to conclude the investigation having secured only a few minor convictions. Dewey may have succeeded with organized crime in New York City, but he failed with the O'Connell machine in Albany.[10]

Why did Dewey fail in Albany? Could it be that there was little corruption to uncover? Or could it be that the O'Connell organization was exceptionally adept at covering up its chicanery? Perhaps, as one knowledgeable observer who was close to Dan O'Connell has suggested, it was that Dewey was looking for the wrong thing. Fresh from crimebusting in New York City, Dewey believed the O'Connell machine to be a Mafia-type organization engaged in gross criminal conspiracies and strong-arm tactics, while in reality what existed in Albany were much lower-level and less well-organized voting irregularities and petty, politically oriented crimes. In other words, Dewey uncovered just about what there was to uncover, but he expected to find much more. Dewey could not accept the possibility that the Albany Democrats could gain such large majorities at the polls without widespread corruption.

During a fair portion of the time that Dewey was engaged in battle with the Albany Democrats, Mayor Corning was away from that action. In April 1944, Albany's mayor was drafted into the army, and served as a PFC in the Infantry. He was with a combat unit in the Rhineland and Central Europe campaigns. Corning had had the opportunity to apply for Officer's Candidate School, but he decided not to do so because, as he wrote to his mother, "feeling the war will be over soon, I don't want to spend my entire service *training*. Going to O.C.S. would have another 17 weeks at Fort Benning which would bring my training up pretty much to the end of the year."[11] While Corning was in the army, Albany was administered by an acting mayor, whom Corning appointed under the terms of a law that had been engineered through the state legislature by Fiorello LaGuardia, who had expected it would apply to him. Erastus returned home a local hero in September 1945, just in time to win that year's mayoral election by an overwhelming margin.

As the Democratic mayor of the city that was the most secure Democratic stronghold in the state north of New York City, Corning was of considerable importance in state politics. His name became especially prominent in 1946, as his party was putting together a ticket to challenge Thomas Dewey for the governorship. At the July Democratic State Committee meeting in New York City, Corning proposed Albany as the site for the state convention to be held in early September. This proposal was adopted unanimously. By August, rumors were circulating of a move to put Corning on the Democratic state ticket, but he appeared to be uninterested, and privately confided that he hoped to avoid being chosen. Nevertheless, at a time when many of the state's voters were recently returned servicemen, a politician who was a member of that group himself would be a great asset to the ticket. The convention's choice for governor was Senator James Mead, whom the O'Connell organization had unsuccessfully backed for that position four years earlier. The nomination for lieutenant governor went to Corning, who accepted it with reluctance. He ran a spirited campaign, however, accusing Dewey of not doing enough for veterans, and generally was considered to be a stronger candidate than the lackluster Mead. When the results were in, Corning had won by a large majority in the city of Albany, but statewide he and his party were soundly defeated. From then on, Mayor Corning devoted all his attention to Albany and never sought any elective office other than mayor.

The fifties were not especially difficult years for the Albany Democrats, but the sixties and early seventies were another matter. A number of factors contributed to the organization's problems during those years. With the exception of those located in the Sunbelt, most cities in the United States were faced with serious economic problems during those years, and Albany was no exception. There, as elsewhere, people were flocking to the suburbs, and business—especially retailing—was following them. There was little that Corning, or any mayor, could do about this. Nonetheless, Corning did try to secure a place for downtown Albany as a regional retailing center. For example, when plans were being made by Sears Roebuck to build a large shopping mall in the centrally located suburban town of Colonie, and to attract Macy's as the other principal anchor store, Corning met with Macy's executives to try to induce them to locate in downtown Albany instead. However, those meetings proved fruitless, since Macy's realized that, even if Albany met all their demands—and to do so would have been very difficult, if not impossible—it would take some time to open a facility. In the meantime, another national chain would become an anchor at the Colonie site and would gain a competitive advantage.[12] Despite these and other efforts, Corning and the Democratic organization were blamed for the city's economic woes.

Also, the sixties and early seventies were volatile years. The civil rights movement and the Vietnam war spawned protests and the formation of action groups, and this activity had its counterpart on the local level in the organization of a variety of civic action groups. In Albany, these local groups saw the source of most problems in a political organization that had been in control for more than four decades. And, with the state government in Republican hands under Governor Nelson Rockefeller, local Republicans and independents were encouraged. Of course, the Albany Democrats did not help themselves. In power for so long, they had become overconfident and assumed they would win no matter who they ran for office.

And so, during the sixties and early seventies, the O'Connell organization was faced with challenges from relatively young and vigorous opponents: independent groups demonstrated an ability to organize effectively, and the local Republicans seemed to take on a new vigor. The first major inroad came in 1966, when a hard-campaigning Republican candidate for Congress defeated a Democratic stalwart, and then succeeded in winning reelection two years later. The toughest year for the Albany Democrats was 1968. Not only did the Republicans retain their recently won Congressional seat, but they also succeeded in winning two seats in the New York State Assembly and one in the state Senate. Even worse, a Republican now held the important office of Albany County District Attorney.

All of this forced the Democratic organization to do some soul searching—and they demonstrated their resiliency. By 1974, they had regained their seats in Congress and the state legislature, and they had recaptured the district attorney's office. Elections were now taken seriously, and candidate choices were no longer based solely on party loyalty. Still, Erastus Corning ran into trouble as late as 1973. In that year's mayoral election, he was challenged by Carl Touhey, the owner of a local automobile dealership. Touhey was popular, and he ran an effective campaign; he was aided by a State Investigation Commission probe of the Albany police department that was in progress at the time. For the first time in his career, Corning engaged in door-to-door campaigning. When the results were in, Corning had won—but not by much. It was the toughest election he had ever faced.

What appeared to be the end of an era came on 28 February 1977, with the death of Dan O'Connell. The big question on just about everyone's mind in Albany was whether the Democratic machine would survive without "Uncle" Dan. Who would assume the leadership, and would that person be able to run the organization with a firm hand and keep it in power? True, Erastus Corning had shown considerable strength and intelligence as mayor, but everyone knew that while Erastus ran the government, Dan ran the party—no decisions of a political nature were made without first consulting the party's "boss." In recent years, though, Corning had been entrusted with more political power, and now he moved rapidly to retain the title of chairman of the Albany County Democratic Party, which he had assumed upon O'Connell's death. He did meet stiff opposition from the Ryan brothers—Charles and James—who had been close to Dan, but he won out over that opposition in short order. From that time until his death in 1983, Erastus Corning was the unquestioned "boss" of the Albany County Democratic organization.

THE END OF AN ERA

When Mayor Corning was elected to his eleventh term of office in 1981, many people speculated on whether it would be his last. But if it were to be, who would be his successor? Thomas Whalen, a member of a prominent Albany law firm and former City Court judge, was interested in the job and saw the presidency of the Common Council as a stepping stone. Corning obliged and supported him for that position. It was widely believed that this made Whalen Corning's choice to succeed him as mayor, but many party insiders deny this, and Corning never made any public statement to that effect. Whether Corning would have run again or not is a moot question. In June 1982 he entered Albany Medical Center for treatment of emphysema, and after a stay of several months he was transferred to Boston University Hospital.

With Corning in the hospital, who was running the city? It was pretty clear that as long as he was in Albany, Corning was running the city from his sickbed. After the shift to Boston, Thomas Whalen, as president of the Common Council, became acting mayor, assisted by an advisory committee of party insiders. Yet, as the public learned after Corning's death, Erastus was still making the important decisions from Boston. Mayor Corning had every intention of returning home to assume his duties, but, on 28 May 1983, he died.

With both Dan and Erastus gone, what would happen to the Albany Democratic organization? Whalen continued to act as mayor until the next election, when he succeeded in winning election to that office, virtually unopposed. But Whalen did not seek the party chairmanship; that post went to Leo O'Brien of neighboring Watervliet, who was not generally regarded to be a strong leader, and who was succeeded by Harold Joyce, a party stalwart. Whalen has achieved considerable popularity in some circles—particularly the business community. However, many of the old party faithful have strong negative feelings about him, although most publicly support him. For a time, at least, the Albany Democratic organization seemed to be firmly entrenched, but it was dealt a serious blow in the 1991 elections when the office of Albany County Executive was won by a Republican. Clearly, the O'Connell-Corning era is gone.

Maintaining a Democratic Stronghold

How has Albany's Democratic organization managed to retain uninterrupted power for such an incredibly long time? Some factors are reasonably clear. Very important to this or any political party is effective organization, with a system of committee members who are responsible for the voters in their districts. The pressure placed on committee members to deliver the vote during the O'Connell years seems occasionally to have led to excesses, some of which were uncovered during the investigations of the Dewey years. Padded registration rolls and repeat voting were some of these. Many voters in Albany were convinced that the party knew how they voted. While this may have been true at some times and at some polling places, it is mostly a part of local mythology. Yet such a mythology works to the advantage of the machine : if voters *believe* the machine knows how they vote, they will vote for the organization.

Another part of the Albany mythology involves property assessments. It was widely believed that homeowners who registered Republican would find that they had higher property assessments than their Democratic neighbors. While this may have been true in the early years, it was not the practice during the later years. State investigators found no evidence that party affiliation determined the amount for which property was assessed. Nonetheless, few homeowners were willing to take a chance, and so most dutifully registered with the Democratic party.

Central to the operation of the Albany organization was the extensive use of patronage. It was firmly believed and publicly stated that patronage was essential to the political process. How else were those who worked hard for the party to be rewarded? Patronage helped to maintain party loyalty, and nothing was considered more important than party loyalty. No matter how much one might disagree with policies or individuals, such disagreements were not to be made public, and every effort was to be made to support the organization. As one long-time party stalwart put it, she learned early in life to "never put the knock on a Democrat."[13] Deviators were dealt with severely.

Similarly, the city rewarded cooperative vendors with contracts, and gave no business to their opponents. In the sixties the city withdrew its official advertising from Albany's two newspapers because it believed that those papers were not supportive of the party. When queried about why city contracts were not let out for competitive bidding, Mayor Corning is reported to have said: "We like to do business with our friends."

Another reason for the Albany Democratic organization's longevity was that it had very shrewd leaders. Dan O'Connell's political acumen was legendary, and he was frequently consulted by major state and national political strategists. Erastus Corning carried on the tradition; it is well known that Mario Cuomo's success in winning the governor's office was due in no small part to Erastus Corning, and Cuomo publicly acknowledged this the morning after he first won election. And even such a dominant figure as Nelson Rockefeller found that he often had to yield to Mayor Corning's desires.

Of no small importance in explaining the longevity of

the Albany Democratic organization is the emphasis that organization placed on serving individual citizens. This was especially true during the Corning years. The development of programs and the establishment of agencies were less important than having personal knowledge of what people needed and tending to those needs on an individual basis. This did not mean that Albany failed to take advantage of federal funds available for social, economic and environmental purposes. Quite the contrary: the city's administration was quick to seize every opportunity to tap into such funds. For the most part, though, rather than dealing with government bureaucrats and filling out forms, citizens could take their problems to committee members for resolution. And, if an individual so desired, he or she could write, call or personally see Mayor Corning. Corning responded to all letters immediately, he frequently answered his own phone, and he held open house every Saturday morning in his office. He tried, as much as possible, to be helpful—even going to the extent of "fixing" parking tickets. It should be noted that party affiliation may have been important for securing city jobs and contracts, but those who wrote asking for the mayor's assistance were never asked if they were Democrats. Favors result in votes, and Corning was well aware of that; but he also genuinely seems to have liked being helpful.

The Albany Democratic organization may, on occasion, have engaged in intimidation and other improper practices. But the evidence encountered in my ongoing study indicates that the organization remained in power so long because it pleased most of the people most of the time.

Notes

Notes to Chapter 1 / Pinkham

1. Among the earlier historians who have studied communities and appear to ignore the rise of urban centers in their works are: William Haller, *The Puritan Frontier: Town Planting in New England, 1630–1660* (New York, 1951); Anne B. Maclean, *Early New England Towns: A Comparative Study of their Development*, (New York, 1908); John Sly, *Town Government in Massachusetts, 1620–1930* (Boston, 1930); and Roy H. Akagi, *The Town Proprietors of the New England Colonies*, (New York, 1924).

2. Haller, 18.

3. Jon C. Teaford indicates in *The Municipal Revolution in America: Origins of Modern Urban Government* (Chicago, 1975) that the city governments at this early stage were still dominated by vested business and proprietary interests, the change to democracy coming later.

4. Teaford, 129.

5. Among the works that have been of most influence in the formulation of this approach are Carl Bridenbaugh, *Cities in the Wilderness: Urban Life, 1625–1742* (New York, 1938) (hereafter cited as *Cities in the Wilderness*); Richard L. Bushman, *From Puritan to Yankee: Character and Social Order in Connecticut, 1690–1765* (New York, 1967); Bruce C. Daniels, "The Colonial Background of New England's Secondary Urban Centers," *Historical Journal of Massachusetts* 14 (January 1987): 11–24, Daniels, *Dissent and Conformity on Narragansett Bay: The Colonial Rhode Island Town* (Middletown, Conn., 1983) (hereafter cited as *Dissent and Controversy*), Daniels, *The Connecticut Town: Growth and Development, 1635–1790* (Middletown, Conn., 1979) (hereafter cited as *Connecticut Town*); Daniels, ed., *Town and Country: Essays of the Structure of Local Government in the American Colonies* (Middletown, Conn., 1978) (hereafter cited as *Town and Country*); Henry Doherty, *Society and Power: Five New England Towns, 1800–1860* (Amherst, Mass., 1977); Henry C. Binford, *The First Boston Suburbs: Residential Communities on the Boston Periphery, 1815–1860* (Chicago, 1985) (hereafter cited as *First Suburbs*); Francis X. Blouin, *The Boston*

Region, 1810–1850: A Study in Urbanization (Ann Arbor, Mich., 1980); and Paul Boyer and Stephen Nissenbaum, *Salem Possed: The Social Origins of Witchcraft* (Cambridge, Mass., 1974). The dynamics of community subdivision has been especially highlighted by Kenneth A. Lockridge, *A New England Town: The First Hundred Years* (New York, 1970) and Douglas R. McManus, *Colonial New England: A Historical Geography*, (New York, 1975).

6. *Journal of the Massachusetts Constitutional Convention of 1820* (Boston, 1820).

7. The writers most effective with the idea of maturity have been Bridenbaugh, *Cities in the Wilderness*, and Richard C. Wade, *The Urban Frontier: Pioneer Life in Early Pittsburgh, Cincinnati, Lexington, Louisville, and St. Louis* (Chicago, 1959).

8. *Boston Globe*, 25 Sept. 1986 and 3 Oct. 1986; of interest in this last phase is that, over 120 years after Roxbury relinquished its city charter in 1867, present efforts by that locality, a predominately black community, are underway to secure another charter and secede from Boston as the city of Mandela. Examining present-day Roxbury, however, is beyond the scope of this paper.

9. Jon C. Teaford, *The Municipal Revolution in America: Origins of Modern Urban Government, 1650–1825* (Chicago: University of Chicago Press, 1975), 38 (hereafter cited as *Municipal Revolution*).

10. *Acts and Resolves of the State of Connecticut in America*, New London, 1784, 164–80; and *Rhode Island Acts, Resolves, and Reports*, 1784.

11. Teaford in *Municipal Revolution* finds that Boston's influence begins to be felt after the Revolution had stripped the city governments to the south of New England of their vested rights and privileges. Thus in 1784 its influence is only beginning.

12. *Rhode Island Acts, Resolves, and Reports*, May 1787–March 1789.

13. *Acts and Resolves, Connecticut*, 1784, 164–80; Benjamin Trumbull, *A Complete History of Connecticut, Civil and Ecclesiastical*, 2 vols. (New London, Ct., 1898) and Benjamin W. Labaree comp. *The Public Records of the State of Connecticut, 1783 and 1784*, 343–373.

14. *Municipal Revolution*.

15. The subcommunities dividing from New Haven were: Woodbridge (1784), East Haven (1785), North Haven (1786), Hamden (1796) and Orange (1822).

16. *Connecticut Town; State of Connecticut Register and Manual, 1939*; and the subcommunities dividing from the four Connecticut cities were from Hartford: East Hartford (1783) and West Hartford (1854); from Middletown: Chatham (1767), Cromwell (1851) and Middlefield (1866); from New London:

Groton (1705), Montville (1786) and Waterford (1801); from Norwich: Bozrah (1786), Franklin (1786), Lisbon (1786) and Sprague (1861).

17. David Thomas Konig, "English Legal Change and the Origins of Local Government in Northern Massachusetts," in *Town and County*, 13.

18. *The Public Records of the State of Connecticut.* May 1800–Oct. 1801, vol. 10, Hartford, Conn., 1965, 105–11.

19. *Public Statute Laws of the State of Connecticut*, 1821, 108–23.

20. *Public Statue Laws of the State of Connecticut.* Hartford, 1821 (hereafter cited as *Statutes of Connecticut*; and George C. Waldo, Jr. ed., *History of Bridgeport and Vicinity* (New York, 1917), 63 (hereafter cited as *History of Bridgeport*).

21. *Statutes of Connecticut*, 1821, 94–105.

22. *Rhode Island Acts, Resolves, and Reports*, May 1787–March, 1789, 4–5; and for background information on Newport, see Lynn Withey, *Urban Growth in Colonial Rhode Island: Newport and Providence in the Eighteenth Century* (Albany, NY, 1984).

23. *Acts and Resolves of the General Assembly of the State of Rhode Island and Providence Plantations, 1853–1855*, May 1853, 21–29.

24. Josiah Quincy, *Municipal History of Boston*, (Boston, 1852) (hereafter cited as *History of Boston*; and *Journal of the Massachusetts Constitutional Convention*, 1821, 67 and 97.

25. Teaford in *Municipal Revolution*, chapter 8, saw the revolution as having been complete by this time.

26. *Laws of the Commonwealth of Massachusetts, 1818–1822*, 734–51; Josiah Quincy, *History of Boston*; *Journal of the Mass. Convention.*, 1821; and John Koren, *Boston, 1822–1922: The Story of Its Government* (Boston, 1923).

27. *Connecticut Register and Manual*, 1939.

28. The communities becoming boroughs between 1800 and 1870 were Bridgeport (1800), Stonington (1801), Guilford (1815), Essex (1820), Killington (1820), Danbury (1822), Colchester (1824), Newtown (1824), Waterbury (1825), Stamford (1830), Norwalk (1836), New Britain (1850), Derby (1851), Danielson (1852), Wallingford (1853) and Greenwich (1854). *Connecticut Register and Manual*, 1939.

29. *Acts and Resolves of the General Assembly of the State of Rhode Island and Providence Plantation*, January 1830, 33–45; and Richard M. Bayles, ed. *History of Providence County Rhode Island*, vol. 1 (New York, 1891).

30. *Legislative Documents of Maine, 1831–1832.* Portland City Charter, 2–11; *The City Charter and Ordinances of the City of Bangor*, Bangor City Charter of 1834, 1839, 2–21; and for general background information of the new cities of northern New England, see A. J. Coolidge and J. B. Mansfield, eds., *A History*

and Description of New England (Boston, 1859).

31. Waldo, *History of Bridgeport*, 87–88.

32. *Acts and Resolves of Massachusetts*, March 1836, 686–99; and *Laws of Massachusetts, 1834–1836*, Boston, 1834, 1835, 1836, 788–807.

33. John Haywood, ed., *New England Gazetteer*, 1840, Boston, 1841; Frederick W. Cook, Secretary of the Commonwealth, *Commonwealth of Massachusetts, Historical Date Relating to Countries, Cities, and Towns in Massachusetts*, 1948 (hereafter cited as *Historical Data of Mass.*); *Maine Register, 1921–22*; George J. Varney, ed., *Gazetteer of the State of Maine*, Boston, 1882; and Stanley B. Attwood, ed., *The Length and Breadth of Maine* (Augusta, 1946) (hereafter cited as *Length and Breadth of Maine*).

34. *Historical Data of Massachusett*s; the two subcommunities dividing from Boston were Brookline (1705) and Chelsea (1739); the subdivisions of Salem were Wenham (1643), Manchester (1645), Marblehead (1649), Beverly (1669) and Danvers (1757); for Portland the principal source is *Counties, Cities, Towns, and Plantations of Maine: A Handbook of Incorporation, Dissolutions, and Boundary Change*s, Maine State Archives, Augusta, 1940 (hereafter cited as *Counties and Cities of Maine*); and the subdivisions of Falmouth were Cape Elizabeth (1765), Portland (1786) and Westbrook (1814).

35. *Historical Data Related to Massachusetts*; and Lowell was carved from Chelmsford in 1822.

36. *Dissent and Controversy; Rhode Island Register and Manual, 1898–99;* and the subdivisions of Providence were Glocester (1731), Smithfield (1731), Scituate (1731), Cumberland (1747), Cranston (1754) and Johnston (1759).

37. *Counties and Cities of Maine;* and the subcommunity separating from Bangor was Veazie (1853).

38. *Historical Data Related to Massachusetts; Counties and Cities of Maine; Length and Breadth of Maine; Connecticut Register und Manual, 1939; Rhode Island Manual, 1898–99;* Edwin A. Charlton, ed., *New Hampshire As It Is*, Claremont, N. H., 1855; and *Conant's Vermont*, Seventh Edition, 1905.

39. The 25 new city charters written between 1846 and 1855 were Manchester (1846), Roxbury (1846), Bath (1847), Charlestown (1847), New Bedford (1847), Cambridge (1848), Worcester (1948), Portsmouth (1849), Augusta (1849), Gardiner (1849), Calais (1850), Hallowell (1850), Lynn (1950), Newburyport (1851), Springfield (1852), Belfast (1853), Concord (1853), Nashua (1853), Waterbury (1853), Newport (1853), Lawrence (1853), Rockland (1854), Fall River (1854), Biddeford (1855) and Dover (1855).

40. *Acts and Resolves of Massachusetts, 1846*, 50–59.

41. *Massachusetts Statutes*, Roxbury Charter, 1846.

42. Although Binford in *First Suburbs* focuses upon Cambridge and Charlestown, it is obvious that Roxbury, too, was on Boston's "urban fringe."

43. Sam B. Warner, Jr. *Streetcar Suburbs: The Process of Growth in Boston, 1870–1900* (Cambridge, MA, 1962).

44. *Acts and Resolves of Massachusetts, 1854*, 172–83; and *Acts and Resolves of the State of Maine, 1855*, 442–53.

45. Justin Winsor, ed., *Memorial History of Boston*, Cambridge, 1881; and Quincy, *History of Boston*.

46. *Acts and Resolves of the State of Maine, 1849*, Gardiner City Charter, 374–87; and *Acts and Resolves of the State of Maine*, Augusta City Charter, 1849, 316–27.

47. *Historical Data of Mass.; Conant's Vermont; Counties and Cities of Maine;* and *Length and Breadth of Maine*.

48. *Acts and Resolves of Maine, 1850*, Charter for Hallowell, 584–93; *Historical Data of Mass.; Counties and Cities of Maine;* and *Length and Breadth of Maine*.

49. *First Suburbs*.

50. *Historical Data of Massachusetts*; the towns that subdivided from Charlestown were Medford (1754), Malden (1649), Stoneham (1725) and Somerville (1842), of which Medford, Malden and Somerville became cities; the communities that separated from Hallowell were Augusta, Chelsea, Manchester and Farmingdale, Augusta separating as a city in 1849.

51. *Length and Breadth of Maine;* and *Counties and Cities of Maine*.

52. *Acts and Resolves of the State of Maine, 1850*, Charter of Belfast, 496–507; *Acts and Resolves of the State of Maine, 1850*, Charter of Calais, 550–61; Cook, ed., *Historical Data of Massachusetts;* and *Counties and Cities of Maine;* and Attwood, ed., *Length and Breadth of Maine*.

53. *Acts and Resolves of Massachusetts, 1866–1867*, Boston, 1867, 754–60.

54. *Historical Data of Mass.*

Notes to Chapter 2 / Martin

1. "The City Police and the Firemen," Pittsburgh *Morning Chronicle*, 3 June 1842.

2. "Progress of Purification—Improvement in Public Morals," *Morning Chronicle*, 4 June 1842.

3. "Riotous Conduct," *American Manufacturer* (Pittsburgh), 11 June 1842.

4. See, for example, John C. Schneider, "Riot and Reaction in St. Louis, 1854–1856," *Missouri Historical Review* 68 (January

1974): 176; and Schneider, *Detroit and the Problem of Order, 1830–1880* (Lincoln: University of Nebraska Press, 1980), 26–31; David R. Johnson, *Policing the Urban Underworld* (Philadelphia: Temple University Press, 1979), 22, 27; Philip D. Jordan, *Frontier Law and Order: Ten Essays* (Lincoln: University of Nebraska Press, 1970), 118, 126; Edward H. Savage, *Police Records and Recollections* (Montclair, NJ: Patterson Smith, 1971 (1873)), 26, 107–12; Roger Lane, *Policing the City: Boston 1822–1885* (Cambridge, MA: Harvard University Press, 1967), 24; Barbara M. Hobson, *Uneasy Virtue: The Politics of Prostitution and the American Reform Tradition* (New York: Basic Books, 1987), 23–24; Timothy J. Gilfoyle, "Strumpets and Misogynists: Brothel 'Riots' and the Transformation of Prostitution in Antebellum New York City," *New York History* 68 (January 1987), 45–65. Accounts of local action against brothels by fire companies can be found in James Hadden, *A History of Uniontown, Pennsylvania* (Uniontown, PA, 1913), 573; Charles Dawson, *Our Firemen* (Pittsburgh, 1889), 24, 32; "Purification," *Pittsburgh Mercury and Democrat*, 8 June 1842.

    5. Population figures from U.S. Census population schedules (statistical summary volumes) for 1800–1850.

    6. *Harris' Directory* (Pittsburgh, 1839), 2.

    7. For discussions of class structure and formation, see Robert Eugene Harper, "The Class Structure of Western Pennsylvania in the Late Eighteenth Century" (Ph.D. diss., University of Pittsburgh, 1969); Solon J. and Elizabeth H. Buck, *The Planting of Civilization in Western Pennsylvania* (Pittsburgh: University of Pittsburgh Press, 1939), 349; Richard Oestreicher, "Working-Class Formation, Development, and Consciousness in Pittsburgh, 1790–1960," in Samuel P. Hays, ed., *City at the Point: Essays on the Social History of Pittsburgh* (Pittsburgh: University of Pittsburgh Press, 1990).

    8. Richard C. Wade, *The Urban Frontier: Pioneer Life in Early Pittsburgh, Cincinnati, Lexington, Louisville, and St. Louis* (Chicago: University of Chicago Press, 1964), 218–19. Henry Mann, ed., *Our Police* (Pittsburgh, 1889) contains an 1804 letter from Presley Neville to the borough Council complaining about "certain houses in the borough kept by free blacks and others, where servants are harbored and countenanced in frolic and dissipation, greatly to the injury of their masters and employers, and to the great encouragement of vice and disorder" (51).

    9. Christine Altenburger, "The Pittsburgh Bureau of Police: Some Historical Highlights," *Western Pennsylvania Historical Magazine* 49 (January 1966), 1: 20–23. For an overview of growing problems of urban order see chapter 3, "The Emergence of Urban Problems," 72–100 in Wade, *Urban Frontier*, especially 87–94.

    10. Pittsburgh *Mercury*, 3 February 1836.

11. See, for example, Mann, *Our Police*, 52, 68–70; Altenburger, "Pittsburgh Bureau of Police," 21; James Waldo Fawcett, "Quest for Pittsburgh Fire Department History," *Western Pennsylvania Historical Magazine 49* (January 1966), 1: 44–45.

12. Dawson, Our Firemen, 19–20; *History of Allegheny County, Pennsylvania* (Chicago: Warner & Co., 1889), 644–45; Wade, *Urban Frontier*, 287–89; Altenburger, *Pittsburgh Bureau of Police*, 21–22, Mann, *Our Police*, 58–60; Pittsburgh *Gazette*, 28 November 1823.

13. *Iron City and Pittsburgh Weekly Chronicle*, 4 June 1842.

14. *Greensburg Gazette*, 7 November 1828; piece reprinted from Pittsburgh *Gazette*.

15. Diary of Charles B. Scully, Darlington Library, University of Pittsburgh, 10 January 1843.

16. L.H. Everts, *History of Allegheny County, Pennsylvania, 1753–1876* (Philadelphia: Everts, 1876), 176. See also Allen H. Kerr, "The Mayors and Recorders of Pittsburgh, 1816–1951: Their Lives and Somewhat of their Times," (unpublished manuscript, 1952, in Carnegie Library of Pittsburgh), p. 4 in section on McClintock (irregular pagination).

17. Pittsburgh *Morning Chronicle*, 2 and 3 June 1842; Pittsburgh *Mercury and Democrat*, 8 Junes 1842.

18. Pittsburgh's fire companies predated the city watch; see Dawson, *Our Firemen*, 19. William G. Johnston describes annual fire company parades as community events in his *Life and Reminiscences from Birth to Manhood* (New York: Knickerbocker Press, 1901), 213–14. For more on volunteer companies generally, see Ernest Earnest, *The Volunteer Fire Company Past and Present* (New York: Stein and Day, 1983).

19. Dawson, *Our Firemen*, 26. Cf. Bruce Laurie, "Fire Companies and Gangs in Southwark: The 1840s," in Allen F. Davis and Mark H. Haller, eds., *The People of Philadelphia, A History of Ethnic Groups and Lower Class Life, 1790–1940* (Philadelphia: Temple University Press, 1973), 76.

20. *Morning Chronicle*, 8 June 1842.

21. Cf. Bruce Laurie, *Working People of Philadelphia, 1800–1850* (Philadelphia: Temple University Press, 1980), 58–59.

22. Dawson, *Our Firemen*, 23, 60. For more on problems with volunteer companies, see Fawcett, "Fire Department History," 47–48.

23. Johnston, *Life and Reminiscences*, 211.

24. Dawson, *Our Firemen*, 60–61, 57. Cf. Laurie, "Fire Companies and Gangs," especially 76–80.

25. Johnston, *Life and Reminiscences*, 212.

26. *Morning Chronicle*, 15 June 1842. See also *Mercury and Democra*t, 8 June and 15 June 1842.

27. Dawson, *Our Firemen*, 24, 32; *Morning Chronicle*, 10 June 1842.

28. Wade, *Urban Frontier*, 271. Cf. Laurie, *Working People of Philadelphia*, 152.

29. Pittsburgh *Gazette*, 7 December 1838. See also Kerr, "Mayors and Recorders," 50.

30. *Mercury and Democrat*, 9 March 1842. See also *History of Allegheny County*, 645–46; Kerr, "Mayors and Recorders," 59.

31. *Harris' General Business Directory of the Cities of Pittsburgh and Allegheny for 1841* (Pittsburgh, 1841), 84.

32. *Morning Chronicle*, 10 June and 15 June 1842.

33. *Iron City*, 21 May, 26 March, 15 January 1842; *Morning Chronicle*, 4 June 1842; *American Manufacturer*, 11 June 1842.

34. *American Manufacturer*, 11 June 1842; Pittsburgh *Sun* article, 7 June 1842, reprinted in the *Morning Chronicle*, 13 June 1842.

35. See, for example, *Iron City*, 15 January, 22 October, 5 November 1842; Pittsburgh *Gazette*, 17, 18, 19 July 1849 for firemen's riots; *Pittsburgh Monthly Museum* 1:7 (August 1846) for an account of a fatal stabbing during a fight between the Allegheny and Niagara companies.

36. *Iron City*, 13 August, 5 November 1842.

37. Altenburger, "Pittsburgh Bureau of Police," 25–26; Fawcett, "Fire Department History," 49; Mann, *Our Police*, 95–97.

Notes to Chapter 3 / Preston

1. Richard Jensen, "New Directions In the History of Social Mobility," Paper Read at the *Organization of America Historians Convention*, St. Louis, Missouri, 8 April 1976.

2. U.S. Department of Commerce Bureau of the Census, "Series A6–8" and "Series A57–72", *Historical Statistics of the U.S.: Colonial Times to 1970*, part 1 (Washington, D.C.: GPO, 1975); Stuart M. Blumin, *The Urban Threshold: Growth and Change In a Nineteenth-Century American Community* (Chicago: University of Chicago Press, 1976).

3. *The* (Frederick, Md.) *Examiner*, 17 June 1863; *The* (Gettysburg, Pa.) *Compiler*, 22 June 1863; *The Adams* (County, Pa.) *Sentinel*, 23 June 1863.

4. Interview with Joseph Elder, Emmitsburg, Maryland, 16 August 1978. Mr. Elder was 93 at the time of the interview and completely lucid. His father owned the store that burned after the stable did.

5. James A. Helman, *History of Emmitsburg, Md.* (Frederick, Md.: Citizen Press, 1906; reprint ed., Emmitsburg, Md.: Chronicle Press, 1975), 69–70.

6. The demographic statistics for Emmitsburg throughout this article, unless otherwise noted, are based on the author's analysis of the manuscript schedules of the U.S Census of 1850, 1860, 1870 and 1880.

7. *The Examiner; The Compiler; The Adams Sentinel* and 1860 *Census.*

8. Helman, 87.

9. Among the works that have contributed to our understanding of mobility are: Stephen Thernstrom, *Poverty and Progress: Social Mobility In a Nineteenth Century City* (Cambridge: Harvard University Press, 1964); Sam Bass Warner, Jr. *The Private City: Philadelphia In Three Periods of Its Growth* (Philadelphia: University of Pennsylvania Press, 1968); Stephen Thernstrom and Richard Sennett (eds.) *Nineteenth-Century Cities: Essays In The New Urban History* (New Haven: Yale University Press, 1969); William G. Robbins, "Opportunity and Persistence In the Pacific Northwest: A Quantitative Study of Early Roseburg, Oregon," *Pacific Historical Review* 39 (1970): 279–96; Peter R. Knights, *The Plain People of Boston, 1830–1860* (New York: Oxford University Press, 1971); Michael H. Frisch, *Town Into City: Springfield, Massachusetts And The Meaning of Community, 1840–1880* (Cambridge: Harvard University Press, 1972); Dean R. Esslinger, *Immigrants and The City: Ethnicity and Mobility In a Nineteenth Century Mid-Western City* (Port Washington: Kennikat Press, 1975); Stuart M. Blumin, *The Urban Threshold: Growth and Change In a Nineteenth Century American Community* (Chicago: University of Chicago Press, 1976); Robert Doherty, *Society and Power: Five New England Towns, 1800–1860* (Amherst: University of Massachusetts Press, 1977); Clyde Griffen, *Natives and Newcomer: The Ordering of Opportunity In Mid-Nineteenth Century Poughkeepsie* (Cambridge: Harvard University Press, 1977); William Silag, "Citizens and Strangers: Geographic Mobility in the Sioux City Region, 1860–1890," *Great Plains Quarterly* 2(3), (1982), 168–83; Elizabeth Hafkin Pleck, *Black Migration and Poverty in Boston, 1865-1900* (New York: Academic Press, 1979); Donald H. Parkerson, "How Mobile Were 19th Century Americans?" *Historical Methods* 15(3) (1982), 99–109.

10. Identifying social and economic factors as "dominant causes" of geographical mobility is not meant to imply that any single individual (or group of persons) was not specifically motivated to migrate because of personal reasons. In his brilliant article, "On Becoming An Emigrant," Leo Schelbert illustrates how a certain set of persons, in his case in the Glarus region of nineteenth century Switzerland, can seem to have a host of well-documented social and economic reasons for migrating, any or all of which could lead historians to announce confidently that

the massive migration from the Glarus Valley was due to these social and economic factors functioning as "dominant causes." In fact, Schelbert finds a series of bizarre personal reasons for why some migrated. Thus "dominant causes" is not used in this article as an exclusive term. See Schelbert, "On Becoming an Emigrant: A Structural View of Eighteenth and Nineteenth-Century Swiss Data," *Perspectives In American History* (1973), 441–95.

11. See note 9 above.

12. Helman, 58, and 1860 *Census.*

13. Helman, 81, and 1860 *Census.* See also John Thomas Scharf, *History of Maryland From The Earliest Period to The Present Day,* vol. 2. (n.p.: n.p., 1879; Reprint ed., Hatboro, Pa.: Tradition Press, 1967) 593; *Adams Sentinel.*

14. John Thomas Scharf, *History of Maryland,* 593.

15. Helman, 75; *Adams Sentinel.*

16. *Adams Sentinel.*

17. Helman, 87.

Notes to Chapter 4 / Ogle

1. The census data tells the story: In 1870, of 663 municipalities (incorporated places with 2,500 people or more), 492 had 9,999 or less and 611 had under 25,000 people. In 1880, or 939 urban places, 716 had under 10,000, while 862 had fewer than 25,000. In 1870 the total urban population of the United States was just over nine million. Slightly more than two million of those people lived in cities of less than 10,000, but if the next category of cities (10,000–24,999) is added, the number rises to four million, almost half of the urban population. In 1880 the urban population stood at just over 14 million. The number in cities under 10,000 was 3.3 million, and the number in cities of under 25,000 was 5.5 million, much less than half, but a sizable chunk nonetheless. Clearly then, while urbanites in very large cities outnumbered those in smaller ones, the smaller city was the more typical institution. Moreover, if one considers the vast numbers of people living in rural areas for whom "the city" was most likely a small market town or county seat, the small municipality played a role whose importance is perhaps obscured by the weight of actual population figures. Census data taken from *Historical Statistics of the United States, Colonial Times to 1979,* vol. 1 (Washington, D.C.: U.S. Bureau of the Census, 1975), 11–12.

2. The most comprehensive survey of services in American cities is in George E. Waring, comp., *Report of the Social Statistics*

of Cities (Tenth Census of the United States, 1880, vol. 19, pt. 1 & 2, Washington, D.C.: 1886), 817–21. Also see Lawrence H. Larsen, *The Urban West At the End of the Frontier* (Lawrence, KS: The Regents Press of Kansas, 1978), 71, passim; Waldo O. Kliewer, "The Foundations of Billings, Montana," in Paul Kramer and Frederick L. Holborn, eds. *The City in American Life* (New York: G. P. Putnam's Sons, 1970), 194–212; Terry S. Reynolds, "Cisterns and Fires: Shreveport, Louisiana, as a Case Study of the Emergence of Public Water Supply Systems in the South," *Louisiana History* 22 (1981), 337–67; Maureen Ogle, "Efficiency and System in Nineteenth Century Urban Services: Volunteer Fire Departments In Iowa, 1870–1890," *Annals of Iowa* 50 (1990–1991): 841–60; Ogle, "Redefining 'Public' Water Supplies 1870–1890: A Study of Three Iowa Cities," *Annals of Iowa* 50 (1990–1991), 507–30.

3. For standard interpretations, see Charles N. Glaab and A. Theodore Brown, *A History of Urban America,* 2d ed., revision prepared by Charles N. Glaab (New York: Macmillan Publishing Co., Inc., 1976), 136–48, 154–57, 164–69; Blake McKelvey, *The Urbanization of America* (New Brunswick, N.J.: Rutgers University Press, 1963), 61–114; Constance McLaughlin Green, *The Rise of Urban America* (New York: Harper and Bros, 1965), 77–80; Zane Miller and Patricia M. Melvin, *The Urbanization of Modern America: A Brief History,* 2nd ed., (New York: Harcourt Brace Jovanovich, Publishers, 1987), 52–59; Bayrd Still, "Establishing a Full Range of Urban Services," in Allen M. Wakstein, ed. *The Urbanization of America: An Historical Anthology* (Boston: Houghton Mifflin Company, 1970), 170–82; Ernest S. Griffith and Charles R. Adrian, *A History of American City Government: The Formation of Traditions, 1775–1870* (Washington, D.C.: University Press of America, Inc., 1983; Praeger Press, 1976); Nelson Blake, *Water for the Cities* (Syracuse, N.Y.: Syracuse University Press, 1956); Stuart Galishoff, "Triumph and Failure: The American Response to the Urban Water Supply Problem," in Martin V. Melosi, ed. *Pollution and Reform in American Cities, 1870–1930* (Austin, Tx. and London: University of Texas Press, 1980), 35–57; Jon A. Peterson, "The Impact of Sanitary Reform Upon American Urban Planning, 1840–1890," *Journal of Social History* 13 (1979), 83–103; Stanley K. Schultz and Clay McShane, "To Engineer the Metropolis: Sewers, Sanitation, and City Planning in Late-Nineteenth-Century America," *Journal of American History* 65 (1978), 389–411. Scholars who have attempted a somewhat different approach to urban development, albeit one that ultimately emphasizes very large cities, are Eric H. Monkkonen, *American Becomes Urban: The Development of U. S. Cities and Towns, 1780–1980* (Berkeley: University of California Press, 1988), esp. 89–110; Joel A. Tarr, "The Evolution of The Urban Infrastructure in the Nineteenth

and Twentieth Centuries," in Royce Hauser, ed. *Perspectives on Urban Infrastructure* (Washington, D.C.: National Academy Press, 1984), 9–34; Geoffrey Giglierano, "The City and the System: Developing a Municipal Service, 1800–1915," *Cincinnati Historical Society Bulletin* 35 (1977), 223-47; Richard B. Calhoun, "New York City Fire Department Reorganization, 1865–1870," *New-York Historical Society Quarterly* 60 (1976), 7–34.

For discussions of the emergence of services in specific cities, see Stuart Galishoff, *Newark: The Nation's Unhealthiest City, 1832–1895* (New Brunswick: Rutgers University Press, 1988); John Ellis and Stuart Galishoff, "Atlanta's Water Supply, 1865–1918," *Maryland Historian* 8 (1977), 5–22; James Boyd Jones, Jr., "The Memphis Firefighters' Strikes, 1858 and 1860," *East Tennessee Historical Society's Publications* 49 (1977), 37–60; Bruce Jordan, "Origins of the Milwaukee Water Works," *Milwaukee History* 9 (1986), 2–16; John B. Clark, Jr., "From Bucket Brigade to Steam Fire Engine: Fire Fighting in Old Louisville Through 1865," *The Filson Club History Quarterly* 27 (1953), 103–18; Geoffrey Giglierano, "'A Creature of Law:' Cincinnati's Paid Fire Department," *Cincinnati Historical Society Bulletin* 40 (1982), 79–99; Kathleen J. Kiefer, "Flying Sparks and Hooves: Prologue," *Cincinnati Historical Bulletin* 28 (1970), 83–107; Arlen R. Dykstra, "Rowdyism and Rivalism in the St. Louis Fire Department, 1850–1857," *Missouri Historical Review* 69 (1974–75), 48–64; Bruce Laurie, "Fire Companies and Gangs in Southwark: The 1840s," in Allen F. Davis and Mark H. Haller, eds. *The People of Philadelphia* (Philadelphia: Temple University Press, 1973), 71–87. Stephen F. Ginsburg, "Above the Law: Volunteer Firemen in New York City, 1836–1837," *New York History* 50 (1969), 165–86.

4. Reynolds, "Cisterns and Fires"; Ogle, "Efficiency and Systems."

5. For discussions of the nature of the early nineteenth century American municipal corporation, see Charles W. Tooke, *Progress of Local Government, 1836–1936* (New York: New York University Press, 1937), 3–13; and Griffith and Adrian, *The Formation of Traditions, 1775–1870*, 23–25, 30–35. An interpretive discussion of these similarities is Alan I Marcus, "The Strange Career of Municipal Health Initiatives: Cincinnati and City Government in the Early Nineteenth Century," *Journal of Urban History* 7 (1980), esp. 17–24. For examples of similarities among municipal charters, see, Iowa, "An Act to Incorporate the town of Davenport," *Laws of the Territory* (1838–39), 265–68; "An Act to Incorporate the city of Keosauqua," *Laws of the Territory* (1841), 210–14; "An Act to incorporate the town of Du buque," [sic] *Acts* (1839), 124–28; Illinois, "An Act to Incorporate the city of Springfield," *Laws* (1839), 6–15; Missouri, "An Act to incorporate

the inhabitants of the town of St. Louis," *Laws* (1825), 198–205; Illinois, "An Act to incorporate the City of Quincy,", *Laws* (1839), 113–22; Illinois, "An act to incorporate the town of Lacon, in Marshall County," *Laws* (1839), 122–27; Indiana, "An Act to incorporate the town of Centerville, Wayne County," *Laws* (1833), 134–41; Indiana, "An Act to incorporate the town of Lafayette," *Laws* (1833), 141–45.

6. See Carl Bridenbaugh, *Cities in the Wilderness: The First Century of Urban Life in America, 1625–1742* (New York: Oxford University Press, 1966, 1938), 55–93, 206–48, 364–407; Bridenbaugh, *Cities in Revolt: Urban Life in American, 1743–1776* (New York: Oxford University Press, 1955): 98–133.

7. For discussions of this phenomenon, see Miller and Melvin, *The Urbanization of Modern America*, 52–59; Griffith and Adrian, *The Formation of Traditions*, esp. 85–92; Glaab and Brown, *A History of Urban America*, 68–81; Monkkonen, *American Becomes Urban*, 100–10; Roger Lane, *Policing the City: Boston, 1822–1885* (Cambridge, Mass.: Harvard University Press, 1967), esp. 59–84; Paul Boyer, *Urban Masses and Moral Order in America, 1820–1920* (Cambridge, Mass.: Harvard University Press, 1978), 67–70, passim; Alan I Marcus, "National History Through Local: Social Evils and the Origin of Municipal Services in Cincinnati," *American Studies* 23 (1981), 23–39.

8. John F. Dillon, *Treatise on the Law of Municipal Corporations* (Chicago: James Cockroft and Co., 1872), note 1, pp. 58–59. Other states adopted general incorporation laws during the next few decades, including Florida, California, South Dakota, Utah, Washington and Wyoming; see Tooke, *Progress of Local Government*, note 53, p. 34. For a general description of this phenomenon, see Griffith and Adrian, *The Formation of Traditions*, 35–39; and Tooke, esp. 15–16.

9. Iowa, "An Act for the incorporation of Cities and Towns," *Acts* (1858), 343–90; Ohio, "An Act to provide for the organization of Cities and Incorporated Villages," *General Acts* (1852), 223–59.

10. Missouri, "An Act for the classification of cities and towns," *Laws* (1877), 41–42; Pennsylvania, "An Act Dividing cities of this state into three classes, regulating the passage of ordinances, providing for contracts for supplies and work for said cities, authorizing the increase of indebtedness, and the creation of a sinking fund to redeem the same, defining and punishing certain offenses in all of said cities, and providing for the incorporation and government of cities of the third class," *Laws* (1874); 230–70; Illinois, "An Act to provide for the incorporation of cities and villages," *Statutes* (1871–72), 218–44; Minnesota, "An Act to authorize the Incorporation of Cities," *Laws* (1870), 56–92; Kansas,

"An Act to Incorporate the Cities of the State of Kansas," *Compiled Laws* (1862), 384–97. Although each of these laws recognized classes of cities, they did not classify them identically. Ohio, for example, delineated cities of the first class, 20,000 and above; second class, from 5,000 up to 20,000. In Pennsylvania every municipality under 10,000 remained a borough, and everything above that number fell into one of three classes.

11. Surveys of the period include Glaab and Brown, *A History of Urban America*, esp. 159–208; Maury Klein, *Prisoners of Progress: American Industrial Cities, 1850–1900* (New York: MacMillan, 1976); esp. 339–94; McKelvey, *The Urbanization of America*, 61–114; Raymond A. Mohl, *The New City: Urban America in the Industrial Age, 1860–1920* (Arlington Heights, Ill.: Harlan Davidson, Inc., 1985), 83–137, passim. An important revisionist view is Jon Teaford, *The Unheralded Triumph–City Government in America, 1870–1900* (Baltimore: Johns Hopkins University, 1984), but see also Monkkonen, *America Becomes Urban*, 89–110.

12. "The Future of Great Cities," *The Nation* 2 (1866), 232.

13. For discussions of the special character of small cities and towns, especially as distinguished from great cities, see "The Government of Our Great Cities," *The Nation* 3 (1866), 312; "The Future of Great Cities," *The Nation* 2 (1866), 232; "Health in Great Cities, *The Nation* 2 (1866), 600–01; "Municipal Government," *The Nation* 13 (1871), 188–90; "A Study of Town Meeting Legislation, *The Nation* 20 (1875), 186–87, 203–04; Charles Nordhoff, "The Misgovernment of New York-A Remedy Suggested," *North American Review* 113 (1871), 321–43; William R. Martin, "Cities As Units in Our Polity," *North American Review* 128 (1879), 21–34; George E. Waring, Jr., "The Sewerage of the Smaller Towns," *Journal of Social Science* 10 (1879), 180–94; "Life in Large and Small Towns," *Scribner's Monthly* 20 (1880), 627–28; George E. Waring, Jr., "Village Improvement Societies," *Scribner's Monthly* 14 (1877), 97–107; "The Contract System in Public Works," *Nation* 20 (1875), 324–25; "Village Improvement Societies," *Scribner's Monthly* 12 (1876), 750–51; "Village Improvement," *The Nation* 19 (1874), 149–50; Nathaniel Hillyer Egleston, *Villages and Village Life with Hints for Their Improvement* (New York: Harper and Brothers, Publishers, 1878); Susan Fenimore Cooper, "Village Improvement Societies," *Putnam's Magazine* 4 (1869), 359–66; Edward S. Philbrick, "Water Supply for Small Towns," *The Plumber and Sanitary Engineer* 2 (1878–79), 5; Charles F. Wingate, "Rural Hygiene," *The Plumber and Sanitary Engineer* 2 (1878–79), 183–86.

14. Although the subject of suburban development has been the subject of some excellent studies in the past few years, the ways in which nineteenth century Americans defined and per-

ceived nonurban areas such as the "suburb," the "town" and the "country" is a subject that has received only limited attention from scholars. See Kenneth T. Jackson, *Crabgrass Frontier: The Suburbanization of the United States* (New York: Oxford University Press, 1985), esp. 12–19, 45–47, 73–86; Margaret Marsh, *Suburban Lives* (New Brunswick: Rutgers University Press, 1990); John Stilgoe, *Borderland: Origins of the American Suburb, 1820–1939* (New Haven: Yale University Press, 1988), esp. 22–48, 69–106, 129–38 and 168–206; John Archer, "Country and City in the American Romantic Suburb," *Journal of the Society of Architectural Historians* 42 (1983), 139–56; Tamara Thornton, *Cultivating Gentlemen: The Meaning of Country Life Among the Boston Elite, 1785–1860* (New Haven: Yale University Press, 1989). For studies of "suburban" growth, see Henry C. Binford, *The First Suburbs: Residential Communities on the Boston Periphery, 1815–1860* (Chicago: The University of Chicago Press, 1985); Sam B. Warner, Jr., *Streetcar Suburbs: The Process of Growth in Boston, 1870–1900*, 2nd ed., (Cambridge: Harvard University Press, 1978); Barbara M. Posadas, "A Home in the Country: Suburbanization in Jefferson Township, 1870–1889," *Chicago History* 7 (1978), 134–49; Michael H. Ebner, *Creating Chicago's North Shore: A Suburban History* (Chicago: University of Chicago Press, 1988).

15. Susan Fenimore Cooper, "Village Improvement Societies," *Putnam's Magazine* 4 (1869), 361. For a variety of discussions about the differences between large and small cities, see Dorman B. Eaton, "Municipal Government," *Journal of Social Science* 5 (1873), 1–35; Nordhoff, "The Misgovernment of New York: A Remedy Suggested"; Martin, "Cities as Units in Our Polity"; Waring, "The Sewerage of the Smaller Towns," 180–94; "Life in Large and Small Towns," 627–28; "The Contract System in Public Works," 324–25; "Village Improvement Societies," *Scribner's Monthly* 12 (1876), 750–51; "Village Improvement," 149–50; Egleston, *Villages and Village Life with Hints for Their Improvement* Philbrick, "Water Supply for Small Towns," 5; Wingate, "Rural Hygiene," 183–86.

16. Eaton, "Municipal Government," 1. For boards of trade, see McKelvey, *The Urbanization of American*, 12. He counted at least 30 such groups in the last quarter of the century; that number is probably an underestimate since many of these boards likely organized only informally. Virtually no research has been done on "improvement" societies, which appear to have originated in New England. According to the *Plumber and Sanitary Engineer*, over 50 such groups had been formed in Connecticut alone by 1878 (*Plumber and Sanitary Engineer*, 2 (1878–79), 245. A brief note published in *Scribner's Monthly* 14 (1877), 110, indicates that a previous article on the subject had led to an

outpouring of mail to the journal, as readers sought more information on the subject. See also Cooper, "Village Improvement Societies"; Egleston, *Villages and Village Life*; George E. Waring, Jr., "Village Improvement Societies," *Scribner's Monthly* 12 (1876), 750-51; "Village Improvement," *The Nation* 19 (1874), 149–150. For discussions of improvement and boosterism, see Carl Abbott, *Boosters and Businessmen: Popular Economic Thought in the Antebellum Midwest* (Westport, Conn.: Greenwood Press, 1981); Glenn Quiett, *They Built the West: An Epic of Rails and Cities* (New York: Cooper Square Publishers, 1965; D. Appleton-Century Co., Inc., 1934), esp. 88–112; Larsen, *The Urban West at the End of the Frontier*; Daniel J. Boorstin, *The Americans: The National Experience* (New York: Random House, 1965), 115–33 and 161–68; Boorstin, *The Americans: The Democratic Experience* (New York: Random House, 1973), 273–80; J. Christopher Schnell and Katherine B. Clinton, "The New West: Themes in Nineteenth Century Promotion," *Bulletin of the Missouri Historical Society* 30 (1974), 75–88; Richard C. Overton, *Burlington West: A Colonization History of the Burlington Railroad* (Cambridge: Harvard University, 1941); John C. Hudson, *Plains Country Towns* (Minneapolis: University of Minnesota Press, 1985); Burton W. Folsom, *Urban Capitalists: Entrepreneurs and City Growth in Pennsylvania's Lackawanna and Lehigh Region, 1800–1920* (Baltimore: The Johns Hopkins University Press, 1981).

17. Population figures are:

	Iowa City	*Marshalltown*	*Boone*
1860	1,250	981	
1870	5,914	3,218	2,415
1885	6,748	8,298	4,331
1895	7,526	10,049	8,845

18. *Boone Standard*, 3 June 1883, 3. For general histories of the three cities, see Judge William Battin and F. A. Moscrip, *Past and Present of Marshall County* (Indianapolis: B. F. Bowen & Company, 1912); Benjamin F. Shambaugh, *Iowa City—A Contribution to the Early History of Iowa* (Iowa City: State Historical Society of Iowa, 1893); *History of Johnson County, Iowa* (Iowa City, 1883); N. E. Goldthwait, *History of Boone County, Iowa* (Chicago: Pioneer Publishing Company, 1914).

19. For local descriptions of firefighting, see, for example *Iowa City Council Minutes* 9 April 1861; 18 April 1862 (hereafter cited as Minutes-Iowa City); *Iowa City Republican*, 1 November 1871, 3; *Iowa City Daily Press*, 19 March 1872, 3; *Marshall County Times*, 14 November 1866, 5; November 1868, 3; 11 September 1869, 2; 11 November 1869, 3; *Marshalltown City Council Minutes*, 13 March

1867; 29 May 1867 (hereafter cited as Minutes-Marshalltown); *Montana* (Boone) *Standard* 30 July 1870, 3.

20. *Marshall Daily Times*, 11 September 1869, 3; 11 November 1869, 3; *Iowa City Daily Press*, 19 March 1872, 3; *Iowa City Republican*, 5 June 1872, 3.

21. *Iowa City Republican*, 23 February 1884, 4. Descriptions of the fire departments are in "An Ordinance establishing a Fire Department," *Marshalltown Ordinance Record No. 1*, 134; "An Ordinance for the formation and government of the Fire Department," in *Boone Ordinance Book No. 2*, 45–49; "An Ordinance for the formation and government of the Fire Department," *Revised Ordinances of 1874 of Iowa City* (Iowa City: Daily Press Job Printing Office, 1874). For signaling systems, see Minutes-Marshalltown, 23 March 1874; 23 October 1876; 3 June 1878; 17 March 1879; *Iowa City Republican*, 11 July 1881, 3; Minutes-Iowa City, 5 December 1873; *Iowa City Republican*, 12 February 1883, 3; 22 June 1883, 4; 25 July 1883; 4; 28 July 1883, 4; 15 October 1886, 3; *Boone County Republican*, 11 August 1875, 3; *Boone City Council Minutes*, 3 October 1878; 7 January 1880 (hereafter cited as Minutes-Boone). For equipment, fire; police and training, see Minutes-Marshalltown, 9 January 1871; 14 August 1871; 13 November 1871; 8 January 1872; 12 February 1872; 19 August 1872; 14 October 1872; Minutes-Boone, 24 July 1872; 1 February 1873; *Boone County Advocate*, 4 January 1872, 3; *Boone County Democrat*, 14 February 1872, 3; *Boone Standard*, 17 February 1872, 3; 11 May 1872, 3; *Iowa City Daily Press*, 2 May 1872, 3; 24 May 1872, 3; 31 May 1873, 3.

22. A broader discussion of fire department formation in these three cities is in Ogle, "Efficiency and System."

23. *Iowa City Daily Press*, 3 September 1877, 4; *Marshall Daily Times*, 1 May 1876, 4. See also *Marshall Daily Times*, 17 April, 4; 19 April, 1876, 4; 5 May 1876, 4; 10 May 1876, 4; 3 August 1876, 4; 28 August 1876, 4; Minutes-Marshalltown, 17 April 1876; 15 June 1876; 28 June 1876; 4 September 1876; *Marshalltown Ordinance Record No. 1*, "An Ordinance in relation to water commissioners and water works for the city of Marshalltown," 308–13; "An ordinance concerning the water works department of the city of Marshalltown, Iowa, and establishing water rates, rules, regulations and penalties for the government of water taking, licensed plumbers and others," 333–45; *First Annual Report of the Water Works Department*, (Marshalltown: Times Steam Book and Job Print, 1878); *Iowa City Daily Press*, 9 April 1874, 4; 11 April 1874, 4; 1 May 1874; 1 May 1879, 3; 17 July 1879, 3; 22 July 1879, 3; Minutes-Iowa City, 5 September 1879; 17 December 1880; 4 February 1881; 20 May 1881; 25 May 1881; "An ordinance to provide a supply of water for the inhabitants of Iowa City, Iowa,

for domestic, fire use protection, and for other purposes,"*Iowa City Republican*, 7 June 1881, 1; *Boone County Republican*, 27 February 1878, 3; 20 March 1878, 3; 30 June 1880, 3; Minutes-Boone, 6 March 1878; 29 May 1878; 7 May 1880; 26 June 1880; 24 September 1880; *Boone Standard*, 10 March 1883, 3; 19 May 1883, 3; 28 July 1883, 3; 1 November 1880; Minutes-Boone, 29 June 1883; 6 July 1883; 19 September 1883; *Boone Ordinance Record No. 2*, "An Ordinance concerning the Waterworks of the City of Boone, Iowa and establishing water rates, rules, regulations and penalties for the government of water takers, licensed plumbers and others," 232–46.

24. For a full discussion of this topic, see Ogle, "Redefining 'Public' Water Supplies."

25. *Iowa City Republican*, 16 August 1871, 3; *Iowa City Daily Press*, 12 March 1873, 4; 28 May 1879, 4; *Iowa City Republican*, 31 October 1882, 4; 14 November 1882, 3; Minutes-Iowa City, 4 February 1881; 9 May 1884; *Iowa City Republican*, 17 December 1886, 3; *Boone County Standard*, 12 April 1884, 4; Minutes-Boone, 14 February 1881; *Marshall Daily Times*, 26 May 1876; Minutes-Boone, 6 September 1881; "An Ordinance to Exempt Certain Manufacturing Interests from taxation for City Purposes for Five Years," in *Ordinance Record Number 2*, passed 7 September 1881; Minutes-Boone, 6 June 1883; Minutes-Marshalltown, 13 January 1873; 10 February 1873; 12 April 1880; 18 October 1880; "An ordinance providing for the Furnishing of Water to Manufacturing Companies for Manufacturing Purposes," Minutes-Marshalltown, 5 December 1881; 12 December 1881; 18 August 1884; 22 September 1885; Minutes-Marshalltown, 17 April 1888; 7 May 1888; Marshalltown *Ordinance Record Number 1*, "An ordinance Remitting Corporation taxes on proposed pork packing house of Brittain Bros."; "An ordinance to Induce Manufacturing Enterprises to Establish Themselves in the City of Marshalltown," passed 23 February 1886.

26. *Boone County Republican*, 9 February 1881.

27. *Iowa City Republican*, 17 January 1887, 3; *Iowa City Republican*, 6 April 1887, 3; 11 April 1887, 3; 15 April 1887, 3; 18 April 1887, 3; *Iowa City Republican*, 7 May 1887, 1; 20 May 1887; Minutes-Iowa City, 19 May 1887; 3 June 1887.

28. In all three cities, the fire companies received funds, equipment and charters from the city, and the city built and maintained the company "houses." The volunteer firemen, however, chose their own officers, including the chief who was paid by the city. In theory, the city councils had final approval over all fire department actions, but in practice they merely rubber-stamped all department actions.

29. For the full committee report, see *Iowa City Republican*, 4 June 1887, 1.

30. *Iowa City Republican*, 4 June 1887, 1. A law that enabled the cities to pay their firefighters was actually not far off. See Iowa, "An Act to establish and maintain a Fire Department in Cities of the Second Class," *Acts* (1890), 17. Boone and Marshalltown acted fairly quickly to take advantage of the law, but at the end of the century Iowa City's firefighters remained unpaid. See Minutes-Boone, 8 September 1891; "An Ordinance to provide compensation for the members of the Fire Department," in *Ordinance Record No. 2*, 251; Minutes-Marshalltown, 8 June 1891, "Ordinance introduced to create a fire fund per Chapter 8 of the Twenty-third General Assembly."

31. *Iowa City Daily Press*, 3 June 1879, 4.

32. Ogle, "Redefining 'Public' Water Supplies, 1870–1890," 528–29; Ogle, "Urban Growth in Iowa: Building Municipal Services in the Small City, 1870–1890," (Master's Research Essay, Iowa State University, 1988).

33. The description of the LAM is in "League of American Municipalities," *Municipal Journal and Engineer* 13 (1902), 57–58.

34. Frank G. Pierce, "The Development of a State Municipal League," *Midland Municipalities* 19 (1910), 10. For convention coverage, see *Marshalltown Times-Republican*, 26 August 1898, 7; 6 September 1898, 7; 11 October 1898, 7; 14 October 1898, 7.

35. Frank E. Horak, "The League of Iowa Municipalities," *Iowa Journal of History and Politics* 1 (1903), 193–208. For League lobbying efforts, see F. M. Norris, "Report of Committee on Legislation," *Midland Municipalities* 8 (1904), 88–93; Pierce, "The Development of a State Municipal League," 11–14. A good discussion of other local leagues and their purposes is in Clifford W. Patton, *The Battle for Municipal Reform, Mobilization and Attack, 1875–1900* (Washington, D.C.: American Council on Public Affairs, 1940), 34–35.

36. *Boone County Republican*, 17 March 1880, 3. Ogle, "Redefining "Public" Water Supplies, 1870–1890," 526–27.

37. *Iowa City Republican*, 26 January 1883, 4; *Boone County Democrat* 15 March 1871, 3.

38. For a sampling of literature that discusses municipal services in the small city, see Philbrick, "Water Supply for Small Towns"; J. Herbert Shedd, "Water Supplies for Large Institutions and Small Communities," *Papers and Reports-American Public Health Association* 3 (1875–76), 109--19, (hereafter called *APHA*); George E. Waring, "The Sewerage of the Smaller Towns"; Elisha Harris, "The Public Health," *North American Review* 127 (1878), 444–55; Stephen Smith, "The Influence of Private Dwellings and other Habitations on Public Hygiene," *APHA* 3 (1875–1876), 53–61; George E. Waring, Jr., "The Sanitary Drainage of Houses and Towns," *Atlantic Monthly* 36 (1875), 339–55, 427–42, 535–53; Eugene Foster, "The Municipal Organization of the American Public

Health Service," *APHA* 7 (1881), 96–113; Cooper, "Village Improvement Societies"; Egleston, *Villages and Village Life;* George E. Waring, Jr. "Village Improvement Associations," *Scribner's Monthly* 14 (1877), 97–107; "Village Improvement Societies," *Scribner's Monthly* 12 (1876); "Village Improvement," *Nation* 19 (1874); George E. Waring, Jr., "Village Sanitary Work," *Scribner's Monthly* 14 (1877), 176–87.

39. Waring, comp., *Report of the Social Statistics of Cities*, 135–39, 541, 537–40; 645–49, 751–56, 817–21. See also Larsen, *The Urban West At the End of the Frontier,* 71, passim; Larsen, *The Rise of the Urban South* (Lexington: The University Press of Kentucky, 1985), 134, passim; Kathleen Underwood, *Town Building on the Colorado Frontier* (Albuquerque: University of New Mexico Press, 1987), 52–71; Kliewer, "The Foundations of Billings, Montana," 194–212; Ebner, *Creating Chicago's North Shore*, 91–92; Reynolds, "Cisterns and Fires, 337–67; Letty Donaldson Anderson, "The Diffusion of Technology in the Nineteenth Century American City: Municipal Water Supply Investments," (Ph.D. dissertation, Northwestern University, 1980); Moses N. Baker, *Manual of American Water-works* 4th issue (New York: The Engineering New Publishing Co., 1897).

40. The "failure" remark, often quoted but seldom cited, is from James Bryce, *The American Commonwealth* (New York, 1888), vol. 1, 608. The second phrase is from Teaford, *The Unheralded Triumph.*

Notes to Chapter 5 / Wilson & Hartman

1. See Harlan Paul Douglass, *The Suburban Trend* (New York: Arno Press, 1970 (1925).

2. See Harold X. Connolly, "Black Movements Into The Suburbs: Suburbs Doubling Their Black Population During The 1960s" *Urban Affairs Quarterly* 9, September 1973, 19–111.

3. It has generally been stressed that black suburban settlement was inspired by the democratization of the suburbs following the Second World War. Amidst the era of the G.I. Bill, F.H.A. loans, the famous Supreme Court Cases of *Shelley vs. Kraemer, Jackson vs. Barrows* and *Brown vs. the Board of Education*, and numerous civil rights marches, it was believed that blacks were able to experience more mobility than in previous times, and as a result were able to pursue all aspects of the American dream, including suburban homeownership. Reynolds Farley was the synthesizer of this previously accepted theory, as his research revealed the development of suburban communities with signifi-

cant black populations at the end of the 1960s. The work of earlier and later scholars did not detract from this belief, essentially because Farley's work identified a highly mobile African American middle class population. For example, Donald Bogue examined census materials from 1930 to 1950 and found a small, but increasing, suburban black population. His work challenged the notion that black suburban settlement began after the war; however, his work did not investigate the social status of African Americans found in suburbia. Separately and collectively, Leo Schnore, Carolyn Andre and Harry Sharp studied black suburbanization from 1930 to 1970. While they also found suburbanized blacks, they concluded that this suburban population was minimal (roughly two to three percent of the total suburban population) prior to 1970. Avery Guest also studied the changing racial composition of suburbia. He too concurred with the efforts of the others that black suburbanization was a national trend, but his analysis focused on the growth of these populations, not the social status of these residents. In such a manner the Farley thesis generally remains intact. While the work of Connolly and others has demonstrated that blacks were in suburbia before the thirties, there still is not a definitive examination of the social status of the earlier black suburbanite. For further information on this subject, consult Avery M. Guest, "The Changing Racial Composition Of Suburbs 1950–1970" *Urban Affairs Quarterly* 14, December 1978, 195–206; Leo Schnore, Carolyn Andre, and Harry Sharp, "Black Suburbanization 1930–1970," in Barry Schwartz, ed., *The Changing Face Of The Suburbs* (Chicago: University of Chicago Press, 1976); Reynolds Farley, "The Changing Distribution Of Negroes Within Metropolitan Areas: The Emergence Of Black Suburbs" *American Journal of Sociology* 75, January 1970, 512–29; and Donald J. Bogue, *Components Of Population Change 1940–1950* (Oxford, Ohio: Miami University Scripps Foundation).

4. If the word suburb denoted any land abutting or beyond the borders of a metropolitan area, the term "modern suburb" provided an additional definition. The modern suburb represented a higher standard of living. These were planned communities that were basically antiurban in design. Men like Andrew Jackson Downing, Frederick Law Olmsted and Alexander Stewart designed landscaped communities, including Llewellyn Park, New Jersey, Riverside, Illinois, and Garden City, New York that were filled with open spaces. These communities were clearly elitist, and in the view of Kenneth Jackson they demonstrated two truths: "that quality single family homes in a planned environment could not be built at a profit for the working classes, and that those who could afford the luxury of a

substantial home on a large plot would not be satisfied with anything less than full ownership.'" See Kenneth Jackson, *Crabgrass Frontier* (New York: Oxford University Press, 1985), 86.

5. Southern centers like Atlanta, Nashville, Raleigh, Savannah and Richmond annexed predominantly black suburban enclaves between 1879 and 1890. See Howard Rabinowitz, *Race Relations In The Urban South* (New York: Oxford University Press, 1978), 97–101.

6. See Avery Guest, "The Changing Racial Composition Of Suburbs 1950–70," *Urban Affairs Quarterly* 14 (December 1978), 196–98. Guest was the first to stress that southern suburbanization is vastly different than northern suburbanization and that it was decreasing rather than increasing. However, the notion of southern African American Suburban communities being more restrictive and less "suburban" is mentioned throughout the literature. Howard Rabinovitz's research offered examples of prosperous blacks who moved away from the core as early as the 1890s, yet many of these blacks still resided within the city limits. See Howard Rabinovitz, *Race Relations In The Urban South*, 97–127. Harold Rose has led the discussions on the nature of the all-black towns. In his earlier discussions he was quick to suggest that these communities were not suburbs just because they happened to fall within a metropolitan ring. However, his later views tend to be moving away from that position. The all-black towns formed in the South were often outposts for African Americans dissatisfied with urban living. Many of their residents had to commute to urban centers to find work, or existed by farming. See Harold Rose, "The All-Negro Town: Its Evolution And Function," *Geographic Review* (July 1965), and *Black Suburbanization* (Cambridge: Ballinger, 1976).

7. There are numerous examples of this trend, but they are generally more visible in the Midwest or the far West. Excellent examples of this trend can be seen along Chicago's North Shore suburbs. Here, few blacks were able to remain by the lake after 1900. See Michael Ebner, *Creating Chicago's North Shore* (Chicago: University Press, 1988).

8. Outside of Los Angeles, the black population increased from 86 in 1880 to 555 in 1890, and then to 910 in 1900.

9. As a result of his views and speeches on land ownership, Washington became the official spokesman for African American realtors. However, it is unknown if Washington ever intended to accept this mantle. Even his son capitalized on his famous name by naming his company the "BookerTee" Realty Company. Yet, for better or worse, and irregardless of his approval or disapproval of the matter, Washington's name continued to be used to promote sales.

10. *New York Age*, Thursday, 30 March 1905, 3.

11. *California Eagle*, 20 June 1914.

12. *Chicago Eagle*, 17 September 1892, 3.

13. *New York Age*, 1906.

14. *New York Age*, 12 July 1906.

15. *New York Age*, 12 July 1906.

16. *New York Age*, 15 July 1907.

17. *Chicago Defender*, Saturday, 16 April 1910, 2.

18. *California Eagle*, 18 April 1914.

19. *Chicago Defender*, 26 April 1919, 20.

20. *Chicago Defender*, 2 July 1910.

21. *New York Age*, 2 April 1914.

22. *New York Age*, 25 June 1914.

23. *New York Age*, 6 October 1910.

24. *California Eagle*, 20 December 1919.

25. *New York Age*, 6 October 1910.

26. *New York Age*, 12 March 1914.

27. *Chicago Defender*, 28 June 1919, 18.

28. *California Eagle*, 5 August 1927, 1, 5; 12 August 1927, 1; 19 August 1927, 1.

29. *California Eagle*, 4 November 1927, 1.

30. Delilah L. Beasley, *The Negro Trail Blazers of California* (New York: Negro Universities Press, 1969), 204.

31. Michael Ebner, *Creating Chicago's North Shore*, 235.

32. See Kevin B. Leonard, "Paternalism and the Rise of a Black Community in Evanston, Illinois, 1870–1930" (Master's thesis, Northwestern University, 1982).

33. *New York Age*, 7 May 1927, 1.

34. *New York Age*, 19 April 1930, 1.

35. *California Eagle*, 8 April 1916, 1.

36. *California Eagle*, 6 May 1922, 6.

37. *California Eagle*, 17 February 1923, 1.

38. *California Eagle*, 10 April 1925, 1.

39. *California Eagle*, 28 October 1927, 1.

40. *New York Age*, 28 December 1929, 1.

41. *New York Age*, 28 December 1929, 1.

42. Mark S. Foster, "The Decentralization of Los Angeles During the 1920s," (Ph.D. dissertation, University of Southern California, 1971), 71.

43. The lawyers representing African Americans based their case on the premise that the fourteenth amendment rights of their clients were violated. In contrast, the courts viewed covenants as agreements between individuals, and therefore saw no violation of these rights as a result of state action. In this manner, the Supreme Court claimed that the law had not been abridged. From 1926 to 1948, this opinion would maintain the validity of

such contracts. Ironically, many African Americans blamed this dilemma on Booker T. Washington, as he allegedly ignored these Constitutional rights in his famous "Atlanta Compromise Address."

Notes to Chapter 6 / Hoover

1. This is an approximation, as Muncie was not separated from Center Township until 1860. For a discussion of the problems inherent in census data for Muncie, see Alexander E. Bracken, "Middletown as a Pioneer Community, " Ph.D. dissertation, Ball State University, Muncie, IN, 1978, 14–15.

2. Frank D. Haimbaugh, ed., *History of Delaware County, Indiana*, 2 vols. (Indianapolis: Historical Publishing Co., 1924), vol. 1, 412.

3. Scott Ray, "The Depressed Industrial Society: Occupational Movements, Out-Migration and Residential Mobility in the Industrial-Urbanization of Middletown," Ph.D. dissertation, Ball State University, Muncie, IN, 1981, 129–30. For a listing of occupations and manufacturers from census listings, see Bracken, 255–59. These include everything from a maker of Bowie knives to a historian.

4. Bracken, 39–40.

5. Ray, 125–26.

6. These numbers are a compilation of census reports, city directories, and county histories made by Sushmita Ghosh in 1987.

7. Ghosh 1987.

8. Ray, 127–28.

9. Ray, 130. This overlooks the attempts made in Muncie by local entrepreneurs to expand into other enterprises. As we shall see, there were new industries created by the Balls and Warners.

10. Ray, 130.

11. Richard Jensen in "The Lynds Revisited," *Indiana Magazine of History*, 75 (December 1979), 301–19, claims that the Lynds failed to understand this transformation of Muncie's economic life.

12. Robert S. and Helen M. Lynd, *Middletown: A Study in Modern American Culture* (New York: Harcourt, Brace, Jovanovich, 1929; Harvest Book, 1956), 9. Both Lynd and his predecessor, Bailey, had used population growth as a criterion for selection of a community. Bailey had set 35 percent growth during a decade as a minimum. Lynd's criterion was "a sufficiently rapid rate of growth to insure the presence of a plentiful assortment

of the growing pains accompanying contemporary social change,"
(7). Had the Lynds begun a study in an earlier decade, they
would have had to omit Muncie.

13. Lynd & Lynd, 252–53.

14. George Washington Harrison Kemper, M.D., ed., *A Twentieth Century History of Delaware County* (Chicago: The Lewis Publishing Company, 1908), Vol. 1, 153.

15. Haimbaugh, vol. 2, 51. See also W. Charles Oursler, *From Ox Carts to Jets: Roy Ingersoll and the Borg Warner Story, A Biography* (Englewood Cliffs, N. J.: Prentice-Hall, 1959).

16. Kemper, vol. 2, 616; Pete Nyggard, "Warner Gear Company," Student Paper, History 338, Ball State University, Fall 1981, 1.

17. Arthur Pound, *The Turning Wheel: The Story of General Motors Through Twenty-Five Years, 1908–1933* (Garden City, New York: Doubleday, Doran and Company, 1935), 487.

18. *Emerson's Muncie Directory 1913–1914* (Cincinnati, Ohio: Williams Directory company, 1914), 806.

19. William Spencer Huffman, "Indiana's Place in Automobile History," *Indiana History Bulletin,* 38(September 1961), 148–49; (February 1967), 18. The Latter is an expansion of the former. Huffman also lists an automobile called the Muncie made in 1910 but has no further information. In addition, see Lloyd E. Baldwin, "The Interstate Automobile Company," Student Paper, History 338, Ball State University, Fall 1981, 2. *Emerson's Muncie Directory 1913–1914* still lists Stratton as an automobile manufacturer.

20. Baldwin, 1; Ron LeMasters, *Muncie Star,* 4 July 1976; Jerry Newland, The Automobile Industry: Muncie, Indiana, 1906–1923," Student Paper, History 600, Ball State University, Fall 1986. 2

21. Kemper, vol. 1, 150.

22. Baldwin, 3; Newland, 3; LeMasters, The same year witnessed a political division between the Hart and Ball families. Mrs. Alfaretta Hart, the wife of Thomas Hart, who was Catholic and a Wet, was a strong supporter of Democrat Rollin C. "Doc" Bunch in his campaign for mayor in 1913. George A. Ball, a Universalist and Dry, had helped form the Citizen's Party, a reform group that fielded a candidate in the same election. For further information see my "Middletown Elects a Mayor, 1913 and 1917: National and Local Issues Intersect," paper read at the Midwest Popular Culture Conference, Kalamazoo, Michigan, 25 October 1986; and "Daisy Douglass Barr: From Friends Memorial to the Ku Klux Klan," paper given at the spring meeting of the Indiana Association of Historians, Franklin, Indiana, 19 March 1987.

23. Baldwin, 3; Newland, 3, LeMasters. There is no explanation as to why the Balls did not push automaking. By this time, the brothers were doing well and expanding in other directions. There is no hint of a reason in Frank C. Ball's *Memories of Frank Clayton Ball* (Muncie, IN: by the Author, 1937). As a matter of fact, Ball never even mentions the Inter-State experience.

24. Haimbaugh, vol. 2, 600; Nayggard, 2.

25. "Middletown Elects a Mayor, 1913 and 1917"; and my "Politics as Usual in Middletown, 1913–1986" paper read at the Great Lakes American Studies Association Meeting, Adrian, Michigan, 4 October 1986; *Muncie Evening Press,* 24 January 1919; 29 January 1919.

26. *Muncie Evening Press,* 14 March 1919.

27. Arthur Pound, *The Turning Wheel: The Story of General Motors Through Twenty-Five Years, 1909–1933* (Garden City, New York: Doubleday, Doran and Company 1935), 149–51. See also Lawrence Gustin, *Billy Durant: Creator of G.M.* (Grand Rapids, Michigan: William B. Eerdmans Publishing Co., 1973).

28. Pound, 179; *Muncie Evening Press,* 21 March 1919.

29. Pound, 179, 183, 203.

30. *Muncie Evening Press,* 9 September 1919.

31. *Muncie Evening Press,* 10 September 1919.

32. *Muncie Evening Press,* 5 September 1919; 19 September 1919.

33. *Muncie Evening Press,* 23 September 1919.

34. *Muncie Evening Press,* 4 October 1919; Pound, 181; Haimbaugh, vol. 2, 51.

35. Pound, 487–88; Arthur J. Kuhn, *G.M. Passes Ford, 1918–1938* (University Park, PA: Pennsylvania State University Press, 1986), 145.

36. Haimbaugh, vol. 2, 51; *Muncie Evening Press,* 28 October 1919.

37. Gustin, 212.

38. Gustin, 218, 223, 230.

39. Lynd and Lynd, 253.

Notes to Chapter 7 / Folsom

1. "Tennessee vs. Truth," *Nation,* (8 July 1924), 58; "Tennessee vs. Civilization," *New Republic,* (22 July 1925), 220–22; "Thought: Free or in Chains?" *School and Society,* (11 July 1925), 44–45; "Foreign Amazement in Tennessee," *Literary Digest,* (25 July 1925), 18–19; Joseph Wood Krutch, "Darrow vs. Bryan," *Nation,* (29 July 1925), 136; Donald L. Brod, "The Scopes Trial: A Look at Press Coverage After Forty Years," *Journalism*

Quarterly (Spring 1965), 220–23; "The Dayton Battle May Have Been Bryan's Doom," *Literary Digest*, (8 August 1925), 44, 46.

2. Alistair Cooke, *The Vintage Mencken* (New York, 1955), v–xii, 153–67.

3. Dixon Merritt, "Bryan at Sixty-Five," *The Outlook* 140 (3 June 1925), 182; George Fort Milton, "Can Minds Be Closed By Statute?" *World's Work* (1925), 323; Joseph Wood Krutch, "Tennessee's Dilemma," *Nation* (22 July 1925), 110; and Krutch, "Darrow vs. Bryan," 136–37.

4. Sinclair Lewis, *Elmer Gantry* (New York, 1927); and T.S. Stribling, *Teeftallow* (New York, 1926).

5. Donald Davidson, "First Fruits of Dayton," *Forum* 79 (June 1928), 898–906; Thomas Daniel Young and M. Thomas Inge, *Donald Davidson* (New York: Twayne Publishers, 1970), 130; Twelve Southerners, *I'll Take My Stand: The South and the Agrarian Tradition* (New York: Harper and Brothers, 130).

6. William H. Nolte, *H. L. Mencken: Literary Critic* (Seattle: University of Washington Press, 1966), 185–88. Mencken rejected some of Davidson's work submitted to the *American Mercury*. For problems between Mencken and the Southern Agrarians, see John Tyree Fain and Thomas Daniel Young, *The Literary Correspondence of Donald Davidson and Allen Tate* (Athens: University of Georgia Press, 1974), 16, 130, 132, 260.

7. Norman F. Furniss, *The Fundamentalist Controversy, 1918–1931* (New Haven, 1954), 76–100; George M. Marsden, *Fundamentalism and American Culture* (New York, 1980) 206–11.

8. Bryan, *Memoirs*, 485–86; Howard K. Beale, *Are American Teachers Free?* (New York, 1936), 229–36. Elbert L. Watson, "Oklahoma and the Anti-Evolution Movement of the 1920s," *Chronicles of Oklahoma* 42 (Autumn 1964), 403.

9. Maynard Shipley, "Growth of Anti-Evolution Movement," *Current History* 32 (May 1930), 330–32.

10. Arkansas *Democrat*, 11 November 1928.

11. Arkansas *Gazette*, 1, 2, 25 November 1928 and Arkansas *Democrat*, 28 October and 4 November 1928. See also Bentonville *Record and Democrat*, 1 November 1928; and Blytheville *Currier News*, 3 November 1928; and Ginger, *Six Days or Forever?* 212–13.

12. Virginia Gray, "Anti-Evolution Sentiment and Behavior: The Case of Arkansas," *Journal of American History* (September 1970), 352–66; Fayetteville *Daily Democrat*, 7, 8 November 1928.

13. C. Allyn Russell, *Voices of American Fundamentalism* (Philadelphia, 1976). My North Carolina data came from Willard B. Gatewood, Jr., *Preachers, Pedagogues, and Politicians: The Evolution Controversy in North Carolina, 1920–1927* (Chapel Hill, 1966), 146. The Kentucky voting is in the *Journal of the House of*

Representatives of Kentucky, 1922, 3–7, 1668–71.

14. *Court Trial,* 321–39; Bryan to S. Edgar Briggs, 5 January 1924, Bryan Papers.

15. Judith Grabiner and Peter D. Miller, "Effects of the Scopes Trial," *Science* (6 September 1974), 832–37.

16. Grabiner and Miller, "Effects of the Scopes Trial," 832–34.

17. George W. Hunter, *A Civic Biology* (New York, 1914), 194–96.

18. *Court Trial,* 174–75.

19. Grabiner and Miller, "Effects of the Scopes Trial," 833–37. The authors discovered the reaction of Hunter to Bryan's attacks by asking Professor A. O. Woodward, one of Hunter's colleagues at Pamona College. See also Hunter, *New Civic Biology* (New York, 1926), 250–51. Hunter, *Civic Biology,* 194.

20. Shipley, "Growth of Anti-Evolution Movement," 330–32; *Quarterly Review of Biology* (September 1929), 423–24.

21. Grabiner and Miller, "Effects of the Scopes Trial," 833–36.

22. Estelle Laba and Eugene W. Gross, "Evolution Slighted in High School Biology," *Clearing House* 24 (March 1950), 396–99 (quotation on 398).

23. Tom Dearmore, "Will Evolution Come to Arkansas," *Reporter* (16 January 1966), 34; Wadsworth Likely, "Evolution Trial Relived," *Science* (29 April 1950), 266–67.

24. For a historian's look at the creation science movement, see Willard B. Gatewood, Jr., "From Scopes to Creation Science: The Decline and Revival of the Evolution Controversy," *South Atlantic Quarterly* 83 (Autumn 1984), 363–83. See also Ronald L. Numbers, "Creationism in 20th Century America," *Science* 218 (5 November 1982), 538–44. I have also learned about creation science from reading issues of *The Creation Research Society Quarterly.*

25. George Gaylord Simpson, *Tempo and Mode in Evolution* (New York, 1944). Chris Pipho, "Scientific Creationism: A Case Study," *Education and Urban Society* 13 (February 1981), 220. Simpson, "One Hundred Years Without Darwin Are Enough," in *This View of Life: The World of An Evolutionist* (New York, 1964), 26–41. *American Men and Women of Science* (New York and London, 1982), xi, 741.

26. Simpson, "One Hundred Years," 32, 33.

27. Simpson, "One Hundred Years," 26–29, 32–34.

28. Simpson, "One Hundred Years," 40–41; Pipho, "Scientific Creationism, 221–23.

29. Grabiner and Miller, "Effects of the Scopes Trial," 836.

30. Pipho, "Scientific Creationism," 219; Gatewood, "From Scopes to Creation Science," 376–77.

31. Bill Keith, *Scopes II: The Great Debate* (n.p., 1982); Janet

Raloff, "Of God and Darwin," *Science News* (2 January 1982), 12–13; William Overton, "Creationism in Schools? The Decision in McLean vs. the Arkansas Board of Education," *Science* (19 February 1982), 934–43; John W. Donahue, "Creation and Evolution: A Balanced Treatment," *America* (6 February 1982), 90–92.

Notes to Chapter 8 / Long

1. James D. Hart, *A Companion to California* (Berkeley, Ca.: University of California Press, 1987), 408.

2. Turrentine Jackson and Alan M. Patterson, *The Sacramento-San Joaquin Delta: The Evolution and Implementation of Water Policy* (Davis, California: University of California Water Resources Center, 1977).

3. These are generally accepted terms in urban history, although some scholars refer to the City Functional as the City Practical.

4 John Reber, "Annals of the Plan," 1955, Reber Papers, San Francisco Bay Delta Hydraulic Model, Saulsalito, Ca. [SFBDHM].

5. U. S. Congress, Senate, Subcommittee of the Committee on Public Works, *Needs of the San Francisco Bay Area, California, Hearings before a Subcommittee of the Committee on Public Works, on S. Res 119*, 81st Congress: 1st session, 1949, 28.

6. The hydraulic fill would have been a strip-like man-made island.

7. "San Francisco Bay Project," *Western Construction News*, March 1942, 103.

8. Jackson and Patterson, 68.

9. "Statement of John Reber," *The Needs of the San Francisco Bay Area*, 28

10 "Statement of John Reber," *The Needs of the San Francisco Bay Area*, 19–20.

11. "Statement of John Reber," *The Needs of the San Francisco Bay Area*, 23.

12. L. H. Nishkian, *Report on the Reber Plan and Bay Land Crossing to the Joint Army-Navy Board* (San Francisco: Real Estate Association, 12–15 August 1946), 7. The work provided for trolleys and interurbans as well.

13. *The San Francisco Downtowner*, 7 July 1948.

14. L. H. Nishkian, letter to U. S. Department of Interior, Bureau of Reclamation, 10 October 1945, Nishkian Papers, Nishkian Engineering, San Francisco, California.

15. An acre/foot is the volume needed to cover one acre of land with one foot of liquid.

16. "Statement of John Reber," *The Needs of the San Francisco Bay Area*, 7.

17. *The Commonwealth: Transactions of the Commonwealth Club of California*, 8 August 1955, 242.

18. John Reber, "Streamlining California," n. d., Reber Papers, San Francisco Bay Delta Hydraulic Model, Sausalito, California.

19. U. S. Congress, Senate, Special Committee on National Defense, *Investigation of the National Defense Program, Hearings Before a Special Committee Investigating the National Defense Program Pursuant to S. Res 71*, 77th Congress: 2nd session, 1942, 5494.

20. John Reber, *The San Francisco Bay Project-The Reber Plan*, 1949, Nishkian Papers, Nishkian Engineering, San Francisco, California.

21. William Dubois (lobbyist for California Farm Bureau), telephone interview by author, 4 April 1988.

22. The idea to create bay barriers as transportation arteries was original to John Reber. As early as 1880, however, Assistant California State Engineer C. E. Grunsky suggested the use of a barrier for salinity control. Throughout the early twentieth century, several organizations promoted the idea. Although Reber was not the first to advocate a barrier proposal, his design apparently owed nothing to earlier ideas and it was the only "master plan" anchored by such a system. (For more on the earlier barriers movements see: Alan Patterson, "The Great Fresh Water Panacea," *Arizona and the West*, vol. 22 (1980), 307–22).

23. The Golden Gate and Bay Bridges were completed in 1937 and 1936, respectively. [Charles Wollenburg, *Golden Gate Metropolis* (Berkeley: University of California Press, 1985), 209.]

24. *The San Francisco Chronicle*, 26 February 1952.

25. *The San Francisco Chronicle*, 3 May 1942.

26. The works of Gerald Nash and Roger Lotchin treat this idea in the context of Western American History. See Nash's *The American West Transformed*. Lotchin's work includes: "City and Sword in Metropolitan California, 1919–1941," *Urbanism Past and Present* (Summer/Fall 1982), 1–16, as well as *The Martial Metropolis: U. S. Cities in War and Peace* (New York: Praeger Publications, 1984) and *Fortress California* 1910–1961: From Warfare to Welfare (New York: Oxford University Press, 1992).

27. The gap that the planner attempted to bridge between the Bay Area and its southern rival was substantial. By 1948, Los Angeles annually attracted 300,000 visitors who stayed for an average of three weeks. The end result was an income of $500 million dollars. In San Francisco, however, those figures were 87,000 people, three days and $33 million dollars, respectively. ("Statement of John Reber," *The Needs of the San Francisco Bay Area*, 25.)

28. "Statement of John Reber," *The Needs of the San Francisco Bay Area*, 28.

29. *The San Francisco Downtowner*, 14 April 1942.

30. For interpretive material about the White City, see: Mel Scott, *Americacn City Planning Since 1890* (Berkeley, CA: University of California Press, 1969), 31–37; John W. Reps, *The Making of Urban America: A History of City Planning in the United States* (Princeton, N.J., 1965), 497–502; and Henry Steele Commager, *The American Mind: An Interpretation of American Thought and Character since the 1880's* (New Haven, CT: Yale University Press, 1966), 394–97. For a more encyclopedic view see: Hubert H. Bancroff, *The Book of the Fair*, 4 vols. (Chicago: Bancroft Company, 1893).

31. For a discussion of the City Beautiful and of its antecedents, see two works by Jon A. Peterson: "The City Beautiful Movement: Forgotten Origins and Lost Meanings," *Journal of Urban History*, vol. 2, no. 4, pp. 415–34; and "The Impact of Sanitary Reform upon American Urban Planning, 1840–1890," *Journal of Social History*, vol. 13, no. 1 (Fall, 1979), 83–103. For material concerning some comprehensive planners in the nineteenth century, see David C. Hammack, "Comprehensive Planning Before the Comprehensive Plan: A New Look at the Nineteenth-Century American City," in Daniel Schaffer, ed., *Two Centuries of American Planning* (London: Mansell Publishing Limited, 1988), 139–66.

32. Scott, *American City Planning*, 33.

33 Charles Moore, *Daniel Hudson Burnham, Architect, Planner of Cities* (New York: MacMillan Company, 1921), 126.

34. Thomas Hines, *Burnham of Chicago: Architect and Planner* (Chicago: University of Chicago Press, 1979), 126.

35. M. Christine Boyer, *Dreaming the Rational City: The Myth of American City Planning* (Cambridge, MA: MIT Press, 1983), 84.

36. Judd Kahn, *Imperial San Francisco: Politics and Planning in an American City 1897–1906* (Lincoln, Nebraska: University of Nebraska press, 1979), 77. *The New York Herald* exclaimed of the area's own City Beautiful plan: "The kind of beauty that makes Paris charming can only exist where private rights and personal liberty are or have been trampled on." (Harvey A. Kantor, "The City Beautiful in New York," *New York Historical Society Quarterly*, vol. 53, 1973, p. 152.)

37. Scott, *American City Planning*, 33. Christopher Tunnard, in commenting on the architectural achievements of the White City, noted that the design actually did represent a new American style that ultimately influenced European architects. Additionally, he believed that the new form was vastly improved over some existing ones, particularly that of the "Picturesque City." See Christopher Tunnard, *The Modern American City* (Princeton,

N. J.: D. Van Nostrand Company, Inc., 1968) 114–55.

38. In Chicago, Burnham found himself defending his work as something "practical," and not simply a "trite 'City Beautiful'." (Michael P. McCarthy, "Chicago Businessmen and the Burnham Plan," *Illinois State Historical Society*, vol. 63, 1970, p. 245.) Indeed, Burnham's previous works in cities such as Washington D. C. and San Francisco were a purer form of the City Beautiful. I chose to discuss the *Plan of Chicago*, however, because it, like the Reber Plan, has a clearly regional focus.

39. Committee on the Regional Plan of New York and Its Environs, *The Graphic Regional Plan* (New York, 1929), 138.

40. Also see Committee on the Regional Plan of New York and Its Environs, *The Building of the City* (Philadelphia: William F. Fell Co. Printers, 1931); Committee on the Regional Plan of New York and Its Environs, *Buildings: Their Uses and the Spaces About Them* (New York, 1931) and Thomas Adams, *Planning the Region of New York* (New York, 1927).

41. See Michael Simpson's *Thomas Adams and the Modern Planning Movement* (New York: Alexandrine Press Book, 1985), 135. For a more general discussion of the typical City "Practical" planning style, see Harvey S. Perloff, *Education for Planning: City, State, and Regional* (Baltimore: The Johns Hopkins Press, 1957).

42. See Robert Fitch, "Planning New York," in Roger E. Alcaly and David Mermelstein, eds., *The Fiscal Crisis of American Cities*, 246–84.

43. In these eras when planning was still evolving as a profession, there was a strong impulse toward finding a transferable set of city planning standards. Thomas Adams, for instance, lamented the absence of a central body of principles for his field (Simpson, 165). Not coincidentally, just as Burnham and Adams completed their projects, the nation's universities began to offer new professional planning educational opportunities. The first distinct course in city planning began with Harvard Professor James Sturgis Pray's "Principles of City Planning" in 1909, the year Burnham unveiled the *Plan of Chicago*. In 1929, just as the first volume of the *Regional Plan of New York* appeared; Harvard created the first distinct degree program in city planning. In the coming years, universities across the country followed Harvard's lead. The proliferation of degree programs, however, had a muted impact upon the world of the practicing professional. By 1959, one study found the only seven percent of the practicing planners were trained specifically in the field. Most came from a variety of related disciplines, such as architecture or sociology. [For discussions of the evolution of city planning education see: Harvey S. Perloff, "Education of City Planners: Past, Present, and Future," *Journal of the American Institute of Planners*, vol. 22, 1956,

pp. 186–217; as well as Frederick J. Adams and Gerald Hodge, "City Planning Instruction in the United States: The Pioneering Days, 1900–1930," *Journal of the American Institute of Planners*, vol. 31, no. 1, 1965, pp. 43–51. Lucien C. Faust's "An Analysis of Selected Characteristics of the American Institute of Planners," (Unpublished Master's Thesis, University of North Carolina, 1959) offers an overview of the training completed by the planning guild's members.]

44. Sir Patrick Geddes, *The Evolution of Cities* from Alan Jacobs, *Making City Planning Work* (Washington/Chicago: American Planning Association, 1980), xiv.

45. Boyer, 230.

46. Alan Altshuler, *The City Planning Process: A Political Analysis* (Ithaca, New York: Cornell University Press, 1965), 299.

47. United States Army Corps of Engineers, *Technical Report on Barriers* (1963), 211.

48. Structures resembling the Streamlining California Plan, such as Interstate 5 and the California Aqueduct, were eventually constructed, albeit without Reber's input.

49. Client Analysis involved the use of market research to ascertain the desires of a community to be planned. See Janet S. Reiner, Everett Reimer, and Thomas A. Reiner, "Client Analysis and the Planning of Public Programs," *Journal of the American Institute of Planners*, November 1963, vol. 29, no. 4, pp. 270–82.

50. Mel Scott, *San Francisco Bay Area* (Berkeley, CA: University of California Press, 1959), 264.

Notes to Chapter 9 / Miller

1. The Japanese launched approximately 9,000 balloon bombs in 1944–45, of which only a tiny percentage reached the United States. Some of these bombs traveled as far as Iowa, but most reported incidents were confined to isolated regions of the Pacific Northwest. The bombs set off forest fires and killed several people. See Bert Webber, *Silent Siege: Japanese Attacks Against North America in World War II* (Fairfield, WA, 1984), 224–86 and Richard R. Lingeman, *Don't You know There's a War On?: The American Home Front, 1941–1945* (New York, 1976), 44, 54–55. Several books have focused on the threat of Nazi U-boats on the Atlantic Coast. See Michael Gannon, *Operation Drum beat: The Dramatic True Story of Germany's First U-Boat Attacks Along the Atlantic Coast in World War II* (New York, 1990) and Edwin P. Hoyt, *U-Boats Offshore: When Hitler Struck America* (New York, 1978).

2. Woodring cited in Lee Kennett, *For the Duration: The United States Goes to War—Pearl Harbor—1942* (New York, 1985), 28. See also B. Franklin Cooling, "U.S. Army Support of Civil Defense: The Formative Years," *Military Affairs* 35 (February 1971), 8. President Roosevelt demanded Woodring's resignation in mid-June when he refused to support the administration's policy of aiding Great Britain. For a fuller treatment of Woodring see Keith D. McFarland, *Harry H. Woodring: A Political Biography of FDR's Controversial Secretary of War* (Lawrence, KS, 1975), 103–235.

3. Fiorello H. LaGuardia, "Preliminary Report for Civil Defense Organization and Administration in the United States," Fiorello H. LaGuardia Papers (FHLP), Box 4528 Folder 6, New York City Municipal Archives (NYMA), New York City, New York. See also William M. Leary, "Assessing the Japanese Threat: Air Intelligence Prior to Pearl Harbor," *Aerospace Historian* 34 (December 1987), 272–77. Leary contends that complacency, chauvinism, and ignorance caused the United States to under-estimate Japan's air power. As a result, most civilian protection plans were geared toward the possibility of German air raids.

4. Press Conference No. 736, 18 April 1941, Press Conferences, vol. 17, p. 6, Franklin D. Roosevelt Library (FDRL). The ultimate responsibility for civilian defense was assumed by local authorities. See "Highlights of 1941," in Clarence E. Ridley and Orin F. Nolting, eds., *The Municipal Year Book*, 1942 (Chicago, 1942), 8–10.

5. In order to avoid unnecessary battles with the isolationists in Congress, President Roosevelt erected a great deal of the federal wartime administrative bureaucracy through existing statutory law and by executive order. Just one week after war broke out in Europe in September 1939, Roosevelt signed Executive Order 8248 to create the Office for Emergency Management (OEM), which increased the size and scope of the Office of the President. Several federal wartime agencies, including the Office of Civilian Defense were created under OEM auspices. These agencies were closely supervised by White House officials, but they still relied on congressional appropriations for funding. On the other hand, in May 1940, FDR revived a 1916 statute that had created the World War I Council of National Defense to form the National Defense Advisory Commission (NDAC). See National Defense Advisory Papers, 1940–1941, Box 7 Folder 30 (FDRL) and Elwyn A. Mauck, *Civilian Defense in the United States, 1941–1945*, ch. 2 pp. 1–3, Office of Civilian Defense Papers (OCDP), Record Group 171, Washington National Records Center (WNRC), Suitland, MD. See also Cooling, "U.S. Army Support of Civil Defense," 8 and "States on the Job," *Defense* (a weekly

publication of the Division of Information, a subordinate unit of the NDAC) vol. 1 (30 August 1940), 5. By August 1940, legislatures officially recognized state defense councils in the following states: Arizona, California, Connecticut, Delaware, Indiana, Kansas, Louisiana, Maine, Maryland, Massachusetts, Michigan, Minnesota, Missouri, Nevada, New Hampshire, New Jersey, New York, North Carolina, Oklahoma, South Carolina, South Dakota, Tennessee, Texas, Virginia and Washington.

6. A pattern of corporate leadership in municipal civilian defense planning appeared in several cities, including Chicago, Cincinnati, Los Angeles, Philadelphia, Syracuse and Toledo. See M. L. Waltz to Cambria (CA) Council of Defense, 13 January 1942, OCDP, RG 171, Entry 11 Box 72, Regional File-California, (WNRC); Mary Watters, *Illinois in the Second World War: Operation Home Front*, vol. 1 (Springfield, IL., 1951), 6–7, 10 and 26; Ralph D. Henderson to Chamber of Commerce Secretaries, 24 April 1941 and Charles P. Taft to John W. Bricker, 7 April 1941, Papers of the Hamilton County National Defense Council, Civilian Defense Collection, Box 2 Folder 8, Cincinnati Historical Society (CHS), Cincinnati, Ohio; John C. Nagle to Fiorello LaGuardia, 21 May 1941, FHLP, Box 4171 Folder 4 (NYMA); and "The Toledo Chamber of Commerce: An Interim and Varied Program," *Toledo Business* 19, no. 10 (October 1941), Papers of the Ohio State Council of Defense, Series 2246, Box 1 Folder 19, Ohio Historical Society (OHS), Columbus, Ohio. See also "Defense Council for City and County," *American City* 56 (January 1941), 87; Morris Edwards, "Before and Since Pearl Harbor," *American City* 56 (May 1942), 75; and *What To Do In An Air Raid* (Washington, 1942), 4.

7. "Defense Plans in Our Cities," (reprint of the *National Municipal Review* article), *Defense*, vol. 1 (13 December 1940), 4.

8. "Civilian Defense: Suggestions for State and Local Fire Defense," (Washington, D.C., 1941); Elwyn A. Mauck, "History of Civil Defense in the United States," *The Bulletin of Atomic Scientists* 6 (August-September 1950), 266; "State Plans for Civil Protection," *Defense*, vol. 1, (25 October 1940), 4; "The States and Cities," *Defense*, vol. 1 (1 November 1940), 4; and Milo J. Warner to Lowell Mellett (2 April 1941), Wayne Coy Papers, Box 2 Civilian Defense Folder (FDRL).

9. The British government also evacuated more than 12,000 children during the summer of 1940, sending them to the United States and Canada for the duration of the war. See Public Broadcasting System (PBS), "Orphans of the Storm," 26 December 1989. See also Ward B. Tongue to Fiorello LaGuardia, 28 November 1941, FHLP, Box 4211 Folder 1 (NYMA) and Stanley M. Isaacs to Fiorello LaGuardia, 14 February 1941, Stanley M.

Isaacs Papers, American Jewish Archives, Cincinnati, Ohio.

10. British Ministry of Information films like "Neighbors Under Fire" and Goofer Trouble" indoctrinated American municipal officials and civilian defense workers on the proper methods of air raid defense. See FHLP, Box 4211 Folder 9 (NYMA). Long before Pearl Harbor, the Office for Emergency Management worked with the YMCA Motion Picture Bureau in New York, Chicago, Dallas and San Francisco to distribute films produced by the MOI as well as U. S. government-sponsored films to state and local defense councils. A map (c. 1942) denoting the various regions served by the OEM Film Unit in Washington D. C. and the YMCA Motion Picture Bureaus can be found in the Office of War Information Papers, RG 208, Entry 276 Box 1998 (WNRC).

11. *The United States Municipal News*, vol. 8, no. 11, FHLP, Box 4528 Folder 13 (NYMA); Paul V. Betters, "Mayors Propose Civil Defense Plan," *American City* 56 (February 1941), 5 and Mauck, *Civilian Defense in the United States*, ch. 3, pp. 2–3. In October 1940, the International City Managers' Association had expressed similar concerns about the burden of civilian defense on cities at its annual meeting at Colorado Springs. See "The States and Cities," *Defense*, vol. 1 (4 October 1940), 4. Likewise, representatives of 46 states gathered at the Council of State Governments' fifth biennial meeting, in January 1941, and agreed to take "all necessary steps to promote 'total defense.'" See "State and Local Cooperation," *Defense* vol. 2 (28 January 1941), 12.

12. LaGuardia to Franklin D. Roosevelt, 31 January 1941, FHLP, Box 4528 Folder 6 and Resolutions Adopted at the Regional Meeting, 24 February 1941, FHLP, Box 4528 Folder 9 (NYMA). Also see Mauck, *Civilian Defense in the United States*, ch. 3, p. 9 and Kennett, *For the Duration*, 30.

13. Daniel W. Hoan, "Cities and the Defense Program (Address to the USCM meeting in St. Louis)," 21 February 1941, FHLP, Box 4528 Folder 9 (NYMA). The Roosevelt administration discussed home defense schemes in early January 1941. Most of these early plans focused on national morale rather than civilian protection. See Richard W. Steele, *Propaganda in an Open Society: The Roosevelt Administration and the Media, 1933–1941* (Westport, CT, 1985), 83–92; FDR Press Conferences, No. 710, vol. 17, pp. 75–76 (FDRL); and Milo J. Warner to Lowell Mellett, 2 April 1941, Coy Papers, Box 2 (FDRL)

14. "Conferences with the President," 15 February 1941, Harold D. Smith Papers, Box 3 (FDRL); "Memorandum for the President," Wayne Coy, William Bullitt, and Harold D. Smith, 4 April 1941, Coy Papers, Box 2 (FDRL); "Organization and Duties of Defense Councils Outlined in Supplemental Memorandum," *Defense*, vol. 2 (29 April 1941), 22; and Richard W. Steele, Pre-

paring the Public for War; Efforts to Establish a National Propaganda Agency," *American Historical Review* 75 (October 1970), 1640–653. Smith, Coy and Bullitt referred to the volunteer activities which the home defense agency would monitor as "propaganda of the act." Steele argued that public participation in air raid drills and other government sponsored activities before Pearl Harbor helped unify support for Roosevelt and the defense effort.

15. For the best treatment of LaGuardia's efforts as OCD director, see Thomas Kessner, *Fiorello H. LaGuardia and the Making of Modern New York* (New York, 1989), 492–95, 500–03. See also "Conferences with the President," 14 April 1941, Smith Papers, Box 3 (FDRL); James MacGregor Burns, *Franklin D. Roosevelt: The Soldier of Freedom* (New York, 1970), 116; Larwence Elliot, *Little Flower: The Life and Times of Fiorello LaGuardia* (New York, 1983), 234–36; William Manners, *Patience and Fortitude: Fiorello LaGuardia—A Biography* (New York, 1976), 252–53; Charles Garrett, *The LaGuardia Years: Machine and Reform Politics in New York City* (New Brunswick, NJ, 1961), 281; Mauck, *Civilian Defense in the United States*, ch. 3, pp. 8–9; and Samuel I. Rosenman, ed., "The Office of Civilian Defense Is Established. Executive Order 8757. 20 May 1941," *The Public Papers and Addresses of Franklin D. Roosevelt, 1941,* 162–65.

16. Rosenman, ed., *Papers of FDR. 1941,* 162–65.

17. LaGuardia cited in Robert McElroy, *Narrative History of the Office of Civilian Defense* (unpublished, 1944), ch. 6, p. 5, OCDP, RG 171, Entry 232 (WNRC). Eleanor Roosevelt cited in *The Autobiography of Eleanor Roosevelt* (New York, 1958), 225. See also Lois Scharf, *Eleanor Roosevelt: First Lady of American Liberalism* (Boston, 1987), 121–26; Phillip J. Funigiello, *The Challenge to Urban Liberalism: Federal-City Relations During World War II* (Knoxville, TN, 1978), 39–79; and "President Tells Volunteer Committee to Interpret Defense Policies to People," *Defense,* vol. 2 (29 July 1941), 24.

18. LaGuardia cited in Mauck, *Civilian Defense in the United States,* ch. 4, pp. 4–5. See also Fiorello H. LaGuardia, "Report of the Director of the Office of Civilian Defense," 8–9, February 1942, William H. McReynolds Papers, Box 7 OCD File (FDRL) and Cooling, "U. S. Army Support of Civil Defense," 9.

19. "LaGuardia Tells First Civilian Defense Trainees of the Job Ahead of Them," *Defense,* vol. 2 (29 July 1941), 22; "Second Class in Combatting Bombs to Include Officers from 47 Cities," *Defense,* vol. 2 (15 July 1941), 23; Fiorello LaGuardia, "Why National Defense is a Municipal Problem," *American City* 56 (October 1941), 5; and Leo P. Brophy and George J. B. Fischer, *United States Army in World War II: The Technical Services: The*

Chemical Warfare Service: Organizing for War (Washington, 1959).

20 LaGuardia, "Why National Defense is a Municipal Problem," 5, and *Defense*, vol. 2 (29 July 1941), 22.

21. Kessner, *Fiorello LaGuardia*, 493–95; Karl Drew Hartzell, *The Empire State at War: World War II* (Albany, 1949), 16; "Civil Protection and Economic Problems Stressed in Connecticut Progress Report," *Defense*, vol. 2 (9 July 1941), 23; "The City's Part in National Defense," *American City* 56 (June 1941), 5.

22. Landis cited in James M. Landis, "The Progress of Civil Defense," 14 November 1941, James M. Landis Papers, Box 164, Library of Congress, Washington, DC; "The City's Part in National Defense," 5; and Watters, *Illinois in the Second World War*, 10.

23. Robert Earnest Miller, "The War That Never Came: Civilian Defense in Cincinnati, Ohio During World War II," *Queen City Heritage* 49 (Spring 1992), 2–22.

24. "Tally of Local Defense Councils Reveals 5935 Organized in Nation," *Defense*, Vol. 2 (25 November 1941), 31.

25. *Chicago Tribune* (clipping), 1 December 1941, OCDP, Entry 10 Box 2 (WNRC). The identification of the Midwest with isolationism angered an outspoken minority that supported the Roosevelt administration's foreign policy in Europe. See Watters, *Illinois in the Second World War*, 13.

26. LaGuardia, Report of the Director , 1 (FDRL). The public reaction to, and recollection of, the attack on Pearl Harbor has been well documented. See Richard Polenberg, *The United States at War: 1941–1945* (Philadelphia, 1972), 1–4; Allan M. Winkler, *Home Front U.S.A.: America During World War II* (Arlington Heights, IL, 1986), 25–27; Studs Terkel, *"The Good War": An Oral History of World War Two* (New York, 1985), 17–33; and Roy Hoopes, *Americans Remember the Home Front: An Oral narrative* (New York, 1977), 3–45.

27. Gwenfread Allen, *Hawaii's War Years: 1941–1945* (Honolulu, 1950), 1–28, and 37 and LaGuardia, "Report of the Director," 1 (FDRL).

28. Roger Daniels, *Concentration Camps North America: Japanese Americans in the United States and Canada During World War II* (Malabar, FL, 1981), 38.

29. Lingeman, *Don't You Know There's A War Going On?*, 25–26; G. Thomas Edwards, "The Oregon Coast and Three of its Guerilla Organizations, 1942," *Journal of the West* 25, no. 3 (July 1986), 20–34 and Terkel, *"The Good War"*, 23.

30. LaGuardia cited in James R. Chiles, "How We Got Ready For The War That Was Never Fought," *Smithsonian* 19 (1988), 174–204. See also Eleanor Roosevelt, 14 December 1941, Pan American Coffee Bureau Series, Program no. 12 (broadcast from

Tacoma, Washington), Eleanor Roosevelt Tapes (FDRL); "Los Angeles Gets Ready," *Time* 38 (15 December 1941), 76–77; Kessner, *Fiorello LaGuardia*, 502; Joseph P. Lash, *Eleanor and Franklin: The Story of Their Relationship Based on Eleanor Roosevelt's Private Papers* (New York, 1970), 647; J. T. William Youngs, *Eleanor Roosevelt: A Personal and Public Life*, 194–95; and *The Autobiography of Eleanor Roosevelt*, 229.

31. Phillip N. Guyol, *Democracy Fights: A History of New Hampshire in World War II* (Dartmouth, 1951), 77–78; Lingeman, *Don't You Know There's A War Going On?*, 25–29; Hoopes, *Americans Remember the Home Front*, 18–19; Marvin W. Sclegal, *Conscripted City: Norfolk In World War II* (Norfolk, 1951), 128; Miller, "The War That Never Came," 2–22.

32. John J. Rowe to Phillip O. Geier, 9 March 1942, Civil Defense Collection, Box 2 Folder 6 (CHS) and David Brinkley, *Washington Goes to War: The Extraordinary Story of the Transformation of a City and a Nation* (New York, 1988), 98.

33. Bradley quote in Studs Terkel, *"The Good War"*, 25, and "Army Guns Open on Unknown Foe," *Life* 12 (9 March 1942), 37–38.

34. *What To Do In An Air Raid* (Washington, 1941), 1, 5. OCD officials also recommended that each refugee be equipped with a magazine and a deck of cards. LaGuardia received complaints from ministers who felt that people should turn to the Bible, rather than a deck of cards, for comfort during anxious moments. See Fiorello H. LaGuardia to Robert Zarefoss, 23 December 1941, and S. Howard Evans to Rev. Paul M. Miller, 16 January 1942, OCDP, RG 171, Entry 10 Box 2 (WNRC).

35. *What To Do In An Air Raid*, 1, and James M. Landis, "Block By Block," *Victory* (formerly called *Defense*), vol. 3 (22 December 1942), 3.

36. Farmers offered to convert their property to day nurseries and live-in schools if and when the OCD decided to evacuate children from potential target areas. See Henry Chiappone to Franklin D. Roosevelt, 15 January 1942, and Mrs. Nathan Strauss to Mildred Bruckheimer, 14 January 1942, OCDP, RG 171, Entry 10 Box 85 (WNRC). See also Fiorello LaGuardia, 22 February 1942, Radio Address, FHLP, Box 3859 Folder 15 (NYMA) and Eleanor Roosevelt, 4 January 1942, Pan American Coffee Bureau Series, Program no. 15, ER Tapes (FDRL).

37. Lorenzo B. Gasser to A. B. Williams, 31 January 1942, OCDP, RG 171, Entry 10 Box 119 (WNRC) and "Air Raid Shelters," *American City* 57 (February 1942), 55.

38. Rosenman, ed., *Papers of FDR*, 1942, p. 105 and *What Can I Do?* (Washington, 1942), 1.

39. LaGuardia seldom missed a Cabinet meeting, but he had

ignored many of his OCD responsibilities. Just after Pearl Harbor, Eleanor Roosevelt met with Budget Director Harold Smith and presidential assistants to discuss the possibility of removing LaGuardia as OCD director. The president agreed that the mayor could no longer handle two increasingly difficult positions simultaneously. See "Conferences With the President," 19 December 1941, Smith Papers, Box 3 (FDRL) Mauck, *Civilian Defense in the United States*, ch. 7, pp. 12–13; Elliot, *Little Flower*, 237; and Kessner, *Fiorello LaGuardia*, 503.

40. "Eleanor's Playmates," *Time* (16 February 1942), 49; John Morton Blum, *V Was For Victory: Politics and American Culture During World War II* (New York, 1976), 224–25; Roland Young, *Congressional Politics During the Second World War* (New York, 1956), 47–49; Mauck, *Civilian Defense in the United States*, ch. 4, pp. 13–14; and Melvyn Douglas, *See You at the Movies* (Lanham, MD, 1986), 116–19. Eleanor Roosevelt recruited Douglas to serve as an adviser (without compensation) for an Arts Division. Norman Davis, the head of the American Red Cross, explained the attack on the First Lady best. She had been the innocent victim of an attitudinal change from "complacency which retarded preparedness to one of impatience over winning the war in a hurry. . . ." In essence, during the early part of America's involvement in the war, nonprotective aspects of civilian defense were regarded as nonessential. See Norman H. Davis to Eleanor Roosevelt, 22 February 1942, Reel 5, in Susan Ware and William H. Chafe, eds., *Eleanor Roosevelt Papers* (Frederick, MD, 1988), 20 reels.

41. Local defense councils were active in large cities like New York as well as smaller towns like Murdo, South Dakota. See Dudley M. Irwin, Jr., *The Buffalo War Council: How One City Met the Challenge of Total War* (Buffalo, n.d.), 29–65; Robert Karolevitz, "Life on the Homefront: South Dakota in World War II," *South Dakota History* 19 (Fall 1989), 398; Stephen J. Leonard, "Denver at War: The Homefront in World War II," *Colorado Heritage* 4 (1987), 35–36; Lingeman [on New York], *Don't You Know There's A War On?*, 35–36; Lorraine McConaghy, "Wartime Boomtown: Kirkland, Washington, A Small Town During World War II," *Pacific Northwest Quarterly* 80 (April 1989), 46; Robert Earnest Miller, "The War That Never Came," 2–22; Eugene P. Moehring, "Las Vegas and the Second World War," *Nevada Historical Society Quarterly* 29 (1986), 4–8; Schegal [on Norfolk], *Conscripted City*, 124–147; and Charles William Sloane, Jr., ed., "The Newelletters: E. Gail Carpenter Describes Life on the Homefront: Part I," *Kansas History* 11 (Spring 1988), 66, 71.

42. Office of the Deputy Executive, "Memorandum on Enlistment and Assignment of Volunteers as of 31 January 1942," 26

February 1942, cited in McElroy, *Narrative History of the Office of Civilian Defense*, ch. 7, p. 38, OCDP, RG 171, Entry 232 (WNRC), and Russell Barthell and Robert Ward, "Wartime Organization of Cities," *The Municipal Year Book, 1942* (Chicago, 1943), 317–21. LaGuardia's replacement, Harvard Law School Dean James M. Landis, recalled that by the summer of 1942 "the danger of bombing was gone." See James M. Landis, Columbia Oral History Project (COHP), (1963–64), 324, Columbia University, New York.

43. For civilian defense efforts at flood relief, see "Civilians, Military Worked Side By Side to Combat Potomac River Flood," *Victory*, vol. 3 (27 October 1942), 30; "Flood Tests CD in Many States," *OCD Newsletter* no. 27 (25 January 1943) in Official File 4422, Office of Civilian Defense, 1943–45, Box 2 (FDRL); Lt. Colonel H. J. Patterson, Report on Activities in the Cincinnati Area During the Flood Period of January 1, 1943 to 4 January 1943," Papers of the Ohio State Council of Defense, Series 2247, Box 4 (OHS); *Cincinnati Enquirer*, 5 and 6 January 1943; and Landis, COHP, 326. See also Guyol, *Democracy Fights*, 78–79. For firefighting and emergency rescue recue work, see Foster Rhea Dulles, *The American Red Cross: A History* (New York, 1950), 386–87; Watters, *Illinois During the Second World War*, 65–67; and John F. Zwicky, "A State At War: The Illinois Homefront during the Second World War," (Ph.D. dissertation, University of Loyola, Chicago, 1988), 55. See also Willett Wilson to Sinclair Hatch, "Memorandum on the Role of the New York City Civilian Protective Forces in the 'Harlem Incident'," 7 August 1943, OCDP, RG 171, Entry 16 Box 118.

44. Mauck, "History of Civil Defense in the United States," 267. As nominal head of the civilian protection forces in New York City, Mayor LaGuardia criticized the War Department's decision to suspend protective activities. See Fiorello H. LaGuardia, FHLP, Box 3862 Folder 5 (NYMA)

45. For example, during the summer of 1943 the Emergency Child Care Committee of Hamilton County's "National Defense Council," in greater Cincinnati, coordinated the activities of 27 nurseries that cared for 1,067 children. See Maude Neeley Ross, Report of the Director of the Emergency Child Care Office, 3 December 1942 to 1 January 1944, Civil Defense Collection, Box 1 Folder 4 (CHS). See also Memorandum, "Day Nurseries, Nursery Schools, Kindergartens," 26 February 1942, (FHLP), Box 4191 Folder 12, (NYMA); James M. Landis, OCD Operations Letter No. 79, 15 October 1943, Children's Bureau Papers, RG 102, Box 182 (NA); "The Day Care Program of the Federal Government: A Statement Issued By the Office of Defense Health and Welfare Services, 27 July 1942, OCDP, RG 171, 38 Box 44

(WNRC); John B. Blandford, Jr., "Administrative Organization," in *Municipal Year Book, 1943* (Chicago, 1944), 311–14; Guyol, *Democracy Fights*, 83–84; Irwin, *The Buffalo War Council*, 131–42; and Marvin W. Schlegal, *Virginia On Guard: Civilian Defense and the State Militia in the Second World War* (Richmond, 1949), 253–54. For general remarks on national trends in child care during the war, see Florence Kerr to Thomas Devine, c. February 1944, OCDP, RG 171, Entry 32 Box 1 (WNRC); Susan M. Hartmann, *American Women in the Forties: The Home Front and Beyond* (Boston, 1982), 58–59; Polenberg, *War and Society*, 148–49; Doris Weatherford, *American Women and World War II* (New York, 1990), 167–74.

46. For more detailed information about victory gardens, see Doris Weatherford, *American Women and World War II* (New York, 1990), 225–28. After the race riots in Detroit during the summer of 1943, the National Urban League issued an "antiriot" directive to its local affiliates, encouraging them to make use of local defense councils to promote positive ideas about race relations. See James Garfield Stewart, Memorandum, 8 July 1943, Greater Cincinnati Urban League Papers, Box 24 Folder 5 (CHS).

47. Blandford, "Administrative Organization," 311–14.

48. Louis Wirth quoted in Funigiello, *The Challenge to Urban Liberalism*, 187.

49. Walter H. Blucher, "Planning and Zoning: Developments in 1944," *Municipal Year Book, 1944* (Chicago, 1945), 268. Previous volumes (1942, 1943) of this yearbook provided extensive data on the composition of local defense councils and the amount of money appropriated for civilian defense activities. See Barthel and Ward, "Wartime Organization of Cities," *Municipal Year Book, 1942*, 317–21. By 1944, "defense" was no longer even a top priority among urban planners. The same pattern of growing disinterest about civilian defense was present in other publications by and for urban officials. See Paul V. Betters, "Federal Highway Aid Urban Cities" in *American City* 60 (January 1945), 5, 125 and "The Federal Highway Act of 1944" in *The United States Municipal News*, vol. 12, no. 4 (15 February 1945), FHLP, Box 4531 Folder 12 (NYMA).

50. I. M. Labovitz and John W. Field, "Federal–City Relations in 1944," *The Municipal Year Book, 1945* (Chicago, 1946), 124–33; "Executive Order 9562, Termination of the Office of Civilian Defense," 5 June 1945, Harry S. Truman Papers, Official File 29, Truman Library, Independence, MO; and Mauck, *Civilian Defense in the United States*, ch. 16, p. 16.

51. "Preparedness and Prevention—Both Essential," *American City* 63 (March 1948), 83; "Federal Aid Asked for Local Civil Defense," *American City* 63 (May 1948), 4; and Mauck, "A History

of Civil Defense in the United States," 267.

52. *This Is Civil Defense* (Washington, 1951), 4.

53. *This Is Civil Defense*, 8–9. See also "Our Cities Must Fight," RG 171, OCD Film No. 67, (Archer Productions, 1953), 10 mins., and "Duck and Cover," RG 171, OCD Film No. 66 (Archer Productions, 1953), 10 mins., National Archives, Motion Picture Branch, Washington, DC. "Duck and Cover," which was cosponsored by the National Education Association and targeted at school children, deemphasized and minimized the bomb's destructive capabilities. The narrator of the film, "Bert the Turtle," conceded: "We all know that the atomic bomb is very dangerous. . . ." The bomb, he added, could burn you "worse than a terrible sunburn." Bert assured children that "ducking" under their desks and "covering" their faces would provide adequate protection in the event of a nuclear attack. For a detailed analysis of these well-intentioned, though misguided efforts, see Joanne Brown, "'A Is For Atom, B Is For Bomb': Civil Defense in American Public Education, 1948–1963," *Journal of American History* 75 (June 1988), 68–90. See also Allan M. Winkler, "A 40-year History of Civil Defense," *Bulletin of the Atomic Scientist* 40 (June/July 1984), 16–22, and Ann E. Larabee, "Ground Zero: The City, The Bomb and The End Of History," *The Canadian Review of American Studies* 22 (Fall 1991), 263–279.

54. "Conference of Mayors Recommends 600 Millions for Civil Defense," *American City* 66 (July 1951), 95; "For Defense Or Disaster, *National Municipal Review* 41 (June 1952), 294–99; and Brown, "'A Is For Atom, B Is For Bomb,'" 89.

Notes to Chapter 10 / Fairbanks

1. For a sampling of this literature, see Mark I. Gelfand, *A Nation of Cities: The Federal Government and Urban America, 1933–1965* (New York: Oxford University Press, 1975); Arnold R. Hirsch, *Making the Second Ghetto: Race and Housing in Chicago, 1940–1960* (Cambridge: Cambridge University Press, 1981); Kenneth T. Jackson, *Crabgrass Frontier: The Suburbanization of the United States* (New York: Oxford University Press, 1985); Jo Ann Argersinger, *Toward a New Deal in Baltimore: People and Government in the Great Depression* (Chapel Hill, NC: University of North Carolina Press, 1989).

2. Even a recent special issue of the *Journal of the West* devoted to aviation in the West included only one entry from its 13 articles dealing with airports and urban development. See Thomas J. Noel, "Unexplored Western Skies: Denver International

Airport," *Journal of the West* 30 (Jan. 1991), 80–100. Probably the best book on Texas aviation, a 288-page volume, contains no more than ten pages worth of material about airports and urban growth. See Roger Bilstein and Jay Miller, *Aviation in Texas* (Austin: Texas Monthly Press, Inc., 1985). The most important article on the subject of cities and airports to date is Paul Barrett, "Cities and Their Airports: Policy Formation, 1926–1952, *Journal of Urban History* 14 (Nov. 1987), 112–37.

3. Blaine Brownell, *The Urban Ethos in the South, 1920–1930* (Baton Rouge, Louisiana: Louisiana State University Press, 1975).

4. Stanley H. Scott and Levi H. Davis, *A Giant in Texas: A History of the Dallas-Fort Worth Regional Airport Controversy, 1911–1974* (Quanah, Texas: Nortex Press, 1974), 3; *Dallas* 7 (July 1928), 15.

5. Federal legislation in 1926 specifically prohibited federal financial aid to public or private airports. American Public Works Association, *History of Public Works in the United States 1776–1976* (Chicago: American Public Works Association, 1976), 192; *Dallas Morning News (DMN)*, 16 Dec. 1927; Scott and Davis, *Giant in Texas*, 3.

6. "Forward Dallas. Report of the Ulrickson Committee, 1925–1926," n.d., n.p., 46; Andy DeShong, "The Dallas Chamber of Commerce: Its First Seventy Years," (typescript, Dallas Public Library *[DPL]*).

7. *DMN*, 15 Dec. 1927.

8. American Public Works Association, *History of Public Works*, 193.

9. Dallas, Texas, *Progress: An Official Report of Municipal Achievement in Dallas, 1934*, 22.

10. Julian Capers, "From Aviation Outpost to Air Mail Center," *Dallas* 28 (Dec. 1928), 16–17; Edward H. Landreth and Bill E. Cohlmia, "An Analysis of the Progress and Status of General Aviation in the U. S." (Norman Oklahoma: Bureau of Business Research, 1951), 28, Office Files of the Regional Administrator, Fort Worth, Record Group (RG) 237, Federal Records Center, Fort Worth, Texas.

11. Landreth and Cohlmia, "Analysis of General Aviation," 28.

12. *Dallas Dispatch Journal*, 21 (?) Nov. 1939.

13. For more on the Dallas Citizens Council, see Robert B. Fairbanks, "The Good Government Machine: The Citizens Charter Association and Dallas Politics, 1930–1960," in *Essays on Sunbelt Cities and Recent Urban America*, Robert B. Fairbanks and Kathleen Underwood, eds., (College Station: Texas A & M University Press, 1990), 125–50. *Dallas Journal*, 23 Dec. 1937 (?); B. B. Owen, "Dallas Stake in Aviation," *Southwest Business* (April 1939), 11.

14. Donald R. Whitnak, *Safer Skyways: Federal Control of Aviation, 1926–1966* (Ames, Iowa: Iowa State University Press, 1966), 166–67.

15. Whitnak, *Safer Skyways,* 159–60.

16. "Regional Airport—Story With Many Chapters," *Fort Worth Star Telegram (FWST),* 19 Aug. 1962; *FWST,* 2 Oct. 1940; Scott and Davis, *Giant in Texas,* 5–6.

17. *FWST,* 29 Oct. 1940.

18. *FWST,* 19 Aug. 1962; Scott and Davis, *Giant in Texas,* 6.

19. Scott and Davis, *Giant in Texas,* 6–7; *FWST,* 10 Sept 1941, 16 Sept. 1941, 17 Oct. 1941, 8 Jan. 1942.

20. Robert Weer, "A Dream Dies," *Dallas Times Herald (DTH),* 17 March 1974; Scott and Davis, *Giant in Texas,* 7–8.

21. *DMN,* 1 March 1943, 2 March 1943; *FWST,* 23 March 1943.

22. *DMN,* 2 March 1943.

23. Scott and Davis, *Giant in Texas,* 9–12.

24. Harland Bartholomew and Associates, *A Master Plan for Dallas Texas, Report No. 6, Transportation Facilities: Rail-Air-Highway-Water* (July 1944), 43.

25. Scott and Davis, *Giant in Texas,* 11; *DMN,* 5 Nov. 1943, 5 Dec. 1943.

26. Scott and Davis, *Giant in Texas,* 10, *DTH,* 1 April 1943; *DMN,* 9 Dec. 1945.

27. Scott and Davis, *Giant in Texas,* 18.; *DMN,* 30 Oct. 1947.

28. *DMN,* 3 Feb. 1948; *DTH,* 11 Feb. 1948.

29. *DMN,* 6 March 1948, 1 June 1948, 2 June 1948.

30. *DMN,* 4 July 1948, 7 July 1948, 16 Sept. 1948.

31. *DMN,* 24 April 1948. According to one source, the airlines could save over $900,000 yearly by serving a single regional airport instead of two local ones.

32. *DMN,* 13 Sept. 1948, 18 May 1945; Dallas, Texas, Departments of Aviation and City Planning, "The Dallas Urban Plan for Aviation," 1948 (typescript); *DMN,* 17 May 1948.

33. *DTH,* 15 April 1951, 26 June 1951.

34. *DTH,* 5 Aug. 1951.

35. Since the city planned to finance part of future airport development by selling revenue bonds backed solely by the revenue from airport income, bond brokers also strongly urged city officials to retain outside help to evaluate Love Field's future. Interview, George Coker, 12 Sept. 1989; *DMN,* 20 Oct. 1957; DeShong, "The Dallas Chamber of Commerce."

36. *DMN,* 10 Dec. 1951; *New York Times,* 1 April 1949; Jameson W. Doig, "Coalition-Building by a Regional Agency: Austin Tobin and the Port of New York Authority," in *The Politics of Urban Development,* Clarence N. Stone and Heywood T. Sanders, eds. (Laurence: Univ. Press of Kansas, 1987), 73–104.

37. James C. Buckley, Inc., "Report of the Future of Love Field Dallas Texas with Respect to Service by Scheduled Air Carriers, March 1952 (typescript, DPL).

38. James C. Buckley, Inc., "Air Service Requirements for the City of Dallas, Texas. A Study for the Dallas Chamber of Commerce," 15 Oct. 1952 (typescript, DPL). According to Buckley, this was "the first time . . . that a major community has undertaken to review its entire present and prospective air service requirements" (p. 2).

39. Dallas, City Council Minutes, 1 July 1952, Resolution 52–2510; *DMN*, 23 Jan. 1953, 27 Jan. 1953.

40. *DMN*, 25 Jan. 1953; *DTH*, 26 Jan. 1953.

41. *DTH*, 20 Jan. 1953; *DMN*, 21 Jan. 1953.

42. The Doolittle Report (*The Airport and Its Neighbor*) was made by a presidential commission headed by World War II hero Jimmy Doolittle. It was formed in response to three separate airplane crashes that occurred within a one square mile area of residential Elizabeth, New Jersey (near the Newark Airport) in a six week period in 1952. *The Airport and Its Neighbors: The Report of the President's Airport Commission* (Washington, D. C.: U. S. Government Printing Office, 1952); *DMN*, 24 Jan. 1953, 26 Jan. 1953, 28 Jan. 1953.

43. James C. Buckley, Inc., "A Master Plan Study of Love Field," (New York, 8 Feb. 1954); *DTH*, 28 Dec. 1954.

44. Scott and Davis, *Giant in Texas*, 23; *DMN*, 22 Nov. 1954.

45. Draft of Proposed Report of the Aviation Department to George Coker, Appendix D.; Dallas Chamber of Commerce, *Annual Report*, 1953, 9 (DPL); Scott and Davis, *Giant in Texas*, 28–29.

46. *DMN*, 14 Aug. 1953; *DTH*, 4 Sept. 1953, 7 Sept. 1953.

47. *DTH*, 7 Sept. 1953, 21 May 1954.

48. *DTH*, 8 Aug. 1954.

49. Chan Gurney, Chair CAB, to W. O. Jones, Fort Worth City Manager, 5 Nov. 1954, Earle Cabell Papers, DeGolyer Library, SMU; *DMN*, 1 July 1954; *DMN*, 14 Nov. 1954.

50. Scott and Davis, *Giant in Texas*, 30; Dallas, City Council Minutes, 29 Nov. 1954, Resolution 54–5498; *DMN*, 26 Nov. 1954, 28 Nov. 1954.

51. *DMN*, 26 Nov. 1954.

52. *DTH*, 15 Dec. 1955, 9 Feb. 1956; *DMN*, 21 March 1956; 18 Nov. 1951; James C. Buckley, "The Effect of Airport Distance on Traffic Generation," *Journal of the Air Transport Division: Proceedings of the American Society of Civil Engineers* 82 (May 1956): 978-1-19. Scott and Davis, *Giant in Texas*, 32–36.

53. *DMN*, 20 Oct. 1957.

54. The first commercial jet landed at Love Field on 10 No-

vember 1958. Regular jet service started the following February. *DMN*, 11 Nov. 1958. Dallas's longest runway at this time was 7,500 feet. Scott and Davis, *Giant in Texas*, 34.

55. *DMN*, 31 March 1959; *DTH*, 13 Nov. 1959, 22 Nov. 1959.

56. Draft of Proposed Report of the Aviation Committee for George Coker, 1960; *DTH*, 9 Oct. 1962.

57. In March 1960, the FAA approved a $907,500 grant to lengthen Carter Field while at the same time denying a Dallas request. James Winchester, "The Great Dallas-Fort Worth Controversy," *Flying*, May 1961, 85; *DMN*, 1 March 1963.

58. Telegram to Najeeb E. Halaby from Earle Cabell, Aug. 1962, Cabell Papers, SMU; *DMN*, 17 Aug. 1962; *DTH*, 30 Aug. 1962.

59. CAB to City of Dallas, 21 April 1962; CAB, "Initial Decision of Ross I. Newman," 7 April 1964, Dockett 13959, Cabell Papers, SMU.

60. *DMN*, 23 Aug. 1962; Dallas Aviation Council, Fact Digest #4; Earle Cabell and Avery Mays, to Sen. Warner Magnusion, n.d., Cabell Papers, SMU.

61. Earle Cabell News Release, 22 Aug. 1962; H. L. Nichols, to membership of Chamber of Commerce, 31 Aug. 1962; Love Field Advisory Committee Data, 20 Aug. 1962, Cabell Papers.

62. T. R. Mansfield to Earle Cabell, 4 Sept. 1962, Cabell Papers, SMU.

63. *DMN*, 7 July 1963, 20 Sept. 1963.

64. *DMN*, 16 July 1963, 17 July 1963, 18 July 1963.

65. *DMN*, 5 Aug. 1963; 18 Sept. 1963.

66. *DMN*, 24 July 1963.

67. *DMN*, 23 July 1963; Memo on testimony of Dallas non-technical witness in CAB, "Initial Decision of Ross I. Newman," 7 April 1964, Dockett 13959, Cabell Papers, SMU.

68. CAB, "Initial Decision of Ross I. Newman," 7 April 1964, Dockett 13959, p. 45, Cabell Papers, SMU.

69. Scott and Davis, *Giant in Texas*, 49.

70. Scott and Davis, *Giant in Texas*, 49–50; Maurice Carlson to Eric Jonsson, 9 Jan. 1965, Dallas Citizens Committee Papers, Special Collections, UTA.

Notes to Chapter 11 / Steen

1. The principal manuscript sources that have been consulted for this paper are:

> Papers of Mayor Erastus Corning, 2nd, Albany County Hall of Records;
> Edwin Corning Papers, Albany Institute of History and Art.

Oral History Interviews:
Judge Francis Bergan (Interviewer: Ivan D. Steen);
Daniel Button (Interviewer: Dorothy Bross);
Rena Button (Interviewer: D. Bross);
Assemblyman Richard Conners (Interviewer: I. D. Steen);
Mayor Erastus Corning (Interviewer: I. D. Steen);
John Cross (Interviewer: D. Bross);
Judge James Foley (Interviewer: I. D. Steen);
James Gallagher (Interviewer: D. Bross);
George Harder (Interviewer: Kate Gurnett);
Bishop Howard Hubbard (Interviewer: Robert Ward);
Victor Lord (Interviewer: D. Bross);
Assemblyman Arnold Proskin (Interviewer: I. D. Steen);
Judge Harold Segal (Interviewer: I. D. Steen).

NOTE: Most of these interviews are not yet available for consultation.

Also, Albany's principal newspaper, the *Times Union*, has been examined daily for the period 1932–1983.

For the most part, sources have been cited only for direct quotations.

The only book-length study of Albany's O'Connell machine is: Frank S. Robinson, *Albany's O'Connell Machine: An American Political Relic* (Albany: The Washington Park Spirit, 1973). This is a very biased, nonscholarly book. Robinson, an attorney employed by the State of New York, has been active in Republican politics in the Albany area.

2. Irene D. Neu, *Erastus Corning: Merchant and Financier, 1794–1872* (Ithaca: Cornell University Press, 1960).

3. On Parker Corning: *Biographical Directory of the American Congress, 1774–1971* (Washington, D. C.: U. S. Government Printing Office, 1971); *New York Herald Tribune*, 25 May 1943; *New York Times*, 25 May 1943; Albany *Knickerbocker News*, 24 May 1943; Parker Corning to Mrs. Edwin [Louise] Corning, 17 July 5 Aug. 1936, Edwin Corning Papers.

On Edwin Corning: *New York Times*. 16 Jan., 28 June 1926; 16 July 1927; 14 Jan., 13 May, 15 Aug. 1928; 27 Nov. 1929; 6 Jan. 1932; 8 Aug. 1934; *New York Herald Tribune*, 8 Aug. 1934; *Albany Evening News*, 7, 8 Aug. 1934. Also, many letters in the Edwin Corning Papers.

4. James McLachlan, *American Boarding Schools: A Historical Study* (New York: Charles Scribner's Sons, 1970); Peter W. Cookson, Jr. and Caroline Hodges Persell, *Preparing for Power: America's Elite Boarding Schools* (New York: Basic Books, 1985); Frank D. Ashburn, *Peabody of Groton* (New York: Coward McCann,

1944); *Catalogue of Groton School, 1923–24; The Grotonian,* vol. 40 (1924)–44 (1928); *Groton School Quarterly,* vol. 4 (Oct. 1928), 5 (June 1930), 6 (Jan., Apr., June, Dec. 1931, Apr., June 1932); Geoffrey C. Ward, *Before the Trumpet: Young Franklin Roosevelt, 1882–1905* (New York: Harper & Row, 1985), chap. 5.

5. Erastus Corning to Mother [Louise Corning], ? Oct. 1926, Edwin Corning Papers.

6. Erastus Corning to Father [Edwin Corning], 1934 [no month or day], Edwin Corning Papers.

7. Erastus Corning to John J. O'Connell, 31 Dec. 1942, Mayor Erastus Corning, 2nd Papers.

8. Erastus Corning to "Eddie" [Corning], 22 Sep. 1943, Erastus Corning, 2nd Papers.

9. Erastus Corning to Kirk [Broaddus], 17 Dec. 1943, Erastus Corning, 2nd Papers.

10. The Dewey investigations are discussed in Richard Norton Smith, *Thomas E. Dewey and His Times* (New York: Simon and Schuster, 1982), 379–80; and in Robinson, *Albany's O'Connell Machine,* as well as in contemporary newspapers.

11. Erastus Corning to Mother [Louise Corning], n.d. [1944], Edwin Corning Papers.

12. These, and other efforts, are revealed in the Mayor Erastus Corning, 2nd Papers. In particular, Box 11 and Box 12 contain items related to the negotiations with Macy's.

13. Dorothea Noonan Interview on *The Longest Hurrah: A History of the O'Connell-Corning Years,* WMHT (Schenectady, N. Y.) Television Production, Aired 25 February 1987.

Index

power, 48–66; small cities and service, 4–5
Murphy Hannah, 27, 36

National Airport Plan, 171
Nebraska, league of cities, 62
Newark California, 127
Newark, New Jersey, 87
New Britain, Connecticut, 20, 23
New Castle, Indiana, 101
New England, 2, 14, 25, 65: civil defense, 151
New Hampshire, 15, 22, 154
New Haven, Connecticut, 16, 18
New Jersey, 14: evolution and, 199; homeownership in, 74
New London, Connecticut, 16
Newman, Ross L., 182
Newport, Rhode Island, 16–20
New Rochelle, New York, 70–73, 76–80, 89, 92, 95
New York City, 5, 75, 87, 94, 159: civil defense planning, 143, 154; Fire Department, 146; plan of, 138–39, 140–41; World War II, 153
New York State, 14
Nichols, H. L., 181
Nishkian, L. H., 130
Norfolk, Virginia, 3, 154
Norris, J. Frank, 116
North Tarrytown, NY, 92
Northwestern University, 83
Norwich, CT, 16
Nyack, NY, 92

Oak Cliff, Texas, 175
Oakland Estuary, 126
Oakland, California, 125
O'Brien, Leo, 198
Oceanside, California, 78–79
O'Connell, Daniel, 186–87, 191–93, 195–97, 199
O'Connell, Edward, 186–87
O'Connell, John J., 192–93
O'Connell, Jr., Joseph J., 177
Office of Civilian Defense, 143–63
Office of Home Defense, 147–48
Ohio: city classification, 51–52; flood relief, 159; incorporation,

51; city classification, 51–52; civil defense, 151
Olmsted, Frederick Law, 142
Orange, New Jersey, 75, 92
Osburn, Henry Fairfield, 120
Ossining, NY, 92
Overton, W. W., 177
Owens–Illinois, 108

Paducah, Kentucky, 113
Pasadena, California, 71, 76, 80–81, 87–89, 91–92
Patterson, Alan, 123
Patterson, William, 45
Peabody, Endicott, 189
Pearl Harbor, Hawaii, 143, 152–53
Pennsylvania, 14: flood relief, 159; incorporation, 51
Petaluma, California, 127
Philadelphia, 14
Philp, John W., 166
Pierce, Frank, 61–62
Pittsburgh, Pennsylvania, 3, 26–47, 150
Plainfield, New Jersey, 74–75, 92
Plan of Chicago, 136–38, 140
planning, urban: charter, 2–3, 14–25; civil defense, 143–63; classifications, 51–52 history, 12; residency, 17; San Francisco Bay Area, 123–42
plantations, 2, 14–25: compared to municipal governments, 23–24
Playa Del Ray, California, 79
Point San Quentin, California, 131
police: departments, 50–51, 64–65, 79–80; reform, 34–35, 37–38
politics, 79–80: African Americans in, 79–80; in Albany, New York, 185–200; corruption in, 53–54
Portland, Maine, 20, 21
Portsmouth, New Hampshire, 21
Posen, Illinois, 89
Potomac flood, 158
press, 84–85: black, 80; racial unrest, 85–86
Price, G. W., 85
professionals, and mobility, 43
property: assessments, 199; loss, 46; ownership and value, 43

About the Contributors

ROBERT B. FAIRBANKS is associate professor of history at the University of Texas at Arlington. Dr. Fairbanks, who earned his Ph.D. in American urban history from the University of Cincinnati in 1981, is also the author of *Making Better Citizens: Housing Reform and the Community Development Strategy in Cincinnati, 1890–1960* (1988) and the coeditor of *Essays on Sunbelt Cities and Recent Urban America* (1990). He serves on the Board of Directors of the Urban History Association.

BURTON W. FOLSOM is professor of history at Murray State University. His publications include *The Myth of the Robber Barons: A New Look at the Rise of Big Business in America* (1991), *Entrepreneurs versus the State* (1987), *Ethnoreligious Response to Progressivism and War: German-Americans and Nebraska Politics, 1908–1924* (1983) and *Urban Capitalists: Entrepreneurs and City Growth in Pennsylvania's Lackawanna and Lehigh Regions, 1800–1920* (1981). He is also the editor of the journal *Continuity: A Magazine of History*.

VALERIE S. HARTMAN is a lawyer and an adjunct professor of business law at Passaic County College in Paterson, New Jersey, as well as an adjunct professor of political science at William Paterson State College in Wayne, New Jersey.

DWIGHT W. HOOVER is professor of history emeritus and director of the Center for Middletown Studies emeritus at Ball State University. In 1991–92, he was a Fulbright professor of American studies at Jozsef Attila University in Hungary, and during 1992–93, he will be a visiting professor of American studies at Doshisha University in Japan.

Dr. Hoover was also a consultant for the Middletown Film Project, which produced a five-part series shown nation-wide on PBS. He is the author or editor of over 20 books, the latest of which is *Middletown: The Making of a Documentary Film Series* (1992).

DAVID R. LONG is an instructor in the University of North Carolina at Chapel Hill's Division of Continuing Education, and he is a doctoral candidate at the University. He is also the coauthor of a forthcoming article concerning the impact of World War II on the American urban South.

SCOTT C. MARTIN is a visiting assistant professor of history at the University of California, Riverside, where he teaches social and cultural history. Dr. Martin received his Ph.D. in U.S. history from the University of Pittsburgh in 1990. He is currently working on a book concerning leisure in southwestern Pennsylvania, 1800–1850, which will be published by the University of Pittsburgh Press.

ROBERT EARNEST MILLER is an adjunct assistant professor of history at the University of Cincinnati. Dr. Miller is also a research historian for the "Julia Dinsmore Project" of the Dinsmore Homestead Foundation and for the Cincinnati Historical Society's museum exhibit, "Cincinnati Goes to War: A Community Responds to Total War." He received his Ph.D. in history from the University of Cincinnati in 1991.

MAUREEN OGLE recently received her Ph.D. from the History of Technology and Science Program in the department of history at Iowa State University. Her previous publications include "Efficiency and System in Nineteenth Century Urban Services: Volunteer Fire Departments in Iowa, 1870–1890" and "Redefining 'Public' Water Supplies, 1870–1880: A Study of Three Iowa Cities" (*Annals of Iowa* 50).

HAROLD A. PINKHAM, JR. is professor of history at Salem State College. His publications include *An Architectural History of a Summer Community: Ocean Point, Maine, 1876–*

1992 (1992), and he is currently completing *The Rise of Urban New England: The Granting of City Charters, 1650–1850* (forthcoming). Dr. Pinkham, who earned his Ph.D. in history in 1980, was also on the Board of Directors of the Bay State Historical League from 1985–1989 and served as editor of *Bay City History* from 1987–1989.

ROBERT M. PRESTON is professor and chair of the department of history at Mount St. Mary's College in Emmitsburg, Maryland. He received his doctorate from the Catholic University of America in 1969. Dr. Preston is currently working on a book concerning the development of public housing from the time of Franklin D. Roosevelt to Ronald Reagan. He also served as the elected mayor of Emmitsburg from 1982–1992.

JOSEPH F. RISHEL is associate professor of history at Duquesne University and a former director of the Duquesne History Forum. He is the author of *Founding Families of Pittsburgh: The Evolution of a Regional Elite, 1760–1910* (1990). Dr. Rishel's past positions include that of Corporate Archivist for Westinghouse Electric Corporation and Associate Curator of the Archives of Industrial Society at the University of Pittsburgh.

IVAN D. STEEN is associate professor of history at the University at Albany, State University of New York. He also serves as director of the graduate program in Public History and as director of the Oral History Program. His publications include a number of articles for books and journals, including "Ministering to the Poor of Boston: The Work of Rev. Henry Morgan" in *Massachusetts in the Gilded Age: Selected Essays* (Tager & Ifkovic, eds,. 1985). Dr. Steen received his Ph.D. in American urban history from New York University in 1962.

LESLIE E. WILSON is assistant professor of history at Montclair State College, where he teaches American and African history. Dr. Wilson received his doctorate in American history from the Graduate School of the City University of New York. He is the author of *Reaching Out:*

The Epic History of St. Philip's Church (1986) and is the editor of *Introduction to African Civilization* (1988). A work on black urbanization is forthcoming.